WALKING POSSESSION

WALKING POSSESSION

Essays and Reviews

1968–93

Ian Hamilton

BLOOMSBURY

First published in Great Britain 1994
Copyright © 1994 by Ian Hamilton

The moral right of the author has been asserted

Bloomsbury Publishing Ltd, 2 Soho Square, London WIV 5DE

A CIP catalogue record for this book is available from the British Library

ISBN 0 7475 17126

Typeset by Hewer Text Composition Services, Edinburgh
Printed in Great Britain by Clays Ltd, St Ives PLC Bungay, Suffolk

Contents

Acknowledgments

Acknowledgment is made to the following periodicals: *GQ*, *The Listener*, *The London Review of Books*, *New Society*, *The New York Review of Books*, *The New York Times Book Review*, the *Observer*, *The Times Literary Supplement*, the *Sunday Times*, and *The Washington Post Book World*. The essay on Robert Frost was written for a Penguin Books selection of Frost's poems and the lecture 'A Biographer's Misgivings' was first delivered at the YMHA Poetry Center in New York.

Foreword

When the bailiffs come to call, as call they often do down Grub
Street way, your goods and chattels are not immediately carried
off to auction. For fourteen days, you are given a chance to raise
the money owed. During this period, the duns take 'walking
possession' of the things you own, or used to own. For two
weeks, the stuff is not yours but it is also not quite theirs.
Reviewers are sometimes thought of as the bailiffs of literature:
they take walking possession of their subjects; they talk as if they
own them, but they don't. And that's one way of explaining the
title of this book. Another is to confess that many of the reviews
reprinted here were written in less than fourteen days and one
or two of them were done on a typewriter half-owned by the
courts.

I have been writing reviews and literary articles for thirty years
and most of my early work was collected in either *A Poetry Chronicle*
(1973) or *The Little Magazines* (1976). Both books are well out of
print now and there is nothing from either of them in the present
selection.

Many of the pieces in this book were commissioned by Karl
Miller, and it is to him in particular that I would wish to offer my
gratitude.

I.H.

PART I

LIVES AND LETTERS

A Biographer's Misgivings

My life and times as a literary biographer began about fifteen years ago, in 1979, when I started researching a biography of the American poet Robert Lowell, who had died two years earlier, aged sixty, at the height of his considerable fame. In the summer of '79, I was taken by Lowell's widow, Caroline Blackwood, to the house in Ireland where she and Lowell had been lodging during the last weeks of his life. It was a chaotic visit, for one reason and another, and I didn't learn a great deal – but I did come away with a few relics: postcards and letters written to the poet, some fragments of unpublished verse, an old passport, a couple of photographs and several bits of conflicting 'oral testimony', as I believe it's called, from local witnesses – a shopkeeper, a publican, a caretaker and, of course, from the widow herself, who naturally enough found the visit acutely depressing.

When I got back to London I sat at my desk before examining my treasure trove, and I have to say that I felt a bit daunted by the prospect that now lay ahead of me. What did these bits and pieces mean? Where did they fit? Who were these strange – to me – people who signed themselves 'Blair' or 'Frank' or 'Peter'? They were old friends of Lowell's, I supposed. Older, anyway, than I was.

At this stage, I knew little about Lowell beyond what many others knew, from interviews and general gossip and from the evidence of his own heavily autobiographical writings. In my case, the bit extra came from having met him for lunch from time to time during the last half-dozen years of his life, and from a brief and unsuccessful professional collaboration which I will come to in a moment. Did I really want to spend the next half-dozen or however many years of *my* life attempting to inhabit this other, now-dead personality? And what level or quality of habitation was actually possible or desirable?

As I sat there, I got to imagining what it would be like if some biographer were to inspect the contents of the desk in front of me, my desk, as I had just inspected Lowell's. What would such a biographer make of – for example – this note from my mother complaining that she hadn't heard from me in weeks, this letter from my former wife tackling me about some unpaid electricity account, this perfumed postcard from someone called Priscilla, thanking me for a 'wonderful, enriching encounter' and expressing the fervent hope that she and I might 'do it again very soon'. Who *was* Priscilla? I later remembered that she was a research student writing a paper about literary magazines, a subject on which I'd written a book. I'd spent half an hour with her in a noisy London pub, and that had been the extent of our 'encounter'. But if *I* didn't know who she was, some three weeks after the event, what would my biographer make of her? He would probably spend months trying to establish her identity, and the harder it was to do this, the more interesting she would become. He would question all my friends and relatives about her, this mysterious Priscilla 'who clearly meant so much to the ageing Hamilton as he approached the end'. Before long, my friends and relatives would start believing in her too. 'If it hadn't been for that curious Priscilla business, who knows what he might not have gone on to achieve.' And so it would continue.

I ripped up the postcard from Priscilla, sent my former wife a cheque, and telephoned my mother to tell her that I'd be coming to see her next weekend. Biography, or the idea of it, had made me a better person – if only for an afternoon.

But it was not I who was under investigation; it was Robert Lowell, and I was not at all sure that I would become in any way more virtuous by attempting to track down *his* Priscillas, of whom there had been several dozen in his life, by all accounts. By whose accounts? Lowell's life had been of the sort that gives rise to anecdotal reportage. There were dozens of Lowell stories, most of them to do with his conduct during one or another of the manic episodes that afflicted him throughout his life. I knew the stories and had no doubt passed around one or two of them myself, but it was different now. Lowell dead would carry on being gossiped about, but not by me. It was my job to write the stories down, with footnotes, to authenticate.

Up to this point, I had, I supposed, held the usual ambivalent views about literary biography. I read biographies of writers with some pleasure but I was not always certain that knowing about the life was necessary to an understanding of the work. Lowell, it could be argued, was a special case. He was categorised as a 'confessional poet', a writer who had gone beyond customary bounds of reticence or personal embarrassment. There seemed to be a sense in which, more than most, he used his art to master and survive the often terrible circumstances of his life.

Much of Robert Lowell's celebrity since the publication of *Life Studies* in 1959 had had to do with people seeing in him a sort of literary heroism: a willingness to be led by Life into realms of experience that would exert the maximum pressure on his Art. John Berryman once said, 'The artist is extremely lucky who is presented with the worst possible ordeal that will not actually kill him. At that point he's in business.' Lowell himself might not have agreed with this, but a number of his admirers thought he did, and he was not always disposed to contradict them. By the early-seventies, there was nothing that Lowell would not *say* in a poem even though the saying of it might cause serious damage in his life – damage which would in turn provide the subject matter for more poems. In a sense I was embarking on a biography that had already been written, or made up. This meant, or so I thought, that there would be no problems of secrecy, no suppression of materials, no challenging of the essential biographical endeavour. On the other hand, it raised the question: since we knew so much already, did we really need to be told more?

On this, I was unsure. The best I could say was that I was curious to measure the self-created, self-nourished Lowell version of the Lowell life against other, less well-scripted versions: versions that might be provided by those who had muddled up their lives with his. One can never write a Life without also writing, or touching on, several other subsidiary or lesser lives. And in doing this, how judicious, how fair-minded could one actually hope to be? Just by calling such lives 'lesser' one was treating them rather as Lowell himself had treated them in reality. And yet how else could this biography get written? One might, for instance, wish to reprove Lowell's destructive self-absorption; at the same time, though, my narrative could hardly deny him centre-stage. It would be a weird sort of biography that made heroes of its subject's victims, if victims was indeed the right way to describe those who had, at some cost to their own tranquillity, elected to serve the poet's cause.

People would say of Lowell, as they have often said of many other artists, that he caused suffering to others and that no work of art, however marvellous, could compensate for what he did. But then, without the art, we would probably not care much what he did. And why not, in Lowell's case, see the poems as having mitigated the harmfulness rather than having in some way been the cause of it? On the other hand, if the art had not been so admired would he have felt licensed to believe that his life mattered more than those of his admirers? And did the work prosper because of that belief?

Lytton Strachey called biography 'the most delicate and humane of all the branches of the art of writing'. Someone else called the biographer 'an artist on oath'. Biographers love to quote these tags, and no wonder. Contemplating the difficulties of investigating Lowell's life, I could indeed at moments feel myself to have been nobly challenged: we all like to think of ourselves as 'delicate and humane'. But in some other part of my memory I could hear W.H. Auden's dictum about biography being 'always superfluous . . . usually in bad taste' – or, more tellingly, T.S. Eliot's even more magisterial pronouncement that 'curiosity about the private life of a public man may be of three kinds: the useful, the harmless and the impertinent'. If my Lowell project turned out not to be useful, I could hardly be sure that it would also manage to be harmless. Nor could I guarantee that it would not be 'impertinent' – an impertinence of some sort lurks at the heart of all biography, it seemed to me.

These, then, were some of my initial reservations. Perhaps more important was another question: what were my credentials for the task? Well, here I didn't feel too uncomfortable. I had seen quite a lot of Lowell since his move from New York to London in 1970. I had published his poems, I had interviewed him, I had visited him now and then at home and in hospital. We weren't friends, exactly, but we were friendly enough allies, of a sort.

A couple of years before he died, Lowell told me that he was thinking of writing a prose autobiography. He was having difficulty in getting started, he said, and we agreed that maybe if he spoke his recollections into a tape-recorder and then worked on

8

the transcripts, this might get him going. I was editing a magazine at the time, *The New Review*, and we agreed that in exchange for my asking the questions and then getting his responses typed, and so on, he would give me first opportunity to print instalments from the work, as it proceeded. This seemed to me a good arrangement – all I had to do, really, was to give him a few prompts and then sit back and listen. Any magazine at the time would have been happy to print chapters from Robert Lowell's own version of his life.

We had two sessions of tape-recording, and the second was – if anything – more disastrous than the first. In each session, Lowell so rambled and digressed and parenthesised that when we came to type up what he had said it read like the night-mumblings of a drunk. Perhaps he *was* drunk. More likely, though, there was something wrong with our whole method of enquiry. In our two sessions, which dealt with Lowell's student years at Kenyon College, and his friendships with John Crowe Ransom, Randall Jarrell, Peter Taylor and others, we managed to cover about ten days of his life. At this rate of progress, it would have taken about fifty-seven years to cover the whole story. And Lowell was fifty-seven at the time.

Anyway, it didn't work out, and we abandoned it. A number of poems in Lowell's last book, *Day by Day*, to me show signs of having been encouraged by these sessions, so it was not a complete waste of time. And there was a lesson to be learned: biography and autobiography are not close bosom friends. For Lowell, almost every name and date that came up in our conversations was saturated with feeling and significance and mystery. For him, the whole process seemed painful and bewildering. Was he remembering, or misremembering; how much had been forgotten, how much had been embellished, altered by later experience? He would remember a door opening, a pair of shoes, the sound of a voice on a particular afternoon, in a particular sunlight. How to get *that* across, that mixture of the too-blurred and the too-precise, was the sort of challenge that might sponsor the writing of a poem. For a biographical essay, though, it was exasperating that Lowell couldn't remember whose door it was that opened, who the pair of shoes belonged to, what the voice said that afternoon. Why had these images lingered when so many others had been lost? On another day, talking to someone else, would he remember it all differently? For the biographer, seeking a narrative outline, it was important to find answers to these questions, or to propose answers to them. But the autobiographer, the authentic rememberer, would know that there was no point in seeking patterns. The only way to know more was to remember more; and some things had, yes, been forgotten. Which things, though? What sort of things?

And this was Lowell's method, or non-method, with the tape-recordings. He spoke his memories as they came back to him and, host-like, was courteous and welcoming – curious, even, to see how they were dressed, how they looked these days, and so on. And yet at the same time, for him the whole act of remembering was full of sadness, sadness for what had been lost – not just to memory, but lost. From my point of view, sitting there with my editor's tape-recorder and my editor's wish to have all this material explained, the whole thing was both touching and infuriating. I was half-priest, half-torturer, and in neither role was I much of a success. Although I still have the tapes, I have played them back just once, as his by-then biographer, and they were almost completely useless – incomprehensible without a yard or two of explanatory footnotes (not all of which I would be able to provide) and even then too disjointed to be accurately quoted.

For a year or two after Lowell died, there was talk of appointing a biographer. When the time came, it happened that my magazine had folded and I was vaguely looking for some kind of job, or occupation. Caroline Blackwood, together with some other London friends of Lowell's, might well have remembered those tape-recording sessions. If Lowell had entrusted me with the role of his recorder, or sound-man, then maybe he would not have objected to the idea of me as his biographer. I really don't know the background, but when the job was offered I said yes.

This makes it all sound splendidly straightforward, but of course it wasn't. With biographies nothing ever is. Indeed, having said yes, I was immediately pitched into the centre of the very conflict which was to dominate the final chapter of the book I would eventually write. In case you are not familiar with the story, Lowell in 1970 had left his American wife Elizabeth Hardwick and set up house in London with the Anglo-Irish writer Caroline Blackwood. It was an acrimonious transfer, hugely complicated by the poet's long history of mental illness. Was this English adventure just another manic episode from which he would emerge, chastened and apologetic, as so often in the past, or was it the 'real thing', whatever, in his case, that may mean? In America Lowell had a loyal and, it might

10

be said, heroically sympathetic wife and a number of good friends – these people had, so to speak, served time in the Robert Lowell saga: they had rescued him from police stations, sat with him for hours in hospitals listening to him talk lovingly of Hitler and Napoleon, extricated him from absurd romantic and financial entanglements, repaired or tried to repair whatever damage had been done during his various mad periods. They had done all this out of a love and admiration for the man which even now seems awesome. And then, in 1970, he was announcing that he had left America (and them) behind: he had a new life, a new woman, a new house, a new team of helpers, English helpers. Most of his American friends had heard this kind of thing before and expected the episode to be over in six months. Indeed, some of them carried on not quite believing in his new life even after he divorced, got remarried and had a son with Caroline. Others recognised quite early on that this time Lowell meant it. There had become, in many people's minds, two Robert Lowells: the American Lowell and the post-1970 English Lowell. There had become two camps: essentially the Hardwick camp and the Blackwood camp – with overlaps, of course.

For Elizabeth Hardwick there was much to be endured – not least the suspicion that Lowell in England was a dangerous absurdity: he was going against his nature, his background, the true grounding that had kept him sane and creative for long stretches during their marriage and before. For Caroline Blackwood, on the other hand, it was America that drove him mad. In England, away from his own chaotic history, away from the 'glare' – as he himself described it – he would be healed and renewed. It was a terrible situation and Lowell often felt that it was tearing him apart. It might even have shortened his life. Certainly it is hard to forget the very last moments of that life and hard not to find in them a perfect image of the conflict which he had come to feel was both insoluble and inescapable. Lowell died of a heart attack in a taxi cab on his way from Kennedy airport to Elizabeth Hardwick's apartment on West 67th Street, their former home. He had quarrelled with Caroline, the last of several quarrels they had been having over the past few months, and he had probably determined to return to his American life – or to try to, because he was by no means out of love with Caroline. But he was dead on arrival at the house. Elizabeth Hardwick found him in the back seat of the taxi. In his arms there was a brown paper package: inside was a portrait of

Caroline by Lucian Freud, *her* former husband. Lowell had brought the painting to New York, it was said, 'to be valued'. Somehow Lowell, the great self-mythologiser, had contrived to write, or stage, the last, marvellously chilling paragraph of his biography, his Act Five, Scene Five. There was a prosy, common-sense reason for him having that picture in his arms; there was also a poetic aptness. It would be up to me to register the one without diminishing the other.

For the biographer entering this complicated world of recrimination and counter-recrimination, there was straightaway what one might call an 'innocence' problem. I had spent many hours in London, in pubs and restaurants, listening to Lowell fret about his two worlds, his two lives, and the unbearable tension that was building up between them, and I had no more idea than he did about what he should or shouldn't do. What I did have was a much more vivid grasp of his English unhappiness than I did of whatever it was that had driven him from America in the first place.

It was natural enough, then, that in the eyes of Lowell's American friends I would be seen as belonging to his 'English' world, a world which they believed had finally destroyed him. And this was the most daunting of the many obstacles I found when I presented myself in New York in 1979 as the prospective chronicler of Lowell's life. Which Lowell life? was the obvious first question that sprang to people's minds.

At first, doors were opened with great caution. I was given lists of names from Lowell's past, introductions to X and Y, but at this stage I didn't really know what questions to ask. And Lowell's American friends, although they were polite and amiable, were not eager to answer anything they did not have to answer. I soon realised that information was not going to *originate* from any of these so-called 'living witnesses'. Before approaching a witness I needed to know a lot more than I did about the history of that witness's relationship with Lowell. But how would I find out?

A typical situation was that I would approach A (who had been recommended to me by B) and he would ask me 'what I wanted to know' – actually he was trying to find out what I already *knew*. He would then, unfailingly, ask me who else I had seen and who else I was planning to see. 'Well, tomorrow I intend to visit C,' I might say. 'Oh no. Not C. Don't talk to him or, if you do, don't believe anything he says. He resented Lowell. He'll pretend he didn't but

12

he did.' Or it would be: 'I wouldn't bother with D. You won't get anything out of him. He adores Caroline and Lizzie quarrelled with him years ago.' Now and then, I was even told: 'I'd be careful when you talk to X. He's totally on Lowell's side.' What, I had to wonder, could *this* mean: on Lowell's side. And whose side did they think I was on?

Anyway, so much – at first – for the 'living witness' method of research. Later on, I read with much sympathy a comment by Mark Schorer on his researches into the life of Sinclair Lewis. Schorer said:

> Sometimes I wished that I had ten years more, for in that time most of these people would have gone away and I would no longer be confused by their conflicting tales and would in fact be free to say what I wanted about *them*.

I left New York for Harvard and spent the next three months or so in the Houghton Library. A few years before his death, Lowell had sold his 'archive' to the Library – an extensive collection of his manuscripts and notebooks and a vast pile of correspondence: the bulk of it, of course, being letters that had been addressed to him. From these letters I was able to build up a chronology of his life and a fairly reliable map of his relationships over the years. The Priscilla factor, as I now called it, had to be kept in mind. Not having Lowell's side of the correspondence made it difficult to know quite what was going on or – as in the case of his turbulent first marriage to the novelist Jean Stafford – to know who to sympathise with.

The Stafford letters, in fact, cast an interesting sidelight on the whole business of biography. They are superb pieces of marital polemic, detailed and lengthy and almost – though never quite – hysterically high-pitched. They are full of anger and resentment. There are no replies from Lowell – indeed, this is partly what is making Stafford so angry. But I knew, when I read these Stafford letters, that I had heard this voice somewhere before. And sure enough I had – in Lowell's long poem, *The Mills of the Kavanaughs*, written not long before the breakup of the Lowell–Stafford marriage.

It was a poem that had always rather puzzled me, not just because there were a number of local obscurities and a narrative that was extremely hard to follow but also because it gives so many of its best, or at any rate its most ferocious lines, to a vengeful, recriminating female. Women, up to this point, had not featured other than passively in Lowell's verse. Without the Stafford letters, I would now contend, the peculiar energies and intensities of *Mills of the Kavanaughs* would have remained mysterious, without any graspable source or context: although they would not have lost the slightly artificial or transplanted tone that worried me when I first read the poem.

Knowing the source of the poem also tells us something of Lowell's methods as a poet, about his habits of assimilation and mimicry. Lowell, it seems, was as much impressed by the *literary* power of Stafford's letters as he was troubled by their judgements on him as a husband who'd deserted her. After all, the desertion had already happened and he had no intention of going back on it: the poetry had yet to be written. Is this mean self-servingness or is it the icy detachment of the genuine artist? Later on, Lowell would once again make use of a wife's wounded letters in his poetry, with rather more controversial results. Finding the Stafford correspondence made it possible for me to view this process more as a literary compulsion than as an isolated personal outrage – although it was that, too. But I'll come back to this in a moment.

The experience of reading other people's private correspondence is always faintly thrilling and delinquent. Biographers, if they are honest, will admit that the pleasure they take in this branch of their research is not all to do with literary scholarship. In the Lowell case, there was a slightly embarrassing example. In the Harvard Library I came across a handful of letters written to Lowell by a woman we'll call G. It was evident from these letters that G and Lowell had had an affair, an affair that had meant a lot to her at the time – the late-forties. What it had meant to Lowell was, as usual, not entirely clear. I later tracked down G – in London, as it happened, although she was American – and I asked her if she would be interviewed about her relationship with Lowell. She agreed, and I – and my tape-recorder – went along to see her. Not knowing what I knew, she had prepared a presentation in which she and Lowell had been, as she put it, merely 'literary friends'. They had talked a lot about books, they had admired each other's writings, and that was all there was to it. She knew 'very little', she said, about his 'private life'. The interview proceeded along these genteel lines for about half an hour, until I could stand it no longer. I had to tell her: *But*

I've seen your letters. There was a silence, and G's mind was evidently racing: 'Which letters?' 'How?' 'What did they say?' After all, they had been written thirty years ago, in haste. Maybe, since she wrote them, she really had come to believe that she and Lowell had been no more than literary soul mates. She seemed genuinely stricken, as if I had callously, or stupidly, broken an important spell. The silence went on for a bit longer and then I switched off the machine. 'You mean, he actually *sold* them to Harvard University?' she said. I tried to make it better by explaining that he had also sold several thousand other letters, and that most writers did the same, but she was half-listening. 'All right, I'll tell you what really happened,' she said. But she told it with bitterness, and one could not be sure that this bitterness did not have more to do with Lowell's treatment of her *letters* than with his treatment of *her* thirty years before. But then opening old wounds is something else that the biographer needs to be good at. I did not tell G that in the same Harvard Library I had come across some gossipy letters to Lowell by supposed friends of my own – a couple of them making not very friendly reference to me. After all, I was in no position to claim any sort of fellow feeling in the matter.

One of the arguments in favour of writing biographies of the recently dead is that, if you leave it too late, the living witnesses will not be living. But the eagerness to get hold of testimony while it is still hot does have its, shall we say, unseemly aspects. 'The quick in pursuit of the dead', as Elizabeth Hardwick once put it. People don't write letters in the way they used to, and public figures have become more sophisticated in their efforts to forestall and thwart biographers. In the nineteenth century it was possible for a public figure to think of his biographer as a friend – in fact he usually *was* a friend. Nowadays it is taken for granted that, at the very least, there will be a degree of tension between the life-writer and his subject. Thus, in future, there will be an increased reliance on the testimony of contemporaries, and no doubt these 'living witnesses' will themselves acquire a skill and sophistication in the practice of their craft. Their affidavits will become ever more polished and composed; the raggedness of what actually happened will be tidied up. And some witnesses will learn to be expert in biographical double-talk: blackening a name they are pretending to revere. A lot will depend on who, among the witnesses, dies first. If best friend A dies without having been asked to say his piece, we will be forced to rely on second-best friend B for a ranking of A's actual involvement in the studied life. For all we know, B might have resented A and might now wish to downgrade him. And to check this out, we would really need to talk to C, if he is still alive. When it comes to lovers, wives, children even, the competitiveness between the witnesses becomes of course even more hazardous. The closer you are to the action, the more delicate the choice you're obliged to make. In the case of Lowell, I actually suppressed mention of more than one involvement because there was a clear possibility of damage, and I also left out other material because it was put to me that there was a need to protect the Lowell children. But of course it is not always possible to judge the damage, or the misery, that can result from biographical writing.

With Lowell, there were moments when the biographer had to be far more circumspect than Lowell himself had ever been. I often felt that Lowell might find my reticence a bit feeble-spirited. After all, he had pulled no punches. When in the seventies, he took passages from Elizabeth Hardwick's brilliant, angry letters and incorporated them into poems about their separation, he was widely attacked – this was surely the ultimate betrayal. But Lowell could never quite see what the fuss was all about. In quoting Hardwick's letters in his verse, he was responding to them, to her, not as an ex-husband but as a co-writer, a maker-over of pain into poetry. In some important way, he was proud of Hardwick's letters, as he had been proud of Stafford's. And he had found them painful to read, so in this sense they were to be seen as *his* experience, and thus material for art. For Elizabeth Hardwick, at the time, there was nothing in all this except bitterness. Twenty years later, she may be feeling differently. After all, without the lines from her letters, some of these Lowell poems are not very good.

My Lowell book was completed in 1982 and appeared in the winter of that year. After I'd finished it, my publishers immediately began asking me *who* I would be doing next – not what but who. The assumption was that my next book would be a biography. I was now, it seemed, a biographer-elect. Ahead of me lay a possible new career in which I would move from one 'case' to another. It was suggested to me that I might write a life of Ezra Pound, then the name of John Berryman was mentioned. A quite different publisher wrote to ask how I would feel about tackling the life of Sylvia Plath. I described this last proposal to a sardonic friend of mine who said that I should agree to it, of course, but only on condition that the very last sentence of the finished book should read: 'As to her final months, I believe that we should draw a decent veil' – and 'then see what they say'. The common factor in these propositions was, it seemed to me, insanity. I was in danger of being set up as an expert on mad poets. As a bit of a mad poet myself, from time to time, I was not at all sure that this would be good for me. So I declined these offers, or semi-offers, and returned to London – where I had another career of sorts waiting for me, as the reviewer of other people's books about mad poets.

It was during this period that the subject for my next adventure was presented to me, quite by accident. My sixteen-year-old son came home from school one day and announced that he had just read this 'terrific book'. His face wore the look it sometimes had when he came back from a heavy-metal concert. 'Terrific books' were not, at that time, part of his cultural curriculum. 'And what terrific book would that be?' I asked, hoping – at best – for Stephen King or Robert Ludlum. 'It's called,' he said, struggling somewhat to remember, 'It's called *The Catcher in the Rye*.' I was genuinely stunned. *The Catcher in the Rye* was a book I hadn't thought about for a long time. Once, though, about thirty years ago, it had been the key 'terrific book' of *my* adolescence. I'd read it so many times that I almost knew it off by heart. For months, I had gone around *being* the book's hero, Holden Caulfield, until I learned that thousands, perhaps tens of thousands of other adolescents were doing the same thing – and had been doing it since 1951, when *The Catcher* first appeared. I had then followed Salinger's subsequent career, through *Franny and Zooey* to *Raise High the Roof Beam, Carpenters*, trying hard to sustain the same level of enthusiasm, as a devout disciple should. Then Salinger had stopped publishing; he'd disappeared from view and, after a bit, I'd more or less forgotten about him – although every so often, whenever I heard myself come out with a phrase like 'big deal' or 'goddam phoney', I would half-remember where it came from.

And now, years later, here was my adolescent son telling me that he had fallen victim to the same infatuation. I was, of course, delighted; and impressed too that the book still had this power to charm the young. We began comparing notes: 'Remember the bit when old Stradlater leaves his razor in the washroom?' 'What really happened with Mr Antolini?' and so on. And then, a bit later, my son asked me the question that would determine, for me, the shape and substance of the next four years. He asked me, 'Who *is* J.D. Salinger?'

Well, I told him what little I knew, most of it remembered from my own junior researches thirty years before. Salinger was a New Yorker, from a prosperous half-Jewish business background; he was born in 1919; he had attended military college as a boy; he was in the US Army during World War Two, possibly working in Intelligence; he had published short stories in the *New Yorker* during the forties; *The Catcher* was his first novel; it had been a best-seller when it appeared and became a cult text for rebellious teenagers from the mid-fifties to the early-sixties. Salinger had then embarked on a long fictional saga about a family of geniuses called Glass – one of these, Buddy Glass, seemed to have been modelled on Salinger himself. Buddy was a novelist who had written a successful book about an adolescent and who was now greatly troubled by the attentions of his fans. With the publication of *Franny and Zooey* in 1961, Salinger's celebrity had reached such a pitch that, for reasons partly to do with this and partly unknown, he had withdrawn completely from the public arena – not just refusing to give interviews or answer fan-mail but refusing even to publish what he wrote – if indeed he did still write.

To my son, this last bit, the bit about refusing to publish, was the most interesting. In his culture, the pursuit of celebrity was crucial to any so-called creative undertaking. Fame was the sharpest spur. The idea of popular success being voluntarily rejected was perhaps more strange to him than it was to me, but this did not mean that I was able to give him any persuasive account of what Salinger was up to. I muttered a bit about the corrupting effects of collaborating with the media, I threw in a bit about Salinger's Zen Buddhism, I recalled the passage in *The Catcher in the Rye* where Holden Caulfield yearns to go off into the woods and live as a deaf mute. But I could tell he wasn't impressed and, after we'd stopped talking, I found that I was asking myself the question he'd asked me: Who *is* J.D. Salinger?

I then re-read the books and I lingered particularly over the long story, *Seymour: an Introduction*, the story in which Buddy Glass, Salinger's supposed alter-ego, talks directly to his audience – the audience he says he wants to reject. Buddy's manner, rather like Salinger's own manner in the one or two odd statements he had made in his own person over the years, was not the grouchy, inattentive manner of the misanthrope. On the contrary, it was energetically playful and flirtatious. Salinger the author seemed to be using Buddy Glass as a means of both fostering and toying with the curiosity of his worshipping young fans. It was a deeply social, or even a theatrical manner – the manner of one who is sure enough of the affection of his readers that he can afford to play games with it. It was the manner, so I thought, of one who wanted, and expected to be loved – but loved on his own terms, even though the terms might turn out to be more harshly absolute than those which normally prevail between a writer and his readership.

This at any rate was how I read it at that point. Having just emerged from spending three years inside the psyche of a writer to whom reticence meant nothing, and who was intensely involved in all aspects of his fame, I was perhaps over-disposed to be sceptical about Salinger's reclusiveness. I didn't really believe that he wanted to be left alone. It didn't fit with what he'd written. In other words, in this special case, I was ready to project a literary interpretation on to the personality of the author, something I knew in the abstract to be dangerous. But I kept coming back to the idea of play, of theatre, in Salinger's later work. Was his refusal to publish in truth something of a tease? Had we, his readers, failed him in some way? Had we misread him, been insufficiently respectful, not responded ardently enough to his late work? I knew that he had rejected numerous requests for interviews from journalists. Perhaps he was waiting for the really *serious* approach – from *the biographer*. Perhaps he was waiting for *me*.

Some hope. But even so, what if Salinger *was* genuine in his wish to be ignored, forgotten, written off? Did this mean that we, his readers, had to suppress all curiosity about him? I began to get intrigued by the notion of trying to construct a version of Salinger in much the same way as I had constructed a version of Lowell – and using much the same sort of materials: my reading of the works, the testimony of people who knew or had known him, and any documentary evidence that might be there to be uncovered. The difference would be that, with this book, the author under scrutiny was still alive. And yet, so far as biography, or even literary history, was concerned, he would prefer us to think of him as dead. Or so he said.

Without the Lowell experience, with its super-abundance of biographical material, and without the coincidence of my son's encounter with *The Catcher in the Rye*, I don't suppose I would have pursued the matter any further. Fatally, though, I mentioned the idea to my agent, who had also been puzzling over the question of what – or who – I might do next. He suggested, as agents do, that I set down a few thoughts on paper, and I did. I came across this synopsis not so long ago, and in the light of all that has happened since, I was – well – almost reassured by its *naïveté*, its deep *mis*reading of the Salinger conundrum. It starts off with an account of my early attachment to *The Catcher* and it even quotes that line in which Holden Caulfield defines a good writer as someone who makes you feel that you can call him up on the phone. Salinger, in his works, comes across as just that sort of writer. And this observation is not meaningless. After all, who would want to call up the author of *Finnegans Wake* or *The Love Song of J. Alfred Prufrock*? And yet, in life, Salinger had made himself uniquely unapproachable. The synopsis, dated 1983, continued as follows:

What would happen, I wonder, if – without invading his privacy (underlined), without attempting to 'get to' him in any of the obvious ways, one simply set about building a portrait of Salinger's life and personality based on (a) the books themselves (b) records available to the public (c) interviews with people who knew/know/know about him?

The idea would be not to approach Salinger himself until one had reached the end of the 'public' research. He would no doubt hear of one's endeavours, as the thing developed, and he might in the end be tempted out of hiding. The book would not at all depend on his capitulation although the final chapter might well give an account of what happens when, at last, he is approached.

The book's method would have to be one of extreme delicacy and propriety – one should not be seen to push or pry. One should be seen as simply gathering together what is already in the public domain, or recording whatever is willingly, and responsibly offered in the course of the research. In this case, the biographer would be a character in his own book. His rebuffs might be as interesting as his collaborations. The idea would be to arouse in Salinger a sort of grudging curiosity – a counter-curiosity.

Salinger's counter-curiosity was indeed stimulated by my efforts, but it came not in the form of a melting, an unburdening – or whatever it was I had in mind in my painstakingly 'decent' outline for the book. It came in the form of a lawsuit. My book, when it came out, was called *In Search of J.D. Salinger* and it gives a full account of the whole business. The upshot of my attempts to get closer to my admired subject was that I ended up as his arch-enemy. As I say in the eventually published book: 'The book I fell for has at last broken free of its magician author. But even so I can't rejoice that, whatever happens, my name and J.D. Salinger's will be linked in perpetuity as those of litigants, or foes, in the law school textbooks, on the shelves of the US Supreme Court, and in the minds of everyone who reads this, the legal version of my book.'

To sum up, then. I have written two biographies – one of a dead author whom I knew, one of a live author whom I've never met. In each case, though, I have come away from the project with a sense of having failed, with a sense of having got it wrong and of not having greatly liked myself when I was doing it. I am not complaining, nor am I looking for sympathy. I was well paid for this work, and there is clearly something about the whole business of poking around in other people's lives that I quite like. And, in the end, I would probably defend the books I wrote – as books. It is only when I hear biographers talk high-mindedly about the delicate and humane aspects of their calling, or when they refuse to acknowledge that there is in what they do some necessary element of sleaze – it's only then that I remember my own biographer's misgivings: all those letters I read, those tape-recordings I transcribed, those wounds I re-opened, those emotions I guessed at, those lives I plundered or played with so that I could tell my tale.

1990

Jean Stafford

When Jean Stafford died in 1979, she left everything she owned to her cleaning lady, one Josephine Monsell. Mrs Monsell had never read any of her employer's writings, but she was a merry soul, it seems: she used to laugh at Stafford's jokes. Stafford in her will registered gratitude for this service by, so to speak, turning Monsell into a joke. Not only did the unlettered domestic inherit Stafford's almost valueless possessions, she also found herself appointed literary executor, in charge of copyrights, permissions, royalties and all the rest of it. As with so many of Stafford's most memorable jests, there was in this a streak of cruelty.

And Mrs Monsell was not the only victim. Certain of Jean Stafford's closest and most loyal friends were upset that none of them had been asked to look after the novelist's literary estate. But they ought not to have been surprised: the joke was thoroughly in character. Stafford loved to create 'effects' and she enjoyed playing with words: how effective that her own effects should be disposed of in this offhand way. And how sardonically reproachful, too. Even those who had done right by Jean and had stuck by her during her unpleasantly tetchy and demanding final years were made to wonder, in the end, what they'd done wrong.

From the start, Jean Stafford had a way of keeping her friends on their toes, sometimes in a spirit of wit and mischief, but more often – and increasingly over the years – in an attempt to test their loyalty. If they failed the test – and Stafford often saw to it that they did – she would set about them with some of the elaborate, high-intensity invective at which she was so expert, both in life and art. There was almost always a wish in her to have the worst of her bad dreams come true, and much of her most stylish writing issues from a sense of grievance.

The ugly-duckling youngest daughter of a spectacularly failed writer, Stafford was brought up in non-smart Colorado. She married Robert Lowell and thus gained access both to the lower ranks of Boston 'society' and to the notion of literary art as a near-sacred calling. Her first novel, *Boston Adventure*, caused her to be praised for her New England know-how. Prolix and deeply artificial, the book enjoyed a critical and commercial success – a success which many think helped to destroy her marriage to Lowell (he wanted a playmate, not a wife, but what he wanted least of all was a wife whose writing might seriously rival his: in 1944, the year of Stafford's triumph, Lowell's poetry had barely made its mark).

Boston Adventure, it might also be contended, helped to damage Stafford's development as a writer, by misrouting it so early on. It was a large novel pieced together by a brilliant miniaturist, and it won admiration for its scope and structure. From this point (she was twenty-nine in 1944) Stafford was made to feel just a bit dissatisfied with everything she did, with mere stories (however lavishly these were admired), and seemed always to be straining for an American-style *coup*. Needless to say, there was no shortage of encouragers on hand to make sure that she did not settle for the smaller scale.

Stafford's second novel, *The Mountain Lion*, was in fact shorter and a lot more genuine than the Boston book, but it enjoyed nothing like the same success. Her third, *The Catherine Wheel*, did rather better in the market-place but got 'mixed' reviews. By 1952, Stafford had written her last novel; she was thirty-six and she had twenty-seven years of life ahead of her. There were to be short stories, some of them superb, and a quantity of so-so journalism, but the long work of fiction for which she was heavily contracted did not get written.

By the mid-sixties, Stafford was talked of as a figure of the past, and although her *Collected Stories* won a Pulitzer Prize in 1970, dissatisfaction had by then become for her almost a habit of mind; she continued to speak and act as if she had been cheated of some grander accolade. But by then even the short stories had dried up. Stafford was well on her way to full-time eccentricity, a 'character' to be treated with caution and compassion.

In some ways, the most revealing chapter in Jean Stafford's life comes in the early sixties, when her reputation was in decline: she was no longer 'promising' and her ironic conservatism was by no means the flavour of the epoch. She had got married to the journalist A. J. Liebling (there had been another marriage post-Lowell, but it had been brief – 'a marriage of inconvenience', she called it) and for a period of about five years she was apparently content to operate in Liebling's fairly substantial shadow. This did not mean that she stopped writing but it did mean that she was able to relax her make-or-break attitude to what she wrote.

Liebling had money, or could get it, and for Stafford, who had always found it hard to support her not inexpensive tastes, this mattered quite a lot. Also, when it came to writing, he presented himself as a worldly professional – there was none of Lowell's rage for immortality to cope with here. It was all right, *chez* Liebling, not to win the Nobel Prize.

When Liebling died in 1963, Jean Stafford was – in the words of a close friend – 'well and truly stranded': having enjoyed a measure of protection, she found it impossible to resurrect her earlier solo ambitions. And it was hard also for her to operate as Liebling had, in a world of deadlines and commissions. Like a true pro, he had left her just enough money to pay off his debts. The years that followed his death are painful to behold, with Stafford flailing around in search of an 'effective' way to live – or, rather, to present herself. One week she is a hopeless drunk, the next a death-bed invalid; for a month or two she sets up as a crotchety recluse, only to emerge again as a grand dame literary socialite. Whatever the pose, the old dissatisfaction was always ready to bubble to the surface – but in these later years it had a sourer, more retaliatory edge.

After her death, the *New Yorker* published the only publishable fragment of the novel she had been 'working on' for almost three decades. It was a savage account of the break-up of her marriage to Lowell, and it made brilliant mock of the Lowell circle of tormented genius-poets. In ridiculing their narcissistic quest for greatness, she was both seeking to dignify her own abstention and complaining bitterly about having been left out – or cast out, as she saw it.

Stafford was a tireless complainer and exaggerator and one cannot but have some sympathy for her biographer. When Stafford was alive, no one could tell for sure when she was talking straight, even when she was at her most passionately eloquent. Indeed, eloquence was what often urged her into falsehood and distortion. Since many of her lies were told most entertainingly, only a dullard would have thought to pick her up on details. Stafford was also a heavy drinker and in her cups she would be inclined to make for the telephone or the post-box; or, if in company, she would wax confidential, revealing never-before-told secrets of her autobiography. The striving for effect was unremitting, as if she wanted to make her life into the kind of rich, spectacular narrative that was forever eluding her when she sat down to write. For Stafford, there was no such thing as a minor set-back: she traded only in disaster. Imagined slights were written up as major insults. When she was ill (and, according to her, she was ill most of the time) the illness would have to be big-league. As a friend put it: 'She was always having brain tumours and breast cancer.'

And yet she really was ill fairly often. The record shows that she was admitted thirty-four times to one New York hospital and it is established also that her face was badly smashed in a car accident, that her rib-cage broke during a fit of coughing (she was a resolute tobaccophile), and that she frequently manifested symptoms alarming enough to have several doctors sound the red alert. Barely a year passed without some health scare, and Jean was always ready to supply her own lurid, almost exultant commentary on the details of her treatment.

David Roberts knows all this, of course, and most of the time he treads carefully, seeking either to deflate or corroborate the information he has amassed mainly from Stafford's own letters and from the reminiscences of a handful of her friends. There is an odd stretch of the book where Roberts seems determined to prove that Stafford's life was shaped by her having in her youth contracted a venereal disease, and there is more than a touch of prurience in his attempts to work out who she did or didn't sleep with: 'The whole business is of an interest that transcends mere gossip. In virtually all of Stafford's mature fiction, the very fact of sexual relations is ignored.' It is noteworthy that Roberts stops speculating about Stafford's sexual attitudes as soon as she begins to lose her looks.

It is this aspect of the book that will encourage feminist admirers of Jean Stafford to wonder why a woman writer was not asked to write her biography. More than once I found myself wondering the same thing. Even so, Roberts should be given credit for his voluminous research. He is especially good on Stafford's early years and on her Colorado background, which he shares. And when he is not peddling some pet theory, he strikes a balance between admiration and scepticism which Jean Stafford

herself, in kindly mood, might have deemed just about acceptable.

1988

DAVID ROBERTS
Jean Stafford: A Biography
Chatto and Windus

Aldous Huxley's Letters

'I am an intellectual with a certain gift for literary art, physically delicate, without very strong emotions, not much interested in practical activity and impatient of routine.' Aldous Huxley classified himself as firmly and with much the same pedagogic love of paraphrase as he classified most other things. His personality, he believed, had been almost wholly determined by the temporary blindness which afflicted him at the age of sixteen and which left his sight impaired for the rest of his life. If nothing that happened to him afterwards had quite the power to shape him differently, this was because his blindness had rendered him pretty well invulnerable to the kind of ragged human pressures that most people tend to get reshaped by in the course of the years.

Certainly it encouraged him towards a life which, though taking him from Garsington to Hollywood, from Robert Nichols to Timothy Leary, was yet essentially inturned and solitary, preferring Being to beings; it confirmed him in his precocious 'lust for pure knowledge'; it drove him from action to abstraction. It set him apart, and like most people who feel set apart he felt his seat was lofty. And because he was so convinced of what his ailment's various and lasting effects on him had been, it could be said, too, to have shaped some of his more pronounced intellectual biases. For instance, he would not, one is convinced, have had the same hostility to Freudian accounts of how things are if he had not so deeply felt his own nature to have been decided by a physiological accident.

It made him disciplined and self-reliant, but it also taught him to attach an inordinate value to discipline and self-reliance. The first of the acid-heads could be a very heavy father, chastising his errant son for 'letting things slide, forgetting what ought to be remembered, not bothering to do things because you don't happen to feel like doing them, permitting an immediate distraction, such as the purposeless reading of an intrinsically worthless magazine article, to get in the way of a present duty or thinking rationally about the future'.

Huxley's formidably impersonal letters present us with what his novels led us to expect: the apotheosis of arid intellectualism. They are the record – slow-moving and grindingly repetitive and laced here and there with interesting literary chit-chat – of an unusually clever man's unusual mental passions. Where Huxley appears as a human being rather than as an essayist, teacher, medicine man or mystic guinea-pig, he comes across, either as ordinarily decent – efficiently discharging workaday obligations to family and friends – or as extraordinarily desiccated.

Lacking as we do any of his letters to his first wife (when she died he wrote of her: 'In so far as I have learned to be human – and I had a great capacity for not being human – it is thanks to her'), we can't really be sure, but the Huxley who emerges here from letters to his brother, to his parents and his son, just seems incapable of even the most elementary sort of intimacy. Personal matters get despatched in a brusque opening paragraph, and the rest of the letter is more often than not a report on Huxley's current intellectual passion: his new book, or some essay he is working on, gets summarised, a new theory is explained, reading matter is recommended, and so on. Only when the addressee is suffering from an interesting illness does any detailed personal concern begin to show itself, and then only because Huxley usually knows some interesting cure. (He did, after all, distinguish himself as a young man by writing to Ottoline Morrell: 'I wonder if you know what means Bertie Russell employed to cure his piles.') The tone of these often lengthy letters is unswervingly neutral: no one – no one in particular, that is – is being written to.

Huxley would, of course, readily have granted this. But the frequency with which he conceded his own faults does not persuade one that they deeply bothered him. His shafts of self-analysis never quicken far beyond a certain mild despondency: he can't help the way he is, and doesn't anyhow much want to. 'I share with you a fear of the responsibilities of relationships', 'I know how to deal with abstract ideas but not with people', 'I have always tended to be somewhere else, in a world of analysis', 'I sometimes have the

28

disquieting sense that I am being somehow punished by so much good fortune – that it is a scheme to lead me deeper into my besetting sin, the dread and avoidance of emotion, the escape from personal responsibility, the substitution of aesthetic and intellectual values for moral values, of art and thought for sanctity.'

There is something far too pat, I feel, in these over-formulated gestures of self-condemnation, particularly when they are set along-side his more generalised attitudes to the whole world of emotions and relationships. 'One is forced to the conclusion that the men of religious insight were right in insisting that society at large and men and women as they are on the average, in the "unregenerate" stage are doomed to perpetual self-frustration.' Only certain 'individuals' could hope to fulfil their 'enormous potentialities'. Huxley's glibly pessimistic view of events outside his study – the real world he was fond of dismissing as 'a lunatic asylum' – his almost awed contempt for ordinary people, his refusal of even the most obvious kind of political involvement (from Hollywood in 1938 he wrote that 'the persecution of the Jews in Germany is horrible in the extreme; but it is not by proclaiming the fact in a loud voice that this particular persecution will be stopped or that human beings will discontinue the habit of persecution, which is immensely old and which is bound up with habits of thought, feeling, action and belief'): these don't finally amount to anything very passionate or very vicious but are more to be seen simply as ways of inoculating the abstract life against the contaminations of concrete experience.

Rationalistic and scientific in his mental habits, possessed of a vast store of book-knowledge, equipped with all the necessary data, Huxley's thirst for the immaterial never really had a chance, and there is something sad and impressive about the way he tried to make the best of an impossible pursuit. His religious impulse sent him searching for a God whom his scientific impulse insisted must be seen face to face, checked and double-checked. A joyless enterprise to say the least: 'I was born wandering between two worlds, one dead, the other powerless to be born, and have made, in a curious way, the worst of both.'

Reviewers have praised the lucidity, the common sense, of Huxley's later letters about his experiences with mescalin and LSD: but in a way, it is precisely their common sense that makes them depressing reading. Similarly depressing, though touching, too, is his account of his wife Maria's death:

And now she would have peace. And when there was peace and love, there too would be joy and the river of the coloured lights was carrying her towards the white light of pure being, which is the source of all things and the reconciliation of all opposites in unity. And she was to forget, not only her poor body, but the time in which that body had lived. Let her forget the past, leave her old memories behind. Regrets, nostalgias, remorses, apprehensions – all these were barriers between her and the light.

And so it goes on, a strained, guessed-at ecstasy: but an ecstasy of escape, not of fulfilment.

Coming to the end of this, surely far too massive tome, one can't help noting that the more one steps back from Huxley's life and personality the more tragic, or maybe just pathetic, weight they seem to carry. Getting in close, one becomes bored, a bit appalled: one notes, for instance, the way in which Huxley – for all his asserted impracticality – managed to organise his fairly lucrative literary career, one spots the small frigidities, one is in touch with the day-to-day narrowness and thin-bloodedness of the man. But from a distance, his life can seem to have been interestingly plagued by the most drastic of antitheses: light and dark, flesh and spirit, science and religion. All the old enemies were there, with Huxley always studiously stranded between them. And then there were those really punishing ironies of his last years: the bookman's library consumed by fire, the novelist of good talk afflicted by cancer of the tongue. It is a stirring plot, provided that we keep it at arm's length. Again, Huxley would have readily agreed.

1968

GROVER SMITH (Editor)
The Letters of Aldous Huxley
Chatto and Windus

Stephen Spender's Journals

It is rubbed into me by every stroke of my pen that my lack of natural talent, facility, concentration is something to be modest about . . .

Sometimes I wonder if I am so mild through weakness, timidity, conviction, perversity or what. I think it is a mixture of these things.

I'm struggling at the end to get out of the valley of hectoring youth, journalistic middle-age, imposture, money-making, public relations, bad writing, mental confusion.

If any of these three quotations were to be included in a *TLS* competition, few of that paper's poetry-reading readers would fail to spot the voice. The blend of self-censure and contentedness is uniquely Stephen Spender's. In the thirties, as head of the Lyrical Department of MacSpaunday Inc, Spender won high marks for being sensitively muddle-headed when all around him had made up their icy minds, and a kind of wincing bewilderment has been his trademark ever since.

From the outset, he has looked the part. In his youth, he was tousle-headed when his friends were slickly cropped and Brylcreemed; he was gangling and gauche when they were stocky and efficient. All the most famous thirties photographs suggest that in a period of purposeful limb-discipline, of rallies and goose-steps and international brigades, Spender alone knew how to trip over his own fire-hose, and be loved for it. And today, observed at literary gatherings, Sir Stephen still manages to look more attractively boyish than most of the boys, more shyly keen to please, more likely to drift off into some genuinely sweet poetic dream.

Some would say that Spender has made a career out of seeming to be over-sensitive. Poets warm to the image he projects: they too would like to look like that (it's odd, when you think of it, how few tall *and* good-looking poets there are in the world). Non-poets – university professors and cultural bureaucrats – enjoy his company because he puts them at their ease. He looks like a poet but he doesn't behave like one; his diffidence persuades them that it doesn't matter much if they don't read his work. It also pleases them that the work he is most famous for was written a long time ago.

This unkind view of Spender would continue thus: his looks and charm, it would assert, have splendidly equipped him for a cushy, ambassadorial status in the world of letters, and he has been shrewd enough not to rock the boat by publishing new poems that might dim the lustre of his early fame. After all, it was an accident of history that made him seem important in the first place. He is thought now to have 'substance' as a poetry-figure because whenever Poetry of the Thirties is under discussion, he too will be discussed. No anthology of modern poetry would be historically plausible if it did not include half-a-dozen of his early works. Even though he had a good deal less natural talent than, say, Norman Cameron or Bernard Spencer, he was lucky enough to attach himself to a teachable poetic movement, and he has been living off it ever since.

And so on. It is a familiar view, and no one can be more familiar with it than Spender himself. Hence, possibly, these *Journals*. Spender's image might be one of other-worldliness, but he long ago learned how to keep one step ahead of his opponents. His method is quite simple; he forestalls them. He owns up in advance to whatever feebleness or folly he's about to be accused of. And it is thoroughly consistent with his method that he should choose now, in his seventies, to publish not an autobiography (although this is what many would have wished for from the author of *World Within World*) but a carefully edited selection of the journals he's been keeping for some forty years.

The journal is an ideal form for one who might be nervous of final, summarising judgments – his own, or other people's. In a journal, everything is present tense, provisional; no one is going to rebuke the author for some bygone frailty when he himself has so willingly exposed it to the public view. The reader is forced into the role of eavesdropper, and any evidence he picks up is either inadmissible or has already been neutralised by means of a confession. Moreover, a journal isn't really a book; it is something that just happens to have dropped between hard covers. Matters of structure and balance are not relevant: you can't really *blame* the author for jotting down too much stuff about dinner parties and not enough about Vietnam. Who knows what noble thoughts he might have had if he had supped at home?

To our unkind observer, then, it will seem that Spender has pulled it off again. He has appeared before his public bruised, self-knowing and making only the most sheepish of bids for critical forgiveness. 'I imagine the young reading nothing of me but the bad notices other young critics write.' But how could even the youngest of young critics kick a man who keeps on saying, or implying, that – if he'd known better – he would certainly have kicked himself? How can rigour be exercised against a spirit so emptied of vile hubris?

> I am really puzzled and lost when people behave in ways that seem in the least bit self-interested. The slightest degree of self-interest seems monstrous and introduces an element of the incalculable into a relationship.

> I myself have a tendency in my relations with people not to refuse anything and often to undertake far more than I can undertake.

It is easy enough to point to moments when humility shades into saintfulness and it is even possible to isolate brief passages of snobbishness and malice. The journal form decrees, though, that such lapses must be placed in fleeting contexts. All in all, the opposition is thoroughly disarmed.

The trouble with the opposition, however, is that it has all along – in Spender's case – been carrying ridiculously heavy weapons. Also, its motivation has been faulty. The assumption has been that Spender has had a career that can be envied, that he has somehow duped the world of letters into giving him a better deal than he deserves, and that his early success has always worked – or been worked – to his advantage. Accusations of guile and mainchance disingenuousness have tended to be based on suppositions of this kind. In fact, an opposite narrative could just as plausibly be framed, a narrative in which the hero spends a lifetime having to be Stephen Spender, famous poet of the thirties: indeed, famous, young, overrated poet of the thirties.

Spender was only twenty-three when he thought 'continually of those who were truly great', and perceived a resemblance between pylons and 'nude, giant girls'. Now seventy-five, he is thoroughly aware that of all the lines he has composed since 1932, none is likely to lodge in the public consciousness as these have. And this is not a realisation he has painfully arrived at in old age: he has surely known it all along. And he has also known that neither of these lines, nor several others that made him famous as a youth, are really valued as 'good lines' – by him, or by anybody else. If anything, they are remembered because they are so strenuously maladroit – and therefore 'of the period'. When Spender published his *Collected Poems* in 1955, he wrote rather poignantly:

> there seemed an obligation to 'own up' to those poems, like *The Pylons* and *The Funeral* which, when they were written, provided a particular label for some of the poetry of the Thirties: an embarrassment to my friends' luggage more even than to my own. It would perhaps be excusable to disclaim these give-aways now; yet when I come to look at them, they seem to me better than many of the poems I have thrown overboard. In any case, they have a slight historic interest, which, I feel, ought to be represented. Another reason for including them might be that since they are here, the reader can see how uncharacteristic they are of most of these poems.

('The Funeral' he has since referred to as 'my worst poem'.) What to do about his early poems and about his early, famed poetic self has been a problem that has dogged Spender for some forty years. His success was unrepeatable; it was the sort of success that is impossible to build on or develop – it was too deeply tied in with the mythic requirements of the day and too anxious, therefore, to gloss over Spender's essential limitations of both language and technique. A fragile lyric promise was trumpeted as 'new' because it had wrapped itself around a few lumps of industrial machinery. Spender needed only to rest his fevered gaze on 'cripples . . . with limbs shaped like questions/in their odd twist' for him to be hailed as an exemplar of 'compassion'. No one was prepared to say that there was something hideously literary and callous in the use of words like 'shaped' and 'odd'. Nor would anyone – not even T.S. Eliot – rebuke this young bard for the often ludicrous self-centredness

34

that unbalances so many of his flame-eyed excursions into World Events. The age demanded that bourgeois intellectuals agonise in public about their torn sense of responsibility: to art, or revolution? Spender was elected to act out this inner drama in his verse. Cooler heads were happy to nod in approval, happy that someone else had got the job. As Harry Pollitt is supposed to have told Spender when the poet pledged his services to the Republicans in Spain: 'Go and get killed, comrade, we need a Byron in the Movement.'

No one would have thought of saying such a thing to Auden, but then – for all his impact – Auden was never touted as the epoch's spiritual glamour-boy, the 'Rupert Brooke of the Depression'. It was sensed, no doubt, that Auden had the resources of talent and technique to go his own way, and let the others follow. Praise of Spender's warmth was very often a way of measuring an unease about Auden's clinical detachment.

Understandably, Spender began to believe his own publicity. By the time he got to Spain, the awkward, flailing spontaneity that gives a weird glow even to the most silly and pretentious of his *Poems* (1933) had stiffened into a mechanical, spokesmanlike sonority:

> Consider his life which was valueless
> In terms of employment, hotel ledgers, news files.
> Consider. One bullet in ten thousand kills a man.
> Ask. Was so much expenditure justified
> On the death of one so young, and so silly,
> Lying under the olive trees, O world, O death?

And beneath the sonority ('O world, O death') is a doomed effort to assimilate an Audenesque note of sibylline authority to the heart-dominated, narcissistic sensibility of Stephen Spender.

By the outbreak of war, Spender's moment had come and gone. Boyish (not to say girlish) self-scrutiny was no longer in demand; debates about the role of the artist now boiled down to which uniform he ought to wear, and prophecies of doom had turned to prayer. Spender made a token effort to join in:

> Why cannot the one good
> Benevolent, feasible
> Final dove, descend?

And the wheat be divided?
And the soldiers sent home?
And the barriers torn down?

And the enemies forgiven?
And there be no retribution?

The poet's by now well-known attachment to the grand poetic flourish no longer had much power to thrill. 'Scalding lead anxiety', 'skies stained with blood', 'The defeated, filled with lead, on the helpless field', and so on: the adjectives were pumped up as before, but with a stunned, defeated air. Spender's instincts were pacifist, he had had a long love-affair with Germany throughout the late-twenties, and his politics had all along been ruled by a sentimental idealism about personal relationships: 'Under wild seas/of chafing despairs/Love's need does not cease'. The beautiful young comrades of his thirties poems had been acceptable to his audience not because they were socialists but because they were standing in for their older brothers, for the beautiful young comrades-in-arms who had been slaughtered a dozen or so years earlier. 'Born of the sun, they travelled a short while toward the sun': it is no accident that Spender's well-known line echoes Laurence Binyon's 'They shall grow not old, as we that are left grow old'.

They went with songs to the battle, they were young,
Straight of limb, true of eye, steady and aglow.
They were staunch to the end against odds uncounted,
They fell with their faces to the foe.

They mingle not with their laughing comrades again
They sit no more at familiar tables of home;
They have no lot in our labour of the day time;
They sleep beyond England's foam.

As the stars that shall be bright when we are dust,
Moving in marches upon the heavenly plain,
As the stars that are starry in the time of our darkness,
To the end, to the end, they remain.

These stanzas (not in sequence) are by Binyon; re-set as free-ish verse, and with a few minor adjustments, they could easily be passed off as by Spender, c1930. In the thirties, Spender's political poems (and maybe his love poems also) were animated by the elegiac passion of a bereft younger brother. By 'June 1940', these same sentiments necessarily seem frayed and effortful. It was all happening again, and no one needed a poet to tell him so:

Afloat on the lawn, the ghostly last war voices
Gaze for a moment through their serge-grey eyes at this;
England chained to the abyss.

Then, wearied unto death, they begin
In disillusioned chorus: 'We shall win!'

But the ghost of one who was young and died
In the cross-fire of two wars, through the faint leaves sighed:
'I am cold as a winter world alone
Voyaging through space without faith or aim
And no Star whose rays point a Cross to believe in,
And an endless, empty need to atone.'

And this, it might be said, is the fag-end of Spender's public inspiration. From now on, the poems that matter are all personal. To me, this is the period of Spender's career, from the mid-forties to the early-fifties, in which his voice becomes both distinctive and controlled. He is still compulsively adjectival, and he persistently overstates, goes on too long, or strains for profundities in a way that undermines the poems' concrete force, but even so there are stretches where some tender and particular preoccupation insists on its own rhetoric and, so to speak, removes it from the author's charge: one thinks of 'Elegy for Margaret' (and especially Section 3) and 'Sirmione Peninsula' – a poem which, unaccountably, Spender now seems to have disowned.

It is in this period that Spender's *Journal* actually begins, although he also prints his written-for-publication diary, *September 1939*, and gives us a four-page account of what happened to him in the war (not very much, although there are some nice anecdotes about the founding of *Horizon* – it almost got called *Sirius*, *Scorpio*, *Equinox* or *Centaur*). The life that is chronicled here is not the Life of a Poet, but the life rather of someone who now and then writes poems. It is also the rather touching tale of someone who is 'in demand' because of the poems he once wrote. Spender never stops feeling that he 'should' be writing poetry, but the obligation is often made to seem like an annoying irritant in his otherwise busy and rewarding daily round:

> I write poetry for some time each day, getting nowhere. The trouble is I'm not sure I want to get anywhere, to finish anything. The pleasure of not having to write for publication, before critics, and so on is so great. Also my aims are so unattainable. It's more the fascination of the impossible than the difficult. Still the poems themselves nag; they want to get finished. But when they are at the stage where I see what they're going to be, I'm disappointed. Also I suffer always from an excess of ideas for things and at the same time a lack of vitally experienced observation.

Spender edits magazines, attends cultural conferences around the world, gives seminars and poetry readings, writes book reviews and essays, sits on committees, advisory boards, prize panels and so on. Accounts of such experience can be wearisome, but one marvels all the same at this author's willingness to let himself in for so many honorary chores:

> Yesterday an even madder day. After the meeting with the Minister of Education, went to the Christian College. Made two speeches. Then was taken to the Arts College where I gave a lecture. Then was taken to a film studio where there was an immense reception – wreaths, bouquets, etc. After this dinner with pale British Council characters, putting up a brave show in the banter with which they chided their Indian guests.

Admittedly, this was in India and far from home. But then Spender is very often far from home. One of this book's most desolating images is of the poet alone in campus lodgings in America, missing his wife and children, neglected by an English faculty that bores him, and re-polishing his lecture on Auden and the Thirties. Now and then he thinks: But I am Stephen Spender. And now and then we murmur in reply: It sounds good, but what does it mean?

For shortish periods Spender does take regular employment. His editorship of *Encounter* lasted for more than a decade before it was revealed that the magazine had all along been funded by the CIA.

He has taken professorships in universities both in England and abroad – and used these steady periods to produce at least two underrated books of criticism: *The Struggle of the Modern* (1963) and *Love–Hate Relations* (1974). There have been intermittent forays into politics. In 1968, Spender's fondness for the young lured him to the Paris barricades to write *The Year of the Young Rebels*, but his position since the war has been a 'god-that-failed' style of liberal anti-communism. He has toiled manfully against political censorship around the world, and has clearly been a valuable, heartening presence in the international community of letters. One warms to him as he treks around his smart, rich American friends trying to drum up backing for *Index on Censorship*.

The smart and the rich are not always approached cap-in-hand. Spender evidently has a weakness for both species and much of his journal is taken up with tiresome lists of who he has had lunch with, or where he's spending his weekends. Screeds of dreary dinner-table chat have to be waded through before one gets to the odd, anecdotal gem. It is often as if Spender believes that the sheer magic of the names will compensate for the slim diary-pickings that these outings tend to yield.

The book's real anecdotal meat is in its literary portraits, and in its portraits of close friends. Cyril Connolly and Christopher Isherwood are affectionately *there* throughout the book, and there are neat (not so affectionate) sketches of Louis MacNeice, Sonia Orwell, Ruthven Todd, Conrad Aiken, Humphrey Jennings and a dozen others. There is also a superb passage on the death of Allen Tate. Altogether, the loose diary genre gives Spender just the scope he needs to demonstrate both his gift for friendship (in addition to the names we've heard of, there are mysterious characters with names like B and D who make regular appearances throughout) and also his oblique, almost clandestine waspishness. More than once the benign mask is allowed to slip, revealing a useful-looking, if rather dainty, pair of fangs.

The book's overshadowing presence, though, is that of Auden: priggish, bossy, selfish, and a bore, if we are to believe Spender's fond account. Auden from time to time turns up at Spender's London home and takes it for granted that the household will instantly revolve around his every whim. And he's not in the least nice about it. Why – or how – Spender put up with him is hard to say, since Auden gives his old friend absolutely nothing in return. When, at one of his American Auden lectures, a student asks Spender if he ever really 'liked' Auden, the question seems unanswerable. Auden, after all, is Auden. At another point, Spender benevolently advances the theory that Auden was irritable because he wished that he'd had children. He would have made an excellent father, Spender pleads, although everything he has said about him suggests quite the opposite. It's a strange relationship – strange from the start – and one feels that Spender still cannot quite bring himself to probe it very deeply.

Certainly, no attempt is made to do so in his 'Auden's Funeral' – the strongest among several poems of reminiscence that appear towards the end of his reissued and revised *Collected Poems*. The revisions are drastic. Spender has once again left intact the well-known anthology pieces – although 'The Funeral' has gone – but elsewhere the surgery is brutal. Homosexual love poems are either toned down, made more laconic (the 'pretty mouths' of boy-whores become the 'guilty mouths'; 'How strangely this sun reminds me of my love' becomes 'How it reminds me of that day') or they are dropped altogether. I can't imagine that many readers will miss pieces like 'Your body is stars whose million glitter here', or strain to remember lines like 'Even whilst I watch him I am remembering/The quick laugh of the wasp-gold eyes', but even so, it *is* the bold awfulness of works like these that give the young Spender some of his distinctiveness. He was, after all, the bard of wide-eyed affirmation in those days and it does seem a bit like cheating when he now edits poems of young hopefulness so as to make them seem merely resigned. Take a poem called 'The Little Coat', included in a section once called 'Love and Separation' but now called simply 'A Separation'. The poem used to end:

> Hold me in that solemn kiss
> Where both our minds have eyes
> Which look beyond this
> Vanishment: and in each other's gaze
> Accept what passes, and believe what stays.

This stanza has now gone, and the poem is made to end with a dismissive shrug towards 'the Springs of yesterday'.

Throughout, Spender seems to be saying 'O, come off it' to his younger self. 'I corrupted his confidence and his sun-like happiness', he used to say. No longer. 'I am the coward of cowards' now reads 'But fear is all I feel'. The fifty-line splurge of pretentiousness called 'Exiles from Their Land, History Their Domicile' is now six lines of off-hand but grown-up wisdom. There is also a political purging – the image of the hot young revolutionaries is severely doused ('Oh comrades, step beautifully from the solid stone' is now 'O comrades, step forth from the stone') and a good deal of period stuff is hacked away (the whole 'Hitler' stanza of 'The Uncreating Chaos' has now disappeared). Even a famous poem like 'Landscape Near an Aerodrome' does not escape the knife: the Church that used to block the sun is now – timorously? – lower-case. Also purged – the unkindest cut of all? – are all grandiloquent references to the poet's own prospects of high immortality.

The urge, Spender says in his introduction, is towards greater clarity, and in many cases the poems *have* been made a little less obscure. On the whole, though, I think most readers will prefer to stick with their *Collected Poems 1955*, and treat this new book as covering the thirty years of Spender's work since then.

1985

STEPHEN SPENDER
Journals 1939–1983, edited by John Goldsmith
Faber

STEPHEN SPENDER
Collected Poems 1928–1985
Faber

Sylvia Plath: 1

It is now almost a quarter of a century since Sylvia Plath killed herself, at the age of thirty. Since her death, there have been several attempts to write her definitive biography, attempts that at some stage or another have run into trouble with those who safeguard the poet's literary estate: her husband, Ted Hughes, and his sister and agent, Olwyn Hughes. Whenever the 'truth about Sylvia Plath' is discussed, you can be fairly sure that sooner or later the Hugheses will be mentioned with disfavour, as if the pair of them were somehow in the business of suppressing vital data. Nobody ever seems very clear about what kind of data this might be; the innuendoes persist, though, and it is hard to imagine what will put a stop to them.

On the face of it, the Hugheses can indeed be described as overcautious, not to say obstructive, in their dealings with those who wish to write Plath's life. It is known that there are Sylvia Plath writings under seal in libraries, not to be seen by anyone until the year 2013. It is also known that Ted Hughes destroyed a notebook that records Plath's most private thinking during the last months of her life ('because,' he says, 'I did not want her children to have to read it'), and that another notebook from 1962 has simply, according to Hughes, 'disappeared'. There is also the draft of what might have been Plath's second novel, 'Double Exposure'; that too is missing.

These disappearances, coupled with what one hears about the strict way the Hugheses have of granting permissions, can easily be made to sound suspicious, as if Ted Hughes were more interested in protecting himself, or some image of himself, than in letting his dead wife be heard. And since there are many admirers of Plath who have already cast Hughes in a villainous role – as the husband who dominated and then wronged her – such suspicions have gained ground over the years. There is a certain glamour in the projected notion of Plath as a woman posthumously victimised, just as (so it is thought by some) she was victimised in life.

It is difficult, with admirers of this sort, to plead for a more balanced view, and this new biography will not, I fear, make it any simpler. Linda Wagner-Martin is herself in favour of more balance, and she has learned enough about the more intimidating aspects of Sylvia Plath's personality to steer clear of any crudely feminist judgements of Ted Hughes. Indeed, in her presentation, the marriage ended because Sylvia Plath expected too much from it. Even so, her book is prefaced with complaints about her dealings with the Plath estate. Hughes, she says, wanted some 15,000 words deleted from her manuscript. Although she made concessions, she did not go along with all the suggested changes, and she has therefore been denied permission to quote at length from Plath's writings.

What were these changes, and why did they matter so much to Hughes (his list of objections, we are told, runs to fifteen pages)? Were his objections self-interested, or did he straightforwardly believe that this biographer had got things wrong? But surely every biographer gets things wrong in the eyes of those who shared the life under discussion. What did Hughes see in this book that made him want to alter it so drastically? If the author had chosen to give us the details of her differences with him, some useful demystification might have been achieved. As it is, we go on wondering.

But wondering what? After all, it is not as if the world were starved of information on the life and private thoughts of this ferociously self-centred writer. We know about her glittering Smith College record, her precocious successes as a writer in her early twenties, her breakdowns and her first suicide attempt, her move to Cambridge, England, where she met and married Hughes – a poet far more self-assured and successful than she was. During the marriage, Plath did her best to be a 'good wife' to a husband she adored, and her own literary ambition, which was huge, took – or pretended to take – second place to his. The explosive poems of 'Ariel' were written after Hughes left her for another woman, and it is because of these poems that we have wanted to know more about her life. But what more can there be to know? We have in print 500 pages of her journals and 350 pages of 'Letters

Home'. We have dozens of memoirs and one or two full-length biographies. And, of course, we have the poetry, which in its later stages is scorchingly autobiographical. There are, to be sure, unpublished letters and large sections of Plath's journals that were not included in the edition co-edited by Hughes. But do these hold secrets that need to be revealed before we can be satisfied that we possess the truth about Sylvia Plath?

Wagner-Martin has been through all this material and is able to give us some facts we didn't have before. None of these seems wildly controversial, and none reflects all that badly on Hughes – nor, come to that, on Plath herself. Wagner-Martin's additions to the record are minor, circumstantial, and to savour them (or, sometimes, even to register that they are indeed additions) we really need to see her book alongside the published journals. One effect of such an exercise is to make the Wagner-Martin text seem thin, impoverished. Even at her most hysterical, Plath has the intelligence and word power to defeat, or outshine, any paraphrase – and Wagner-Martin is not, in any case, the most subtle of reporters. Another effect is to make us wonder if the journals themselves could not have been less timidly prepared for publication.

For example, in the published edition, there are a number of declared omissions, material plucked from the middle of sentences and paragraphs and replaced by tantalising dots. These censorings have, needless to say, given rise to uncharitable speculation. But whenever Wagner-Martin takes it upon herself to fill in these gaps, the result is invariably so tame as to make us wonder why the original omission was ever thought to have been worth the trouble. To take one instance, in the published journal we have this description of Plath's first meeting with Ted Hughes: 'Then he kissed me bang smash on the mouth (omission) . . . And when he kissed my neck I bit him long and hard on the cheek, and when we came out of the room, blood was running down his face. (Omission.) And I screamed in myself, thinking: oh, to gave myself crashing, fighting, to you.'

Wagner-Martin has been to the source, and she transcribes as follows: 'Then he kissed me bang smash on the mouth and ripped my hairband, my red hairband scarf which has weathered the sun and much love, and whose like I shall never find again, and my favourite silver earrings: ha, I shall keep, he barked. And when he

44

kissed my neck I bit him long and hard on the cheek, and when we came out of the room, blood was running down his face.'

We note that the second of the two original omissions is allowed to stand, so we must still remain ignorant of how, precisely, Hughes responded to that bite, but surely the material that *is* filled in need not have been excluded in the first place.

It is this sort of discussion that Wagner-Martin's book is most likely to provoke. As to Sylvia Plath, the picture we already have of her, and of the marriage, remains essentially unaltered, and Ted Hughes's own brief account of his wife's struggle to determine her 'real self' still seems entirely plausible. One of the problems, though, with any biography of this poet is that Hughes himself has never given his version of the marriage. He has spoken abstractly about Plath's personality, and he has been a loving and scrupulous editor of her poetry, even though the best of it is fuelled by an intense anger against him. He has permitted the publication of journals in which his own private conduct is laid bare in a way that he might well have found intolerable in a biography of which *he* was the subject. How much more discomfiture should be required of him? Plath in her last months was in a vengeful mood most of the time, and one can well imagine that there are unpublished writings that, if released, would seem to invite some sort of line-by-line rebuttal by Hughes. Temperamentally, he is as reticent as Plath was effusive, and that reticence surely deserves more respect than it is usually granted.

And yet does one really want more paraphrase of the prohibited material, more guesswork, more sentences like this one (from Wagner-Martin): 'They spent the night at his second-floor flat on Rugby Street in London, reciting poetry, making love, finding their alter ego in each other – rebellious and isolated, strong and erotic and gifted'? Wagner-Martin's style veers between colourful empathising and businesslike terseness ('Summer was slow, relaxed and – for Ted – productive. Everything he wrote was good'), and her book is somewhat unbalanced by her wish to exhibit the fruits of her considerable research. That is to say, if an event is covered by the published journals, she will tend to skimp it, but if it is 'new', it gets more emphasis than it necessarily deserves. This again brings us back to the problem of permissions, and to the thought that the next Sylvia Plath biography will surely have to be one that enjoys the full co-operation of Ted Hughes. In the meantime, there is a question that is too rarely pondered: what would Sylvia Plath have wished to preserve, if she had lived?

1987

LINDA WAGNER-MARTIN
Sylvia Plath, A Biography
New York, Simon & Schuster

Sylvia Plath: 2

Two years ago, an American professor called Linda Wagner-Martin published a biography of Sylvia Plath that was prefaced with complaints about the behaviour of those who safeguard the poet's literary estate: Plath's husband, Ted Hughes, and his sister and agent, Olwyn Hughes. According to Wagner-Martin, the Hugheses, when they saw her manuscript, demanded extensive revisions and excisions: to oblige, she would have had to remove some 15,000 words from her text.

She stood firm. In retaliation the estate refused her permission to quote from Sylvia Plath's writings. Banished into the realm of paraphrase, the biographer did her best to produce a balanced narrative, but the near-absence of Plath's own voice proved a serious disability. A well-researched book came out looking a bit pinched and shifty.

One effect of the Wagner-Martin dispute was to highlight yet again the possessive habits of the Plath estate. Since Plath's suicide in 1963, Ted Hughes has had good reason to feel touchy: the 'Plath legend', as it gained ground over the years, necessarily engendered a 'Hughes legend' – she the victim, he the male oppressor. Several of Plath's most brilliant poems have served to authenticate this version of Hughes. And since Hughes himself is a poet of some celebrity, there has been no shortage of ill-wishers, eager to see the Champ cut down to size. Such commentators have enjoyed pointing out that, after his wife's death, Hughes destroyed the journal that covered her last weeks.

Nobody without a special interest could fail to sympathise with Hughes. If there was an element of vengefulness in Sylvia Plath's suicide, its success has been spectacular. It is now over a quarter of a century since Hughes thought of ending their

47

youthful marriage and here we are, still chewing over its tiniest details.

How much housework did he do? Was he good with the children? Did he really build that kitchen table? Was his study smaller than hers? Why didn't he type his own manuscripts? Did she really take a torch to his complete Shakespeare? So it has been and so it will continue. Sylvia Plath's 'demon self' might have enjoyed the prospect of Hughes's life-long discomfiture; her 'good self' (the self, as she described it, that 'loves skies, hills, ideas, tasty meals, bright colors') would, let us hope, have been appalled.

During these years of innuendo and recrimination, Hughes and his sister have had to function as the executors of Plath's literary estate. There has been the matter of her texts to be attended to – her letters, journals, manuscripts and so on. The Hugheses might defensibly have slapped an embargo on everything except the poet's poems; indeed, some diary material has been so embargoed, until 2013. The overall decision, though, was to go for a policy of staged and monitored publication, releasing a bit here, a bit there. And whenever a would-be biographer came near, the Estate seemed to flex itself for combat.

To the outsider, much of this vigilance appeared excessive (Wagner-Martin, for instance, fills in some of the 'omissions' from Plath's published journals and they turn out to be thoroughly innocuous). The Hugheses too often seemed to be playing into the hands of the suspicious. Hughes himself remained resolutely silent on the matter of his marriage: his only direct involvement with the 'Plath industry', so far as we could tell, was as editor and admirer of her poems. All the rough and tumble was handled by the formidable Olwyn.

And this may well have been a shrewd arrangement. Even so, some of those who wished to defend Hughes against the legend-mongers were now and then drawn also to wish that he would step into the arena. As Wagner-Martin made clear, he has been ready enough privately to tell Plathologists that they have got it wrong. What, in his view, would be the way to get it right?

Around the time of the Wagner-Martin publication, it was made known that at last an 'official' Life was on the way. It would be written by Anne Stevenson, an American-born poet who was a near-contemporary of Plath's and, by all accounts, not someone to be pushed around. The assumption was that Hughes would now give his side of the story and that Stevenson would enjoy the freedom normally granted to authorised biographers. At least this was my assumption: reviewing the Wagner-Martin book in an American paper, I conjectured that the 'next Sylvia Plath biography will surely have to be one that enjoys the full co-operation of Ted Hughes'.

Is *Bitter Fame* that book? Well, yes and no. It certainly enjoys the full guidance of the Plath Estate, and Anne Stevenson has indeed had access to materials and testimonies unavailable to earlier biographers. The chronology of the poet's final weeks is now much clearer than it was before, and we know more than we did about a number of key episodes in her writing life. At her best, Ms Stevenson writes with a controlled excitement and a genuine, if intermittent, sense of fellow feeling. Left to her own devices, she might well have written the Plath biography that we have been waiting for. Unhappily, the whole enterprise seems to have been crippled by interference from outside.

The book's real guiding influence is Olwyn Hughes. So significant is her presence that Stevenson has felt obliged to attach a prefatory note: 'In writing this biography, I have received a great deal of help from Olwyn Hughes, literary agent to the Estate of Sylvia Plath. Ms Hughes's contributions to the text have made it almost a work of dual authorship.' And in a note to this note, she tells us that Olwyn Hughes has added 'texts', 'paragraphs', 'concepts' and 'introductory material' to the discussion of fourteen Plath poems including 'Daddy' and 'Lady Lazarus'. As if this were not curious enough, we are also instructed that the book carries 'additional material by Lucas Myers, Dido Merwin and Richard Murphy' – three essays, or memoirs, which are printed at the book's rear as 'appendices'.

Each of these essays is extensively quoted in the main body of the text; reading them in full adds nothing very much to what we have already gleaned. Myers, Merwin and Murphy are three 'witnesses' among many. Why are their versions given special status? It has to be observed that each of them reveals some unattractive not to say repugnant aspect of Sylvia Plath's personality: each serves to support a view of her as jealous, success-hungry, manipulative, self-obsessed and – in Dido Merwin's venomous contribution – border-line psychotic.

The message is clear: only a man of saintly temperament and of high commitment to the future of Poetry could have lived with this devil-woman for more than 24 hours. Ted Hughes lived with her for several years but in the end even he had to get some air. I think it is true to say that there is no reference to Hughes in *Bitter Fame* that is not thoroughly approving or border-line reverential – and this in spite of the fact that he refused Stevenson an interview and takes 'no responsibility' for the book's account of his dead wife.

Now it may be that a corrective was needed but this seems a weirdly unsubtle method of providing it. With Olwyn Hughes's influence omnipresent, it is hard for us ever to know whose version we are reading – the biographer's or the Estate's. The book's general drift – that Plath was unstable from the outset and that Hughes did everything he could to help her – might well have been Anne Stevenson's final verdict. It might well be ours. Certainly there seems to be plenty of untainted evidence in support of such a view.

But why is the book dominated by testimony from people who had reason to think ill of Plath, or who simply didn't like her very much (both Olwyn Hughes and Dido Merwin are maligned in Plath's journals, and Lucas Myers and Richard Murphy are manifestly Ted's men when it comes to taking sides)? Why do we hear so little from those who were fond of her and who, pre-legend, believed that it was she who had been given a hard time?

In its treatment of the early years, *Bitter Fame* is competent and brisk, perhaps over-brisk (Plath meets Hughes on page 70 of this 400-page book – in 1956; in Wagner-Martin's 250-page account Hughes makes his first appearance half-way through). It is a little too keen to set up the young Plath as suicidally disposed – which she was, but do we need to be nudged whenever symptoms of her 'life-long obsession with suicide' can be discerned? On the whole, though, Stevenson is intelligent and relaxed in this uncontroversial section of the book, and very good on what it was like to be an American girl student in the fifties.

It is post-Hughes that we begin to feel that we, and Plath, are being got at: sniping asides, ill-natured parentheses, over-definite explanations of Plath's 'motivation'. Thus, for example, when Plath toys with the idea of having her mother come to live near her in Devon, we are told: 'Clearly Sylvia, with her long-term future as a writer in mind, was angling for a babysitter as well as a supportive mother (and typist) who would live close at hand.' It's the 'and typist' that sticks out: did not Plath serve as Hughes's typist during their first years together?

Gradually, as the 'evidence' piles up, Plath comes to seem more and more dislikeable, more and more doomed and destructive: a victim, to be sure, but a victim of her own disordered psyche and, in many instances cited at length, a victim of her own petty, mean-minded, attention-grabbing social personality. A nutcase and a bore.

The poems remain undiminished and, to be fair, the book is unequivocal (and often illuminating) in its acceptance of Sylvia Plath's literary genius. But this very acceptance makes it all the more distressing, somehow, when – after a respectful page or two about the Poetry – the biographers return to their main business. Now, it must be wondered, will we ever see a biography of Plath that is not dictated either by feminist dogmatism or by private rage?

1989

ANNE STEVENSON
Bitter Fame
Viking

Damon Runyon

Damon Runyon is famous for shunning the past tense, as in: 'I am
going to take you back a matter of four or five years ago to an
August afternoon . . . On this day I am talking about, the Lemon
Drop Kid is looking for business.' Even when one of his stories
has been told, is over, and he permits his protagonists a little
late-night deconstruction, there is still this unrelenting attachment
to the present. '"Well, Mrs B," he says. "You almost get a good
break when old Doc News drops dead after you stake his wife to
the poison because it looks as if you have her where she can never
wriggle off no matter what she says. But," Ambrose says, "my
friend Mrs News is cute enough to seek my advice and counsel."'
This speech belongs in the past tense, but the author is determined
not to put it there. By this stage in Runyon's career, to have done
so would have brought professional dishonour.

Runyon did not always write this way, but once he had learned
how to, he never – so to speak – looked back. According to one
commentator, there is in Runyon's New York tales 'only one
single instance of a verb in the past tense [and] I will lay six to
five that it is nothing but a misprint'. Jimmy Breslin reckons that
Runyon caught the habit either from Samuel Taylor Coleridge or
from listening to hoodlums testifying evasively at court hearings.
A more likely bet is that he caught it from Ring Lardner, from
whom he picked up several other hard-boiled/soft-centred tricks
of style. The fact is, though, that the ploy does fit snugly with the
kind of stories Runyon liked to tell, stories whose charm insists that
we are not often invited to reflect on origins and consequences. In
Runyon's wide-eyed gangland, everyone talks as if he has been
taken by surprise. A counsel for the defence can usually plead that
his client was obliged to act before he had a chance to think.

In most of Runyon's tales of Broadway low-life in the twenties, the narrator has no past and not much of a present – or perhaps, like his characters, he has more past than he cares to remember and a future that is, to say the least, uncertain. He is a Mr X, and he functions as a warm-up man for the main action. He can be found most nights in Mindy's Restaurant 'putting on the gefillte fish, which is a dish I am very fond of, when in come these three parties from Brooklyn'. The parties have names like Harry the Horse or Nick the Greek or Johnny Uptown and they are mostly small or medium-time bad guys: thieves, extortionists, kidnappers, racketeers or killers. The word 'killer', however, is a word that's never used. These men with funny names also have funny names for what they do. They speak of giving their foes 'a little tattooing', 'a boff over the pimple', or of whipping out 'the old equaliser' in order to aim some 'whangity-whang-whang at Louie the Lug' or at whoever has been foolish enough to make a party feel 'somewhat disturbed' or 'very much excited'. The narrator does not object to such euphemising because equalisers usually equalise each other – well, almost usually. Like the papers say, innocent bystanders can now and then get caught in other people's crossfire. But then, what's innocent about bystanding at a time like this?

This is a question that is never put to Mr X. Although he knows this world, he is not of it. For some reason, though, the Mindy's hoods practically queue up at his table for the chance to bend his ear: 'Maybe you will like to hear the story'; 'It's a very unusual story indeed, and is by no means a lie, and I will be pleased to tell it to someone I think will believe it.' This hunger to narrate is portrayed as common to all gangsters of the epoch. None of them can read or write 'more than somewhat', and none has even a rudimentary knowledge of life outside his little stretch of urban jungle. On politics and geography, for instance, they are particularly weak. In one story, Harry the Horse and friends find themselves at a political party convention and have no idea what is going on; in another, set in wartime, someone wants to know where – indeed *what* – Europe is. But then, as Mr X would have us bear in mind, these outlaws have long ago handed in their right to vote, travel is not permitted by the terms of their parole, all politicians are owned by the very gang bosses who own *them*, and all foreigners seem to be living in New York, so what's the point?

What the hoods do have, thanks to Mr X, is a natural aptitude for speaking Runyonese, a lingo invented to convey the simultaneous workings of a slow brain and a speedy tongue. The vocabulary is alive with colourful demotic but the syntax is stately, uncertain, pseudo-British. It is as if these self-confident slack-mouths suspect that what they are saying might get written down and used in evidence. Maybe this is why they talk to Mr X: they know – as we are not supposed to – that he is actually a hotshot columnist, that he is an associate of Arnold Rothstein, Al Capone and Mayor Walker, that he can get your name in the papers as easily as he can keep it out, that he has clout in places where it matters: in baseball, boxing, the racetrack, City Hall, the Mob. Certainly, this is how Runyon himself liked to be seen – as the invisible string-puller, the shrewd appraiser on the sidelines. 'I am the sedentary champion of the City,' he once said. 'In order to learn anything of importance, I must remain seated. Why I am the best is that I can last an entire day without causing the chair to squeak.'

Mr X likewise does not often squeak his chair. He also wishes to present himself as an all-knowing neutral. But he is shifty too, and timid, and nothing like as grand-mannered as Runyon, his inventor. He is, he tells us more than once, 'a law-abiding citizen at all times' and 'greatly opposed to guys who violate the law', although he also makes it his business to steer clear of the police: 'Personally, I do not care for coppers, but I believe in being courteous to them at all times.' Luckily, the cops usually steer clear of *him*: 'They know there is no more harm in me than in a two-year-old baby.' Mr X is not 'a guy who goes around much', but now and then he is asked to do small favours for the hoods – he runs errands for them, delivers messages, fixes pow-wows between warring parties, and so on. His chief duty down at Mindy's, though, is to sit still and listen while they talk.

Mr X is sometimes reluctant to do this – maybe because most of the hoods' plotlines turn on a contrived misunderstanding or on some implausible offstage machination – but at such moments he reminds himself that cute guys like Izzy Cheesecake and Rusty Charlie are likely to turn not-so-cute if they don't get to tell the tale. So he listens, and we listen with him: as eavesdroppers, we are even less likely than he is to make sniffy moral judgments or offer to help out with the grammar or even to request a bit more detail when it comes to the descriptive stuff. On dolls, especially, the guys tend not to throw away the words. 'I never see such a wide doll. She looks all hammered down.'

We know nothing about Mr X beyond the very little he lets slip. He seems not to have a regular job, and our guess is that he pays for his meals at Mindy's out of his racetrack winnings, or that he has some fringe role in the bootlegging business – he certainly knows all the joints. Unlike the guys he eats with, though, he wants nothing for himself: he is not in pursuit of money, power or women. He is what Damon Runyon, who pursued all three, would now and then have dearly wished to be: an uncommitted ear.

Runyon, though, according to his biography, dearly wished to be all sorts of things. Born in cowboyland (actually his birthplace is Manhattan, Kansas), he was the son of an ill-tempered Indian fighter turned newspaperman, a drinker and a brawler who, when Runyon's mother died, did not take kindly to the business of towing a small boy from bar to bar. Damon thus early on 'acquired a veneer of hardness covering a heart of loneliness'. He tried his hand at writing poetry, he became a bellhop, a jockey, a boy soldier. But it was not long before Daddy turned him into a small replica of Daddy: he taught the boy boozing, whoring, telling lies, and other necessities of frontier-town living. And little Damon learned fast: by the age of fifteen he was a hardbitten newshound on the Pueblo (Colorado) *Chieftain*, covering lynchings without spilling his whisky and discovering how to hero-worship visiting gunmen celebrities like the ludicrous Bat Masterson, on whom Runyon would later base one of his most dreamy-eyed character-confections, 'The Sky' – or Marlon Brando in the film of *Guys and Dolls*.

Sky Masterson is Runyon's fugitive ideal. As a sportswriter, and as a close-up hanger-on of gangsters and tycoons, Runyon was in the business of constructing heroes, but none of the heavyweight boxers he secretly bought shares in, nor any of the bigshot racketeers he took to ball-games and played poker with, would ever shape up to the image of unfettered manliness embodied by the wondrous Sky. Maybe the fact that Runyon's shoe-size was a near-freakish five and a half or that he lived in daily terror of running out of funds meant that he was in the wrong business from the start. Not so – indeed the money he was earning told him otherwise. As long as he was making such big bucks, he could still reach for The Sky – well, couldn't he?

So far as he was able to, Runyon played the glamorous urban cowboy role: he talked tough, he dressed snappily, he mixed with the right wrong people and tried not to let on that for health reasons he had in young manhood been forced to quit the drink; he married above himself, but not too far, treated his wife badly, took a Mexican showgirl for his mistress (and in time his second wife), telling everyone that she was really a Spanish countess, neglected his children and was nice to animals, especially horses that ran fast (although he did keep a pet cockroach for a time; it slept in one of his bedroom slippers and was considered thoroughly trustworthy). Throughout all this, he drilled out several million words of high-class copy for his lord and master, Hearst.

'I never bite the hand that feeds me' was Runyon's motto as a journalist, and over the years he made sure that he never had reason to fall out with Hearst, even during the proprietor's pro-Nazi phase. By the end of the thirties, he was America's most highly paid columnist, and the Broadway stories – of which there were numerous Hollywood adaptations – made him a millionaire. Indeed, his price was about to go through the roof when, in 1946, he died of throat cancer at the age of sixty-two (or thereabouts; he always lied about his age). For the last months of his life he could not speak. But then he never did speak much. His son Damon Junior records, in a 1954 memoir, that when the dying Runyon was angry about some business having been transacted through a third party, 'I replied: "But I understand he was very close to you." His fingers jabbed emphatically at the keys of the typewriter he was using as a voice. He rolled the paper up so I could see what he had written. "No one is close to me. Remember that." '

Damon Jr did as he was told: he remembered, and his memories, although they labour to achieve a note of fondness, are saturated with resentment. Runyon is blamed for the death by drinking of his first wife, the mental instability of his daughter, and the general fouled-upness of his son, Junior himself, who at the time of writing was emerging from a long struggle with the booze. Runyon's own early flight from the bottle seems to have made him pretty good at driving other people to it.

This certainly would be the view of Jimmy Breslin, who suggests also that Runyon's sense of his own superior detachment must have been well nourished by the atmosphere of Prohibition. In those days, when booze was at the heart of everything, the great spectator was on coffee. This is one of several acute but unfriendly assessments in a biography which, on the whole, is something of a mess. Breslin is for ever jazzing up the action with invented – or is it reconstructed? – dialogue:

> There was a poolroom in the basement of the corner building at 95th and Broadway, and the first day Runyon went in there, one of the guys said to him: 'The people in here are all right. Don't go near Tenth Avenue. They got a lot of killers there.'
> 'Where on Tenth Avenue?' he said.
> He began walking. If there are killers, he reasoned, then that means there are also a lot of crap games and, even better, loose dolls. When he got to the corner of Tenth Avenue and 47th Street, he took one look at the guys standing around and wishing mightily for trouble, and at once he felt at home. Baseball was nice, but murder was the main event.

Jimmy Breslin is himself a big-name New York columnist, and he covers the Runyon low-life beat. For him, too, murder is the main event. Like Runyon, he writes with lots of mush and muscle and he prides himself on knowing the Big Apple right down to its rotten core (hence his six-page digressions on subjects like the construction of the city's subway system). He even wrote a novel called *The gang that couldn't shoot straight*. And he shares many of Runyon's attitudes – to high-brows, Columbia University professors, the Algonquin set; and like Runyon, he always has the dope that's inside the inside dope. For instance, Breslin knows for certain that Jack Dempsey had lead in his gloves when he knocked out Jess Willard, he has the actual *name* of the guy who shot Arnold Rothstein, and he was pretty much *in the room* when Bugsy Siegel watched his screen test.

All in all, the example of Damon Runyon must have guided Breslin's career 'no little and quite some'. His biography, however, is far from homage-ful: on the contrary, it reads more like an attempt by Breslin to get Runyon off his back, once and for all. The disciple misses no opportunity to cut the master down to size: Runyon 'believed in writing only for money, even ahead of vengeance'. 'He wanted phrases that would make the reader think only of him.' 'While he pretended that bellhops were his people, he usually situated himself close to the money.' By the end of it,

Runyon's pimple is well boffed, and Breslin rules. Indeed, there really is a tone of exultation in Breslin's account of Runyon's young second wife's affair with the muscleman Primo Carnera. The by-then aged Runyon, who collected dumb heavyweights and saw himself as 'the ultimate Broadway wise guy', was for years in ignorance of the affair, and there was much chortling at his expense in Mindy's, chortling Breslin now rather nastily sits in on. Breslin might retort that Runyon would have done the same for him. But would he? *Damon Runyon: A Life* tells us plenty about Runyon, but it doesn't tell us this.

1992

JIMMY BRESLIN
Damon Runyon: A Life
Hodder

Kingsley Amis's Memoirs

Kingsley Amis has a reputation for not liking other people, but – these so-called *Memoirs* might seem to permit us to enquire – does anyone, *could* anyone, like him? Is Kingers himself, at the end of the day, the sort of bloke you'd want to run into at – well, at the end of the day, at the club, or the pub, or at some crappy dinner party?

On the face of it, no thank you. The faint hope might have been that, in writing directly about himself, the irascible old shag would come over as somewhat, shall we say, cuddlier than his usual public image makes him seem. To any such tender expectations, though, Amis offers here a close-to-gleeful 'In a pig's arse, friend' – i.e., you bastards will get nothing out of me, or not much, and what you do get you won't like.

For starters, he confides, there will be zero in the book about anything that is private to him. Dodgy material of that sort will be restricted to privacies other than his own. He will tell us nothing of real interest about his wives, mistresses or kids (although he chucks Martin the odd walk-on here and there), or about any living loved-ones – a species defined by him as those 'who have emotional claims on me'. He doesn't want to hurt types like these, he says, or hurt them any more than he already has (mind your own business), and he doesn't want to be boring.

He also promises not to tell us how he thought up the plots of his novels, nor to go on about reviews and sales: writer's-life data that nobody, he thinks, wants to know about – and if anybody does, too bad. As it happens, quite a bit of such data does leak through, and we are two or three times referred to page so-and-so of *Stanley and the Women*, or wherever, and he even lets fall the occasional bibliographer's nugget, if you please: for instance, did you, or *Private Eye*, know that Amis's very first piece of published writing was called 'The Sacred Rhino of Uganda'?

Thirdly, there will be a near-embargo on genealogical bullshit, Tony Powell stuff about the ancient Amises of Virginia, USA. We get a grandad with hairs sticking out of his red nose ('how much I disliked and was repelled by him'), a grandma – 'large, dreadful, hairy-faced' – whom he remembers having 'loathed and feared', and an aunt who was, no question, off her head. A few Pritchettian genteel-weirdos are to be chanced upon around the margins of young Kingsley's suburban London childhood, but the general picture of those years is as blurred for us as it evidently is, and maybe was, for him. (And no, we do not get told whose idea it was to call him Kingsley – something to do with Charles of that name, we conjecture, or perhaps it was Henry, C's blacksheep brother, a figure whose curriculum vitae reads very like some of those that Amis has in store for us: pissed all the time, terrific sponger, no good at writing novels, and so on.)

We are, however, vouchsafed a glimpse or two of Amis's mother and father, whom he seems to have quite liked. Too much on them would have meant having to tell us more about a certain adolescent culture-vulture who used to tick his dad off for not liking Brahms, but we do learn that Amis *père* was a pretty good cricketer (possessing 'a late cut I have never seen surpassed') and had a talent for mimicry 'that made him, on his day, one of the funniest men I have ever known'. And Mum? Well, like many another boot-in merchant, Amis does tend to go a bit trembly on the subject of his Mum: 'She was a jolly little woman for all her nerves, and shortness of breath, fond of a giggle, a fag, a gin and tonic (no more than a couple) and, I am sorry to record, an occasional glass of Empire wine, Keystone or Big Tree, for the "iron" in it. But she was more than that. It was that gentle creature who, when I rendered my first wife pregnant before our marriage, told my father not to be such a fool with his threats of excommunication and persuaded my future parents-in-law not to boycott the ceremony as they had been intending – the first of the appallingly long line of figures in my life who I have come to value altogether more highly, to appreciate the uniqueness of, now they are gone.'

The grumpily workmanlike prose style finds it difficult to cope with unaffected warmth. But this is Kingsley on his Mum, choked up; normally, he is careful to avoid such challenges to his composure. As to that 'appallingly long line' of valued and unique associates, it has to be reported that very few of them put in an appearance in this book. They, too, come under 'privacy', no doubt. Altogether, he vows, we will not be hearing much about 'merely good chaps, or fairly good chaps', nor about 'self-restrained' chaps, or 'secretive' chaps.

And fair enough, we have to say: these are *his* memoirs, after all. But what then is left to tell? Luckily, Amis possesses a good memory for anecdotes, or so he says, and he is also not too choosy when it comes to embellishing what he remembers – in this sphere, he would rate himself as 'fairly conscientious'. He has few scruples, either, about putting words into people's mouths – especially dead people's mouths – if it helps to liven up the narrative or lends support to some malign character sketch. 'Of course,' he says, 'I have invented dialogue', and if this means giving himself some of the more trenchant ripostes, the more dignified silences, so be it. There are moments, though, when we would like to know just how much inventing has been done. Did Philip Larkin really say of John Wain: 'No advantage of birth or position or looks or talent – nothing, and look where he is now'? If I was John Wain, I would want to be sure of the exact words. According to Amis, Wain used to think of Larkin as a friend. And Larkin, although he is here said to have groaned when Wain 'invited himself' to stay with him in Hull, is also said (not here) to have refurnished his house in preparation for Wain's visit. Admittedly, this does not mean he was looking forward to the visit, but even so, he did a bit better than just groan, or so it seems.

Another sort of scruple Amis doesn't have is the sort that might have restrained him from recycling bits of writing from the past. These old bits – always acknowledged – do tend to stop us in our chortling tracks: strange, unexamined reminders of an earlier, more solemn Kingsley Amis: 'His hands looked strong and deft, like a precision mechanic's. But his face held the attention. With its clear blue eyes, thin upper lip above delicate teeth, and generally flattish planes, it was both grim and gay, seeming to hold both these qualities at once when in repose and lending itself to swift alternation between the one mood and the other.' Eh? No parody, this is Amis on Yevtushenko, c. 1962. Amis's point in reprinting such blurbese is not, alas, to show us what a prat he used to be but (I think) to persuade us that there was nothing personal about the

Amis/Levin campaign in 1968 to prevent Yevtushenko's election to the Oxford Professorship of Poetry: 'If successful, it' – the election – 'would have installed a trusted ally, if not a total minion, of the Soviet regime in a highly sensitive and influential slot.' The highly sensitive slot, incidentally, went that year to Roy Fuller, who, when asked, declared himself 'absolutely sympathetic to Marxist ideas' and spoke of his 'fundamental belief in the materialist conception of history'. And five years after that, it went to the highly sensitive John Wain, thus prompting Larkin's sneers, cited above. Oxford undergraduates, take note: Sir Kingsley, CBE, Dip. Booker, is perhaps not so honour-laden that he might not, if pressed . . . etc. Just a thought.

We ought not to downplay Kingsley's sense of his own worth – that's for sure. Wounded or ruffled vanity is the trigger for several of the score-settling tales he has to tell. John Wain has not been forgiven for patronising Amis early on, and both Enoch Powell and Roald Dahl might have been rendered more benignly if, when given the chance, they had evinced a surer grasp of Kingsley's stature. When Andrew Sinclair and James Michie are sniped at for being mean, for not picking up the tab, we get the feeling that Amis's ire comes mainly from his not having been treated with sufficient deference. Surely it wasn't just the *money* – and yet maybe it was: they say it takes one tightwad to nail another. And is there not a certain meanness of – um – spirit in making public a chap's way with his wallet? The retribution seems excessive.

But then it often does. Even Amis's famous right-wing politics seem to be standing in for something else, some deeper enmity. Certainly, they have as much to do with loathing the lefty element in our domestic cultural arena as they have with plotting any new world-orders. And his literary judgements seem similarly tainted with a sort of oppositional vigilance, with protecting his own turf. The writers he likes pose little or no threat – Elizabeth Taylor, Elizabeth Bowen, Anthony Powell: either safely senior or safely underrated by the mob. Philip Larkin used to exhibit the same tendency when asked to name *his* lineup: Barbara Pym, Stevie Smith, Betjeman.

Larkin, of course, is the one contemporary to whom Amis is prepared to yield high marks (Robert Conquest, perhaps the most 'all right' of Kingsley's literary cronies, is shunted off into 'light verse'). Larkin is named as Amis's second-favourite poet (Housman is tops, though he might not have stayed tops, we suspect, if Amis had ever sat next to him at Trinity High Table), and as his 'best friend'. Mysteriously, though, the pair of them seem rarely to have met: in thirty years, Larkin never invited Amis up to Hull – not even to look over his new furnishings. The friendship was given its shape and its vocabulary when they were undergraduates and perhaps each of them was nervous about risking too much adult intimacy. It's odd, though, and it prompts the question of how often Amis got to see his other friends. He says that altogether in his life, he has had seven friends.

Amis's memoir of Larkin is affectionate enough. Most of it was written for a book of tributes, when Larkin was alive. There are now a few posthumous additions and they leave a taste – not a nasty taste, but almost. There are the quoted indiscretions, and there are disclosures that put Larkin in a bad or embarrassing light (it seems he was a tightwad, too). And there is also a wish, not obvious, to take the poems down a peg or two. On the subject of Larkin's much-celebrated 'Aubade', Amis is dead right to pick on that dreadful 'think with/link with' rhyme, but he is surely too heartily commonsensical in his summing-up: 'on first reading "Aubade" I should have found a way of telling you that depression among the middle-aged and elderly is common in the early morning and activity disperses it, as you tell us in your last stanza, so if you feel as bad as you say then fucking get up, or if it's too early or something then put the light on and read Dick Francis.' And then what? Sit and wait for it to go away – the feeling, and the poem? Amis believes it was 'fear of failure' that prevented Larkin from persisting in his attempts to be a novelist. 'No poem of Philip's preferred length lays your head on the block in the way any novel does.' Yes, *any* novel.

Behind so much of Amis's jesting, we discern a rigidly straight face, an obscure but powerful thwartedness. He tells us that he has had a lifelong fear of going mad, and we believe him. Maybe if he was not so afraid of sounding like an American poet, he could have told us in this book what sort of mad he has in mind. We do get a description of some hallucinating he once did when he was in hospital – he calls it 'A Peep Around the Twist' – but this chapter is as boring as most dream-writing tends to be, as boring as Amis himself would doubtless find it, were it not about him. I suppose what's really missing is any sense of Amis as a plausible character in his own narrative. Without wanting him to get stuck into a stretch of fearless self-analysis, we would quite like him to tell us what he thinks is wrong with *him*.

As it is, all the drunks drink more than he does, or can't handle what they drink as well as he can. All the narcissists and time-servers push themselves and try to get ahead, as he does not. All the talent is either wasted early or absent in the first place – not true of his own. To which he might retort: but that's what being a writer of fiction is all about – you get to be in charge, you get to lay *their* heads on the block. Instead of presence, we get authorial persona, by the yard: Amis the observer, the interlocutor, the recollector, the top judge, consistently projected as the shag who got things right that other shags kept getting wrong. And as the shag, moreover, who's been given precious little credit for his efforts, since you ask. Well, actually, we *didn't* ask, but still . . . good God, is that the time? One for the road? We'll pay.

1991

KINGSLEY AMIS
Memoirs
Hutchinson

Evelyn and Auberon

When Evelyn Waugh died in 1966, his son Auberon felt that a 'great brooding presence' had been lifted 'not only from the house but from the whole of existence'. Auberon was in his twenties then, and – as he tells it in his book of memoirs – he had long ago got used to living in the shadow of his famously unpleasant dad. 'It was many years before I could break the habit of viewing every event with half an eye to the bulletin I would send to my father.' 'The strain of living two lives, one on my own, and the other through his eyes, was greatly relieved by his sudden death.'

Indeed he was a most loyally imitative son – and remained so, long after the lifting of the presence. He wrote satirical novels and became a 'grinding snob'. He attended Roman Catholic church services until Cardinal Hume turned them into 'kindergarten assemblies' which would be 'completely unrecognisable' to Evelyn. He secured a commission in his father's regiment and then, as if in some post-Waugh comic fiction, peppered himself with bullets from his own bren gun. He married well and learned to write sneeringly about the working classes. He served time as a downmarket Fleet Street dandy and as an indignant country squire. He went to Africa, he lost hair, trod on toes, and made no secret of one or two ignoble yearnings. 'An ancient name, a stately home and a couple of thousand acres' would, we understand, have had a calming influence on Evelyn. So, too, with the son.

Auberon believes, or so he says, that one of his father's great missions in life was to 'make jokes, to turn the world upside down and laugh at it, to enrich and enliven this vale of tears with a little fantasy'. He also says he believes that the old man's fabled rudeness was no more than the nervous exasperation of an artist whose audience rarely understood what he was up to. Evelyn's

65

great fear was 'incomprehension': 'It was this, more than anything else, which he dreaded, and which made him shun strangers with a rudeness which never failed to make people gasp. "Why do you expect me to talk to this boring pig?" he would suddenly shout at his hostess about some fellow guest. "He is common, he is ignorant and he is stupid, and he thinks Picasso is an important artist."' This story is told fondly by a son who now boasts of himself: 'Looking back over my career and at all the people I have insulted, I am mildly surprised that I am allowed to exist.'

Unhappily, it was also Evelyn's fear of not being comprehendingly admired that caused him so often to rebuff his children's efforts to impress him. Auberon in particular was given the cold shoulder, being treated from infancy with a mixture of indifference and contempt. Although Evelyn's 'desire for a son and heir could not have been stronger if he had been a reigning prince', there was evidently something about the tiny Bron, when he appeared, that fell seriously short of the ideal. The boy was swiftly reckoned to be 'sly, without intellectual, aesthetic or spiritual merit', he was 'mindless and obsessed with social success', a sort of 'defective adult . . . sadly boring'.

Auberon was about seven years old when these character assessments were mailed to Evelyn's friends, but the verdicts were not significantly softened with the passing years – indeed, the older Bron got, the more harshly he was likely to be judged. In his teens, he is said to be a 'queer, morose boy, sloping round the woods with a gun alone and playing light opera on his gramophone'. He gets into scrapes and miniature rebellions, but it takes just a few unforgiving words from father to get him back on track: 'Don't write in that silly tone . . . You have made a mess of things . . . You must help yourself.' And there was never any point – it should perhaps be said – in Auberon running to his mum. Her tenderness, he claims, was reserved for her small herd of cows: 'She loved them extravagantly, as other women love their dogs or, so I have been told, their children.'

What he really wanted was to be patted on the head by pater. So far as we can tell, he never was. His mordant first novel was found to be needlessly offensive to the monks of Downside, its success entirely 'undeserved'. Even his near-death in the Army aroused no more than a flicker of paternal interest. From a bed of pain in Cyprus, Auberon wrote Evelyn 'a maudlin, deeply embarrassing letter telling him how much I admired him'. The letter was intended to be read 'in the event of my pre-decease'. Even as Bron penned it, though, Evelyn was telling Diana Cooper that he had no plans to fly out to his stricken son – unless the boy died, of course, in which event he might feel obliged to put in an appearance. The only marks Auberon managed to win from the whole uncomfortable episode were for having been observed 'quietly speaking the *De Profundis* in his extremity'.

Evelyn, of course, liked to be seen as having a brusque way with the emotions and – as we can deduce from the entertaining *Mr Wu and Mrs Stitch* – he would not have wished the likes of Diana Cooper to think of him as boringly tethered by fatherhood. He would also not have wished his lady-friend's attention to be distracted from his own interesting personal development. Even so, it does seem that his dislike of young Auberon was genuine. ('I think I must have been a difficult child to like,' says the obliging Bron. And here, too, he was just like dad. In *A Little Learning*, Evelyn recalls with some satisfaction 'the dislike in which I was held' in early childhood.) When Bron told 'the august creator of my being' that he, Evelyn, was about to become a grandfather, the response was challengingly gnomic: 'I hope the coming year will find you the father of a son as worthy of your devotion as you have been of mine.' Auberon explains: 'I do not think, as others may decide, that the . . . sentence was intended ironically. Or at any rate, not very ironically. It certainly was not intended as an embittered father's curse.'

Well, he should know – except that, on the matter of his dad, Auberon Waugh is not the most confident of explicators. He would probably wish now to be able to write about Evelyn with the same ease of condescension that he brings to other subjects, but whenever he does try to shuffle free of the intimidating presence ('from that moment, I never treated anything he had to say on faith and morals very seriously'), we know that some counterbalancing obeisance will follow.

The overbearing presence of Evelyn perhaps explains the curious lopsidedness of Auberon's account of his 'First Fifty Years'. The pre-1966 material is rendered with an unusual care for detail. Episodes from infancy and adolescence are recalled with no more than the odd glint of affectation. And the prose in these early sections of the book is more workmanlike than in those which deal with Waugh's own career as a prose-writer, where there is much repetition and clumsiness ('he was not someone with whom I ever established an instant rapport').

Now and again, in the first hundred or so pages, we are in the presence of a genuine investigator of the past; later on, we are gradually introduced to the smirking columnist, the reminiscer; by the end, it is all *Private Eye* buffoonery and gossip. Since Auberon on Evelyn comes under Biography, there isn't, on this subject, the usual scope for jaunty fibs. But Auberon's filial respectfulness goes deeper than any nervousness about being rumbled by Waugh Studies. Even as a grown-up memoirist, he is incapable of being truly Bron-ish so long as – in his narrative – the remembered Evelyn still lives. To have written too saucily of family matters up to the year 1966 might have been to tempt terrible reprisals.

With Evelyn dead, Bron was both released and at a loss. He was gripped by two warring impulses: emulation and escape. Free to become himself, what self should he become? There was still a chance, he at first seems to have thought, that he might turn out to be a novelist with gifts of his own. He published five novels, and then stopped. It was not that the books were rubbish; indeed Bron is at pains to let us know which of them got good reviews or was chosen as a Book of the Year by *Books and Bookmen*. It was just that 'any success which I might enjoy would always be attributed to the fact that my name had already been made famous in literary circles'. There would from him be no 'corpus of beautifully polished writing as a permanent memorial to his genius' (which is how he describes his father's work). How painful the repudiation was we do not learn, but we can guess.

For a time, in the late-sixties, Auberon thought of setting up as a straight-faced man of conscience, and we can measure the absurdity of this ambition by the amount of fuss he still makes over his one flirtation with a Cause. Writing of his efforts on behalf of the Biafrans, he almost brings a tear to the eye – his eye. One of his children, he says, is named Nathaniel Thomas Biafra. Should he have persevered along this high road? He would like us to think that he could have if he'd wished. The Biafran adventure he now presents as formatively souring: 'I think it had a profound effect, convincing me not only of the fatuity of politics – I was already more than half convinced of that – but also of the wickedness of politicians.'

Auberon would now say that his career peaked in the late-seventies, with the Diary he kept for *Private Eye*. 'However ephemeral it is bound to prove, I suspect it will remain my proudest achievement.' Certainly, it was pretty funny at the time, but there is something rather ludicrous in the way he dredges up a string of ancient *Eye* vendettas as if they had been to do with fighting a good fight. More than once, he swells into the cadences of an old general reliving world-altering campaigns: 'The enemies we made were worth making, the battles we fought were worth fighting. I am happy and proud to have been given the chance to serve beside him.'

The comrade-in-arms here is Richard Ingrams, with whom Waugh is now serving on a new journal called the *Oldie*. Ingrams, we learn from a recent interview, also has a father-problem. He told Lynn Barber that 'he could not have worked for *Private Eye* if his father had been alive, because "he would have been so disapproving"'. *Private Eye* humour has often enough been called schoolboyish, and so it is, but perhaps we are close here to discovering its source: a fear of father, or at any rate a need to remain within a dread father's imagined zone of jurisdiction. The fogey aspect of the *Eye* is thus meant to appease the father's wrath; the urchin ingredient is what can be got away with when the old brute isn't looking.

Commercially, it has been a winning formula, having an appeal both to nose-thumbing student types and to reactionary buffers from the shires. The young could be made to feel superior, the old to feel mischievous. Not bad. And for Auberon it was the perfect platform: he could be like his father after all – rude, bigoted, irascible and so on – but in short trousers. If Evelyn were watching, he would see not a grown-up hack journalist but a still-errant schoolboy, the Auberon of whom he wrote (in 1946): 'I have tried him drunk and I have tried him sober.'

Perhaps *Private Eye* served a similar function for the Ingrams psyche. We know little of his father. According to Lynn Barber, Leonard St Clair Ingrams was 'a freelance banker' whose doings are 'shrouded in exotic mystery'. Leonard may or may not have been a great athlete, a fascist and a spy – 'I don't know if he was pro-German or pretending to be pro-German,' Ingrams says. He may even have been put in a novel by Jean Cocteau, 'as the archetype of the dashing English gentleman'. Whatever he was, he died at the age of fifty-three, and Ingrams 'has just passed that age himself'. It has been observed that when a son gets to be older than his dead father ever was, strange things can happen to him. He might buy a house, get married or go gay. He is likely to feel that he has finally 'come into his own': he has no senior. Ingrams has chosen to celebrate his self-ownership by founding a magazine for fifty-three year olds. He resigned some years ago from *Private Eye* because he felt that 'he was losing his grip. He was very tired.' The *Oldie* is aimed at a readership which might have some understanding of this malaise.

Certainly, the magazine seems mightily fatigued. The routine *Spectator* and *Eye* names are there, but wearily, the layout seems to have been borrowed from friends and there has clearly been a how-to-get-the-space-filled difficulty – note the full-page photograph of Lord Deedes of Accrington, seventy-eight, and another of the front door of Kelmscott Manor. And much of the writing needs an early night. Kelmscott is 'a hard place to leave, for it is one of the most peaceful houses I have ever been in, but you can always linger on the way back and look at the Ernest Gimson cottage built for May Morris, William's daughter, in 1915, and the memorial cottages designed by Philip Webb for Mrs Morris in 1902 . . . The village hall was also designed by Ernest Gimson, and is well worth a glance.' Which brochure was this lifted from, we have to ask, and why was Germaine Greer's climactic paragraph not instantly redirected to Pseuds Corner?

> The sunlight has turned faintly rose. A pallid moon like a broken plate is sidling up the sky behind the rags of thinning cloud. The night will be very, very cold. I am so full of joy that I am almost afraid to move in case I spill some.

The *Oldie* pretends to hate the young, but – like *Private Eye* – it actually sucks up to them. Freddie Mercury, Madonna, Heavy Metal and the like are given the expected dressing-down but with a knowing wink: we may be oldies but we're not really out of touch, and nor are you. The Heavy Metal piece, for instance, could only be struggled through by someone who wanted to know, or already knew, the difference between Chuck Shuldiner of Death and Glen Benton of Deicide. There are some nice ideas – an oldies' video column and a 'Still with us' feature about people who we think are dead: but even these have the feeling of a one-off joke, a dummy rather than a magazine that's built to last. Unlike the former editor of *Private Eye*, I am inclined to welcome new periodicals and to hope that they survive. Of this one, though, I'll settle for hoping that it does not die any sooner than it wants to.

1992

AUBERON WAUGH
Will this do?
Century

Oldie. No. 1
Edited by Richard Ingrams

The DNB

On the dustjacket of the latest supplement to the *Dictionary of National Biography* there are photographs of David Niven, Diana Dors, Eric Morecambe, John Betjeman and William Walton. Dors has a leering 'Come up and read me sometime' expression on her face and Niven wears his yacht-club greeter's smile. Morecambe seems to be laughing at one of his own jokes. Amiable images, devised no doubt to lure us into a placidly elegiac mood: death can't be all that bad if it gets you an entry in the *DNB*. But what's the matter with Betjeman and Walton? They look glum and sulky, as if they've been put in the wrong graveyard by mistake.

At a glance, the new supplement (covering the years 1981–5) does seem to be offering itself as something other than librarians have learned to expect, perhaps taking too literally its first editor's charitable dictum: 'It is not upon the lives of great men that the book really depends. It is the second-rate people that provide the really useful reading.' OUP's colourful packaging hints at a sexy, debonair new mix, with tits and Brylcreem replacing the dog-collar and the flared side-burns of bygone days. But dustjackets rarely gather dust and when you throw away the wrapping, all is actually well: the *DNB*'s dignity has not been seriously interfered with. Bishops are still preferred to businessmen, cricketers are still posher than footballers and lengthy military service rates more highly than the sort of thing Dors and Niven used to do. The book still means to satisfy the nation's 'commemorative instinct' but it also wishes to promote along the way some image of the ideal Briton: he who combines self-reliance with a sense of public service.

Of course, in order to prove that your self-reliance is genuinely tough-fibred and that your sense of public service is not just some youthfully liberal flash-in-the-pan, you have to live to a great age. Fifty year olds with blood-pressure difficulties might scan the *DNB*'s roll-call of eminents with divided feelings: although it is cheering to note that for most of the dictionary's entrants, the age of fifty marks Stage Two in a nobly envisaged Five-Stage masterplan, it is depressing to be taught how long, how very long you have to live in order to rack up these near-superman C.V.s.

In the forty–sixty age group, there is but a handful of entrants and these have mostly earned their place by compiling points in relatively vulgar, early-burn-out professions like publishing or pop singing. And even the sixty–seventy grouping carries a faintly sleazy air: poets, comedians, psychiatrists and the like. It is only when we pass the age of seventy that the entrants begin to look as if they've really earned their keep. For one thing, they've been in the war. Even if they didn't actually fight, they performed wonders of crypto-analysis at Bletchley or they blue-printed some devastating weapon. And if they then went into politics, or returned to the diplomatic, they had bags of time in which to serve with exemplary facelessness as second secretaries, or under-secretaries or Ministers of State. At moments, their chief achievement can seem to have been that they somehow got out of being dead. There are as many ninety–hundreds in the *DNB* as there are sixty–seventies, and although seventy–eighty is by far the largest grouping, the eighty–nineties run it a fair second.

It has been complained in the past that the *DNB*, for all its love of private enterprise, has been niggardly in its homage to non-establishment achievers, and maybe the Dors–Niven ploy is meant to be seen as an egalitarian riposte. In this latest supplement (the first to cover a five-year instead of the customary ten-year span), the scientists comfortably outnumber the politicians and parsons; and businessmen are in fact neck and neck with civil servants. The 'media' are now beginning to offer up a few candidates and we find as many entrants from Film/TV/Radio as from the armed services: in ten years' time, admirals will almost certainly have been replaced by anchormen. As it is, fashion designers are close to outstripping the doctors and the lawyers. And it is presumably significant that only one entrant owns enough land to be described simply as 'landowner'. And, sure enough, the attitude to showbiz triumph *is* surprisingly relaxed: even Billy Fury, whose sole gift was that he looked a bit like Elvis Presley, rates a respectful (if lamely written) entry – perhaps in his case an early death worked in his favour.

Women still seem to be getting a raw deal, with only about 10 per cent of the entries, but this percentage is up on previous supplements and although one talks idly of raw deals it is hard to think of a woman who has been wrongly overlooked. I'm sure someone will be able to. The women who do get in tend to be from the arts or from the new-ish social sciences – 'educationist' is a formulation that's used more than once.

Another routine complaint against the *DNB* is that its editors seem to encourage a blandness or stuffiness in their contributors, and that this tendency is helped along by their clinging to old formulas – like insisting on naming a chap's wife's father's job: 'Jackson was married first in 1956 to Sheila Mannion. She was the daughter of John Henry Mannion, unskilled employee of the Gas Board.' It does seem a bit rough on John Henry that he should for ever be remembered as 'unskilled'. We learn of John le Mesurier's three wives that they were daughters of, respectively, a theatre manager, a test pilot and the manager of 'a Ramsgate funfair'. Why does it matter that the funfair was in Ramsgate? We might brood on such details in the hope of discovering some deep obsessive pattern, or the surreptitiously down-turning graph of a career, but of course we know that information of this sort is thoroughly superfluous – a relic, presumably, of the days when a man's shrewdness could be measured by the calibre of his wife's family. For some, the practice adds to the book's charm. For others, it's an irritating affectation. (John le Mesurier, incidentally, appears to have sustained his mock-lugubrious demeanour to the end: on the day of his death an announcement appeared in *The Times* that: 'John le Mesurier wishes it to be known that he conked out on 15 November. He sadly misses family and friends.')

A good test of the *DNB*'s supposed stuffiness is to check out its attitude to wickedness. There used to be a policy of excluding 'sinners' from the 'biographic fold' but, needless to say, it has not been enforced with any rigour. With luck, the entrant will have done a bit of non-sinning in his time, so that, when we are given the whole picture, he can be judged to have gone off the rails. In the present volume, however, it is hard to believe that John Bodkin Adams would have won a slot as a medical practitioner. Indeed, the Adams entry is something of a puzzle. He was acquitted of the murders he is famous for having been accused of, but his *DNB* biographer evidently believes that he was lucky to get off: 'The seams of the Crown's case had started to come apart, and worse was to follow . . . The defence, perhaps wisely, decided not to put the talkative Adams into the witness box.' Is this trial by *DNB*, or do we now know for certain that Adams was guilty? And if we don't, why does he get an entry?

Wickedness, in the case of Anthony Blunt, actually pays off rather handsomely. He gets a four-column entry against the average two, and it is unlikely that this would have been his lot had he been listed merely as 'art historian' and not also as 'a communist spy'. (Donald MacLean, we note, gets less space but is made to sound a little more respectable: his profession is described as 'Soviet spy'.) As it turns out, Blunt's biographer so admires the art historian that he wishes to deal kindly with the spy: thus much of the space that was surely earned by Blunt's espionage is devoted to praising his work as director of the Courtauld Institute: ' . . . a superb director . . . natural authority . . . infectious enthusiasm . . . winning way with students . . . inspired those around him' etc. The spy business was unfortunate, but surely a lot of the agitation against Blunt after his unmasking was prompted by 'class hatred'. The *DNB*'s compassionate and superficial (or compassionately superficial) summing up of Blunt's delinquency might be thought of as his final triumph: 'More immediately, his career can perhaps best be explained by the fatal conjunction in him of his own outstanding gifts and his desire to be at once part of the establishment and against it; or, as an acquaintance put it, "The real trouble with Anthony was that he wanted both to run with the hare and hunt with the hounds."'

In the case of both Blunt and MacLean there is no mincing of words on the question of their homosexuality. On Blunt, it is conjectured that 'at a time when homosexual acts were still illegal in Britain, he seems to have relished the resulting atmosphere of secrecy and intrigue'. Of MacLean we learn that, when head of Chancery in Cairo in the late-forties, he was 'subjected to psychiatric examination for his homosexuality and alcoholism'. It was only when the Foreign Office believed that 'he had recovered' (from *both* ailments?) that they sent him off to his new job in America – where of course he was better placed to pick up secrets than he would have been in Cairo. This career-move is almost as hard to fathom as the one that was arranged for Beverley Nichols: 'While attached to the War Office, his unconventional and indiscreet sex life caused consternation and he was hastily transferred to Cambridge to instruct officer cadets in military strategy.' In the case of Nichols ('He was unmarried') we are allowed some scope for speculation on the matter of his sexual bias and thus there is scope also for some old-style innuendo. When Nichols arrived in Cambridge we learn that:

> Here he was befriended by (Sir) A.E. Shipley (q.v.), vice-chancellor of the university, and was seconded to him as aide-de-camp when he headed the Universities Mission which toured America for the last three months of 1918. Nichols, strikingly handsome in uniforms of his own design, was hailed as a war hero and acted the part with aplomb and charm. Such was his success that he extended his stay in New York for two weeks to cope with social engagements.

This sort of cattiness, if such it is, does not show through too often in the *DNB*. Most contributors are anxious to say the best that can be said, and as a result there is a fair amount of automatic writing: so-and-so's 'deep personal integrity was founded upon his staunch Presbyterianism' and someone-else was 'a very private person with a profound belief in Christian values and the family as the bases of civilized life'. But this is not to say that there is any general reluctance to tick off the dead. Dick Emery was 'a talent sadly unfulfilled', George Brown's career was 'hampered' by 'his explosive temperament, often aggravated by alcohol', Enid Bagnold was 'too fond of the great and the grand to be taken seriously by the literary establishment' and Nigel Birch deserves to be 'remembered for his insistence on retaining the trees in Park Lane when it was widened'.

Sometimes the choice of contributors can seem cosier than it might have been: Ned Sherrin on Caryl Brahms, for example, or Hugh Johnson on his publisher, James Mitchell: '*The World Atlas of Wine*,' Johnson writes, 'became the most discussed and most imitated reference book of the seventies among rival publishers. By the end of the decade it had sold one million copies.' It is also noticeable that ordinarily quite lively writers are not at their most sparky when working for the *DNB*: Geoffrey Wheatcroft on Shiva Naipaul, for instance, or Richard Ingrams on Claud Cockburn (although Ingrams has taken the trouble, it seems, to check through

The Times's files in search of that famous Cockburn headline: 'Small Earthquake in Chile. Not Many Dead.' Unsurprisingly, it wasn't there). Strange that these *Private Eye* types should be hired by the fact-revering *DNB* – and yet not so strange: after all, the *DNB*'s idea of Englishness is in some aspects perfectly in line with *Private Eye*'s. And it is not quite true to say that the *DNB* has muzzled the young buffers. Auberon Waugh's piece on his Uncle Alec has at least one genuinely comic paragraph:

> After this success, in the opinion of his brother Evelyn, Alec Waugh never drew another sober breath, but this was an exaggeration. He lived for much of the year in Tangier, Morocco, where an old-age pension from the State of New York enabled him to equip a house with cook, butler and houseboy; at other times, he lived austerely as writer-in-residence at a mid-western university, eating his meals from divided, plastic plates in a room above the students' canteen, and emerging from time to time to entertain his friends in London at elegant dinner parties, where he wore immaculately tailored but increasingly eccentric suits.

The comedy here is in what is left unsaid, or unexplained. In this sense the paragraph typifies what is perhaps the *DNB*'s chief pleasure: it leaves us to divine the 'real story' that may or may not lurk behind its polite graveside presentations. With the best-known entrants, we will very likely have – or soon be getting – some other, more unbuttoned narrative. For others, though, the *DNB*'s biography may well be the last word. We are thus left to fill out our own versions of the journalist who 'alleviated' his sleepless nights by 'naming an XI of lefthanded clergy in first-class cricket', or the 'devout' Roman Catholic medievalist whose 'first marriage to an Oxford pupil was annulled in 1949', or the Cathedral organist who discovers that he may be going blind:

> . . . playing some difficult Bach at the end of a service, he suddenly found himself unable to see the printed page. Immediately he decided to retire from the great position he had held so long. He also had such an attachment to W.R. Matthews, with whom he had collaborated for thirty-one years, that he did not want to continue after Matthews' retirement from the deanery. He took a

flat near Westminster Abbey which he attended regularly. Weak sight robbed him of the earlier pleasure of reading Victorian novels, and railway timetables, on which he was remarkably expert. (He loved to plan imaginary cross-country journeys with *Bradshaw*.)

And, it might be added, he lived on for another fifteen years. Surely there is somewhere a neo-Victorian novelist who can imagine for us the 'whole truth' about Sir John Dykes Bower. Or is it already written, in the *DNB*?

1990

LORD BLAKE AND C.S. NICHOLS (Editors)
The Dictionary of National Biography, 1981–1985
OUP

PART II

POETS AND POETRY

Robert Frost

Perhaps the chief difficulty in talking about Robert Frost, both for those who talked about him in his lifetime and for those who talk about him now, is the difficulty of separating the poetry from the public personality. During his lifetime Frost was the nearest thing to a 'national' poet that America possessed. His virtues and his wisdom were applauded as representatively, and hearteningly, Yankee – distilled from the soil, his poems spoke of rural labour, of dignified self-reliance, of shrewd, practical and yet respectful dealings with a nature he both loved and hated. They were also, much of the time, unblushingly conservative and patriotic. And better still, they seemed to *talk*; talk in a natural no-nonsense way – a more or less ordinary man talking to more or less ordinary men. Throughout his life, Frost assiduously cultivated this portrayal of himself as the lovable, plain-dealing New England farmer-poet. In hundreds of personal appearances, interviews and poetry readings, he did nothing to disappoint expectations of this sort. Here, for example, are two press cuttings he might well have enjoyed poring over:

> Robert Frost is a poet whose work and personal appearances have moved thousands of Americans to a demonstrativeness that might easily be associated with the presence of a heroic athlete or movie star. When he says his poems . . . it is to standing room only audiences. And the response is based not on superficial idolatry but on a deep set and affection-ate admiration often bordering on awe . . . the impact of Robert Frost on poetry and those who love poetry is possibly less than his impact as a personality on anyone who gets near him . . . he is like no statesman, celebrity or ordinary

human being . . . Robert Frost is quietly but unmistakably overwhelming.

This was written when Frost was eighty-four, four years before President Kennedy sent him to visit Russia as an ambassador of Yankee straightforwardness. Over forty years earlier, though, Frost's personality was being praised in much the same drowsily ecstatic terms:

> Mr Frost has windblown cheeks and clear blue eyes. Yankee of Yankees and glad of it . . . Fresh from his farm on Sugar Hill, Franconia, New Hampshire, where Mt Lafayette towers and the Old Man of the Mountains frowns, Mr Frost is paying his first visit to Philadelphia. Quite recently he's been ski-ing over rugged country, tapping maple trees, and shaping up new poems.

And this for the whole of his career was the way America liked to see Frost and the way Frost wanted to be seen. It was a faultlessly sustained performance.

Needless to say, it was not a performance that everyone enjoyed; there were quite a few dissenting voices, particularly from fellow poets, and not all of them motivated by pure envy. The feeling was that far from doing poetry a service by peddling his rustic charm and by bowing to the patriotic plaudits, Frost was in fact selling poetry disastrously short. Here is a typical expression of that view – by Malcolm Cowley, writing in 1944:

> We have lately been watching the growth in this country of a narrow nationalism that has spread from politics into literature (although its literary adherents are usually not political isolationists). They demand, however, that American literature should be affirmative, optimistic, uncritical and 'truly of this nation'. They have been looking round for a poet to exalt: and Frost, through no fault of his own (but chiefly through the weaker qualities of his work) has been adopted as their symbol. Some of the honours heaped upon him are less poetic than political. He is being praised too often and with too great vehemence by people who don't like poetry. And the result is that his honours shed very little of their lustre on other poets, who in turn feel none of the pride in his

achievement that a battalion feels, for example, when one of its officers is cited for outstanding services. Instead, Frost is depicted by his admirers as a sort of Sunday school paragon, a saint among miserable sinners. His common sense and strict Americanism are used as an excuse for berating and belittling other poets, who have supposedly fallen into the sins of pessimism, obscurity, obscenity and yielding to foreign influences . . .

These two ways of viewing Frost remained fairly constantly in evidence throughout his career – on the one hand, the popular idol, on the other the object of suspicion and some bitterness in the eyes of the highbrow-radical literary world, a world dominated during the period in which Cowley was writing by the ideals of complexity and abstruse wit inherited from T.S. Eliot and encouraged by the New Criticism. Frost, the New Critics could see, was more of a modernist than his popular reputation would allow him to admit, and they resented him for getting, finally, the best of both worlds.

Since Frost's death in 1963, there has been no effective alteration in this balance of opinion – not, at any rate, until two years ago when the second volume of the Frost biography appeared. The author, Lawrance Thompson, was Frost's own appointee, the 'official' choice to write the definitive life, and he had spent many years in Frost's company, apparently as a close friend, during the latter stages of the poet's life. The biography, however, when it appeared – and there is still a third volume to come – turned out to be not the pious tribute that might have been expected, but an elaborate and apparently vindictive essay in character-assassination. Frost emerged from Thompson's pages as anything but the sunny and lovable New England sage of popular legend. On the contrary he was presented as vain, morose, hypocritical and treacherous; as an opportunistic careerist who was prepared to lie, cheat and wound in order to win yet another crumb of adulation. When Frost had a new book coming out, we are told, he deliberately set out to ingratiate himself with prospective reviewers and influential editors; when prizes were in the offing he would make sure that he was on good terms with the jury; when a rival poet seemed to be making ground, he would attempt to impede his progress by a campaign of furtive vilification; when he scented the imminent power of a possibly hostile critic, he would neutralise the threat by making friends with him. All this, of course, went on in private; in the foreground Frost was busily maintaining his air of innocence.

Although one comes away from Thompson's book disliking Thompson rather more than one dislikes Frost, it is none the less a damaging indictment. It is too early to say what the effects of it will be on Frost's popular standing in America but one thing is immediately clear: it will never again be possible for him to be viewed in quite the old way. And this, it seems to me, is all to the good – if Frost's popular following does fall away, as in large part it surely must, this will remove a major obstacle from the path of his genuine, and informed, admirers. It will also make it possible for the poetry to be got at in a new, uncluttered way, much more directly and sympathetically.

And if that happens, then one obvious point about the poetry will emerge more clearly than it has hitherto been able to. It will be seen, in other words, that however devious and self-promoting Frost was in his life, there *never was*, at bottom, anything very lovable about the appearance he makes in his own poems. Even his supposed virtues, the virtues that have been so widely thought to be endearing, are really much more negative than positive. They each have their harsh, misanthropic centre; they are almost always less to do with giving than with taking away. Lionel Trilling once caused a minor scandal by turning a speech of tribute to Frost's eighty-fifth birthday into an examination of what he called the 'terrifying' quality of the best of Frost's work, the utterly uncomforting and resolute sense of futility that much of it bears. He was thought to have behaved disgracefully, insulting the dear old man like that, and of course there has been a long, unthinking conspiracy among Frost's admirers to shut away what even they must have seen to be the essential desperation of much of even his most amiable work.

But before taking a look at what Frost's emotional universe centred on, it is important that one takes into account the stratagems employed by the poet to, as it were, negate his own negations. It is important, that is, to ask what his poetic, as distinct from his personal, charm amounted to. A lot of this charm, it will be readily agreed, has to do with Frost's famous speaking voice. The effort for a truly natural speech, a language of common men, is of course an ancient and rarely successful one. Frost was more successful than most; and at a less propitious time than that enjoyed by earlier contenders. Most of Frost's colloquial rhythms came to him intuitively during the long years of obscurity and neglect that preceded his discovery in England (Frost was in his forties before he won any real reputation as a poet), but his first book, *A Boy's Will*, is full of stiff, literary artificialities – the effort is *for* colloquialism, but at this stage he clearly didn't know how to mould either vocabulary or metre to his purposes. His contact with the English scene at a time when the whole of traditional poetic practice was being called in question – principally by the Imagists but also, in their more cautious way, by the Georgian group which Frost was most involved with – this contact could only have encouraged and focused his ambition for a relaxed naturalness of delivery. What is crucial, though, is that Frost took neither of the obvious or fashionable paths towards this naturalness – neither the path of free verse (for him, he once said, writing free verse would be like playing tennis with the net down) nor the other path of simply dropping in extra syllables here and there or removing them here and there, in order to oil the works of a basically mechanical traditionalism. The challenge he set himself was to risk admitting into a traditional framework what one might call the superfluities of talk – the hesitations, qualifications, repetitions, false starts, parentheses, and so on. His aim was to admit these whilst at the same time maintaining the regularised dignity of metrical speech. He put it this way:

> The living part of a poem is the intonation entangled somehow in the syntax, idiom and meaning of a sentence. It is only there for those who have heard it previously in conversation. It is not for us in any Greek or Latin poem because our ears have not been filled with the tones of Greek and Roman talk. It is the most volatile and at the same time important part of poetry. It goes and the language becomes a dead language and the poetry dead poetry. With it go the accents, the stresses, the delays that are not the property of vowels and syllables but that are shifted at will with the sense. Vowels have length, there is no denying. But the accent of sense supersedes all other accents, overrides and sweeps it away.

There is no question but that much of Frost's charm derives from, quite simply, his over-exploitation of this procedure. It's often as if, having learned to talk naturally, he couldn't stop talking. Some of his long narratives and dialogues are precisely as prolix and tediously self-indulgent as real speech tends to be. But the spectacle of a man jawing on, as if at his own fireside of a winter's evening, and pretending to no degree of intellectualisation or compression or literary artifice – this, and Frost certainly didn't spare himself in his efforts for such cosiness, was irresistible:

> He fell at Gettysburg or Fredericksburg.
> I ought to know – it makes a difference which:
> Fredericksburg isn't Gettysburg, of course.
> But what I'm getting to is how forsaken
> A little cottage this has always seemed . . .

The message seems to be that you can always trust a man who lets you catch him thinking aloud. There are of course huge tracts of Frost's work as irritatingly and wastefully 'colloquial' as this, and they become all the more irritating as, in his late poems, he begins dealing in craggy wisdom. But one can see, and respond to, the appeal. And one can see also that Frost needed this prolixity, this confidence in his freedom to ramble on, in order to achieve the triumphs of concentrated and subtle naturalness that one finds in the best of his shorter poems. 'Birches' is a famous example. Here Frost achieves the extraordinarily difficult task of both mounting the scene, pictorialising it in vivid and exact detail, and at the same time convincing us that he is – *at this moment* – pursuing a complex and precarious course of feeling, a course of feeling which we can observe shifting and developing as the local drama unfolds. What sustains the tension is the poem's achieved state of presentness, and this is made convincing by the authenticity of Frost's spoken rhythms:

> So was I once myself a swinger of birches.
> And so I dream of going back to be.
> It's when I'm weary of considerations,
> And life is too much like a pathless wood
> Where your face burns and tickles with the cobwebs
> Broken across it, and one eye is weeping
> From a twig's having lashed across it open.
> I'd like to get away from earth awhile

And then come back to it and begin over.
May no fate wilfully misunderstand me
And half grant what I wish and snatch me away
Not to return. Earth's the right place for love:
I don't know where it's likely to go better.
I'd like to go by climbing a birch tree,
And climb black branches up a snow-white trunk
Toward heaven, till the tree could bear no more,
But dipped its top and set me down again.
That would be good both going and coming back.
One could do worse than be a swinger of birches.

In these, the poem's concluding lines, one notices in particular the finely calculated balancing of the elevatedly poetic with the low-colloquial. The flatness of 'And then come back to it and begin over' is subtly redeemed by the loftiness of 'May no fate wilfully misunderstand me'. One notices also – and this crops up time and again in Frost's work – his ability to hit on natural or familiar turns of phrase which are in fact regular iambic pentameter – in these lines he is able to use his strict iambics to keep a check on the looser lines, but such is his knack that the iambic lines tend to be among the most natural, the most loose-sounding, in the poem – 'And so I dream of going back to be', 'I'd like to get away from earth awhile', 'And life is too much like a pathless wood', and so on.

The best-known lines in 'Birches': 'One could do worse than be a swinger of birches', 'Earth's the right place for love: I don't know where it's likely to go better', usefully illustrate another important ingredient of Frost's charm – his use of the aphorism, and in particular the aphorism that speaks of a resigned cheerfulness, or a cheerful resignation. Frost is a master of the stoic shrug, the rugged settling for what there is, however less than perfect. Behind this resignation there are in fact deep areas of fear and despair, but only intermittently are these allowed to show through. Frost uses his social manner, his maintaining of a brave face, as a defence against the real meanings (should one choose to follow those meanings right through) of many of his more popular, calendar-bound, aphorisms. Of course, as with his colloquial habit, the habit of nuggety wisdom was a seductive one and Frost was encouraged to indulge it. There is a determined eagerness to charm in lines like:

The melancholy of having to count souls
Where they grow fewer and fewer every year
Is extreme when they shrink to none at all.
It must be I want life to go on living.

or:

If one by one we counted people out
For the least sin, it wouldn't take us long
To get so we had no one left to live with.
For to be social is to be forgiving.

The point in each of these cases is excruciatingly banal and cheaply consolatory. At a more sophisticated level, though, one has a poem like 'The Road Not Taken' – a poem much-celebrated but one which seems to me to make a pretence of doing the bold things it says it's doing; a poem which is ultimately more concerned to be winning than disturbing. The poem's charm is in *seeming* to have engaged with a huge and central problem, the problem of moral choice. But the issues we are presented with are so vague and arbitrary that we are allowed to luxuriate in the delusion that we have actually been made to ponder them. The air of lostness, of irretrievable error that hangs over the poem is a beguiling means of disguising its essentially inert bleakness. To Frost, it doesn't seem to matter much which road he took, or didn't take. It is that indifference which should have been the real subject of the poem.

Much more compelling and infinitely more genuine is this poem's rival in celebrity, 'Stopping by Woods on a Snowy Evening', where the hesitation, the confrontation of the choice, is neither laboured nor inflated but on the contrary is sensitively dramatised in its own slight, fleeting terms. The woods *are* inviting – as death is, or escape is – but the hesitation is momentary; it pretends to be nothing more. And the enormously skilful ending, with the repetition of the last two lines catching the suddenly onward-going, duty-directed, hoofbeats of the horse, is again of precisely the right emotional and philosophic weight. The poem has embodied a faint, awesome, intimation.

The rather picturesque horse of 'Stopping by Woods' gave Frost a few moments' worry but it is, for me, an unusually acceptable member of the poet's often rather twee and cosy bestiary. Frost's gentle way with animals is another feature of his charm. At his best, as in 'The Bear' and 'Two Meets Two', he is very good at catching the mutual, suspicious tentativeness with which animals encounter each other, and these chance meetings are made to carry with them, and in them, a sense of the mystery, the alien and tempting menace of nature as a whole. But here as always, Frost was prone to vulgarise and over-sell one of his best gifts. Thus one comes across the picture-book anthropomorphism of, say, the frogs in 'Pea Brush' or, worse still, the bird in 'The Wood-pile':

> A small bird flew before me. He was careful
> To put a tree between us when he lighted,
> And say no word to tell me who he was
> Who was so foolish as to think what *he* thought.

Having given at least a few reasons for Frost's popular appeal, the most important factor remains – and this has to do with the poet's promotion of himself – in his work – as an embodiment of a lost or threatened rural dream. Sceptics have been quick to point out that Frost only spent five years of his life actually working on the land, and his treacherous biographer has gone to some lengths to establish that Frost was never much good at farming anyway. But it doesn't seem to me that this is a very fruitful, or just, line of assault. The fact is that Frost did know what he was talking about when he talked of country matters – and his poetry is almost exclusively country-based. What *may* be said against him is that he made a bit too much of this knowledge, that there is an element of dressing up in dungarees about his work. Certainly it is the case that, although his poems mount much of their appeal on the illusion that here is a countryman talking to other countrymen, they are in fact aimed at an audience which is of the town. And for the townee, Frost's poems are marvellously full of helpful detail, both of country lore and also of the practicalities of farm labour. The sheer amount of detail rather gives the game away. To go back to 'Birches' – to the first half this time – one finds this:

> Soon the sun's warmth makes them shed crystal shells
> Shattering and avalanching on the snow crust –

Such heaps of broken glass to sweep away
You'd think the inner dome of heaven had fallen.
They are dragged to the withered bracken by the load,
And they seem not to break; though once they are bowed
So low for long, they never right themselves:

It all gets to sound rather like a farm-training manual after a time, but the point is that there is nothing here – in terms of information – that even the most part-time countryman wouldn't know about. And nor is there much edge of excitement or visual beauty in the description – the lines hope to succeed by virtue of their useful factuality, their revelations about an alien mode of existence. Many of Frost's poems are full of lengthy, discursive slabs of pure informativeness – there is often nothing he likes more than wandering off into a chatty parenthesis about how this or that is fixed, how this or that tree or animal behaves. All of it music, of course, to the sluggish, guilty ears of urban America.

If these are some, at least, of the reasons for Frost's popularity, they are also some of the ingredients of his genuine excellence – I hope I've made my belief clear that the bad things in Frost are usually vulgarizations of the good. But this excellence had other aspects too – and very often the reverse side of Frost's charm was altogether uncharming. For example, Frost was popularly admired for his promotion of ideals of separateness, of self-reliance. Many of his nature poems concern the intrusion of one natural phenomenon upon another, and many of his lyric and dramatic poems present situations in which withdrawal, separation, standoffishness, are positively recommended. At his best, Frost's doctrines of self-reliance shaded into very moving confrontations of solitude, of alienation, of a low-spirited sense of exclusion, settling for tough, short-term objectives. Many of the poems in which Frost was truly and desolately himself are those which inhabit, stoically, a friendless realm.

The people along the sand
All turn and look one way.
They turn their back on the land.
They look at the sea all day.

As long as it takes to pass
A ship keeps raising its hull;
The wetter ground like glass
Reflects a standing gull.

The land may vary more;
But wherever the truth may be –
The water comes ashore,
And the people look at the sea.

They cannot look out far.
They cannot look in deep.
But when was that ever a bar
To any watch they keep?

It is difficult to imagine anything more terminally desolate than that. And yet the strain, the edginess, the intelligence of the poem derive really from a whole-hearted resistance to the terminal – a yearning for the conditions to be otherwise. And in some of Frost's finest poems about barriers and separations this wish is always formidably, futilely, present. But there are other poems in which something else, something more sinister, can be detected – indeed, cannot be ignored. I don't mean simply those right-wing poems of his later years in which he could complacently write:

I have none of the tenderer-than-thou
Collectivistic regimenting love
With which the modern world is being swept

nor those crude aphorisms in which he stated his philosophy to be 'Keep off each other and keep each other off'. The poems I'm thinking of are those, equally brutal in their way, but not in the least complacent, in which Frost faces – self-scrutinisingly – the point at which self-reliance is indistinguishable from self-centredness, from simple misanthropy. Typical of this strain is the dramatic poem, 'Out, Out –' in which a boy suffers from a bad sawmill accident. Frost describes the accident as follows:

His sister stood beside them in her apron
To tell them 'Supper.' At the word, the saw,
As if to prove saws knew what supper meant
Leaped out at the boy's hand, or seemed to leap . . .

91

The boy's death is recounted in similarly chilling terms:

> They listened at his heart.
> Little – less – nothing! – and that ended it.
> No more to build on there. And they, since they
> Were not the one dead, turned to their affairs.

There is a nerveless, anaesthetised cynicism here that one can only believe to be calculated and – in a subtle, disguising but revealing, sense – self-examining. It appears in almost equally bald form in poems like 'The Vanished Red' and 'The Self-Seeker'. In each of these the deliberate callousness, the anti-charm, is – Frost being Frost – of real importance, but there are other poems in which the poet allows matters to get even nearer home. Perhaps the most typical of these is the long work 'Home Burial'. This poem is, we now know, central to Frost's work because it is one of the very few directly autobiographical poems he wrote. Its subject is the death of a child. The mother, years after the child's death, is still in mourning and obscurely resents her husband having got over the whole thing so quickly. Frost's own first child died and his own wife was plagued with resentments and frustrations as a result. One might expect the poem, then, to be defensive or apologetic or at worst petulantly complaining. It is none of these things – unless one chooses to see the husband's resolute unfeelingness and self-involvement as constituting a very oblique kind of apologia. The fact is that throughout Frost's poems, women's fears and insecurities are treated with a fair amount of manly impatience – and 'Home Burial' wilfully carries that impatience to the point of a totally damaging blindness and insensitivity. We are never quite sure that Frost, having consciously and convincingly created this insensitivity, is at all interested in judging it. And yet he is the reverse of blind or insensitive to its *presence*.

And here is perhaps the most interesting of all the Frostian paradoxes: wholly alive to the ugly, unloving elements in his own nature, he now and then depicted these elements with maximum accuracy, without any self-forgiving glossing over or (what might have been more forgiving still) moralistic condemnation. Elsewhere, however, there is the spectacle of this same ugliness and unlovingness being transmuted into what have been applauded as courageous strengths. If one regards Frost's separatist doctrines as genuinely believed, and one has to, then a rather knotty conclusion tends to emerge: that Frost knew his own failings, knew what the world would think of them if it found out, and yet believed the world was wrong. Not only believed it, but devoted a whole career to proving it – in secret.

1973

Robert Graves

Robert Graves is in many ways the most British of poets, but Britain has never fully warmed to him. In spite of his stoutly traditional metres and his gruff military demeanour, Graves has always been thought of as a bit unsound. It is not just that he chooses to live on a Spanish island, or that he has been thoroughly beastly about Auden. Nor is it simply a hangover from the thirties when he and Laura Riding used to mount almost weekly guerrilla strikes against the bosses of the British poetry scene. No, the real suspicion is that throughout a rather well-constructed literary career, Graves has carried with him a faint whiff of the bogus. His famous intransigence and aloofness have often seemed to have their roots in an eager-to-be-wounded vanity. His White Goddess theories (although hugely popular with hard-line feminists) are mad enough to be seen as a pious concealment of pensionable lusts. And his dictums on the subject of inspiration (he believes that poets can only write decently if they are in a state of trance) have sometimes looked like the wish fulfilment of a poet whose most 'passionate' work is essentially cold-hearted and literary.

In Britain, Graves's reputation reached its peak in the early- to mid-sixties. This was a period when there was much head-scratching about the destiny of modernism. It was quite common in those days for poets to be told that they must trace their bloodlines back to Eliot and Pound or risk being written off as insular, reactionary, tame. In response to this (and to the Anglo-Americanism that went with it), a number of British poets began looking for an alternative ancestry, for an unbroken native line that – brushing aside modernism on the way – connected the 'traditional' virtues of the stronger Georgians with the metrical common sense of recent figures like Philip Larkin and Kingsley Amis. Graves, as probably the only bona fide Georgian still practising, was thought by such patriots to exemplify a sturdy British self-reliance. (It was forgotten that he would once have seen himself as a key if lonely modernist, and that he had done much to push the work of e.e. cummings and Gertrude Stein.)

A disciple of Graves, James Reeves, put together a *Penguin Book of Georgian Verse*, which aimed to show that it was not all tea and muffins on those sunlit lawns, and a resurgence of interest in the poets of the First World War (1964–1968 being the fiftieth anniversary) made much of Wilfred Owen's very 'modern' use of assonance. Captain Graves, the old soldier and author of *Goodbye to All That*, was for a time promoted to the rank of Major Poet.

Since the sixties, Graves seems to have slowly drifted back to the marginal/eccentric niche that he had occupied since the days of Laura Riding, although he still does have his ardent champions. (Graves's champions, it must be said, have always been ardent, not to say bellicose.)

In 1975, Graves stopped writing altogether. Instead, he began devoting his time to long chats with Martin Seymour-Smith. Seymour-Smith is a Graves acolyte of long standing (since ca. 1943) and, in the effortful debunkery of his own critical writing, has aped many of his master's attitudes and mannerisms. Not surprisingly, this biography leans heavily on its subject's interpretation of the way things were. Seymour-Smith is sometimes rough with Graves, in the manner of an exasperated friend, but he invariably gives him the benefit of the doubt in matters of importance, and is utterly unshakable in his admiration for his work. Seymour-Smith regards Graves as 'the foremost English-language love poet of this century – and probably of the two preceding ones, too'.

Love poet. The category is insisted on by Seymour-Smith throughout, as is the 'foremost' and the 'of this century'. The insistence seems politic, since Seymour-Smith has some fairly unpleasant things to reveal about the love poet's conduct in the field. His book begins with this uncompromising diagnosis:

One of the keys to Graves's personality, and therefore to his poetry, lies in the fact that he is in a continual state of terror; he relieved this, challenged it, by an increasingly sophisticated romanticism – but a romanticism that is wilfully designed to punish him for his pride, which prevents his loving wholly . . .

According to Seymour-Smith, Graves's 'continual state of terror' began (where else?) at his English public school. The boy Graves, it seems, was a fearful prude and prig. From his German mother he had inherited a moralistic, cautious streak; from his father, an element of Celtic turbulence. At first the mother's influence prevailed and the virtuous young R. von Ranke Graves was to be seen in fierce pursuit of 'purity', of flesh-transcending moral excellence. This was not, alas, a posture all that easy to maintain in English public schools in 1910, and before long Graves found himself sneaking shy glances at one of his more comely fellow students.

The two were soon firm friends, in the *Boys' Own Paper* manner. Nothing 'happened', but for Graves that was not the point: the seeker after purity had discovered in himself the worm of sexual guilt. He became, says Seymour-Smith, 'convinced that underlying his idealisation of Dick there was desire. His notion that this desire existed hurt his immense pride. It was a terrible bogey in the ever-fearful back of his mind.' And it remained so, for the next sixty years of Graves's life. From these first stirrings, the Graves story develops into a saga of sexual timidity – a saga with ingredients both comic and sad, and always with Graves in the role of abject swain – ready and willing to be trampled on by the Strong Woman he could never quite be worthy of.

Seymour-Smith does much brooding on the Dick incident (as Graves himself does in *Goodbye to All That*). We learn that after Graves had left school to join the army, Dick became involved in a minor homosexual scandal. When Graves heard of this, he was appalled: if Dick was queer, did it not follow that Graves, who had harboured a pure but powerful love for him, must be similarly afflicted? Seymour-Smith would have us regard Graves's nervousness with women as having to do with his deep fear that he really preferred men. Of course, he didn't prefer men; Seymour-Smith somehow contrives to be quite certain on this point. But we should never forget that he was frightened that he might.

Graves's first marriage was to Nancy Nicholson, who was something of a pioneering feminist, it seems. Graves met her while he was still serving in the army; indeed, while he was recovering from wounds and shell shock. Nancy, however, was not impressed by her new husband's scars. She 'would tell him that his experiences in war were as nothing compared to the general sufferings of women at the hands of men'. Although Martin Seymour-Smith believes that Nancy was 'not, perhaps, a very interesting person', it is unlikely that he would have dared to say this to her face. As a sex warrior, she was about fifty years ahead of her time and thus of extreme 'interest' to the guilt-ridden Graves. She loathed her wedding service, she refused to take her husband's name, and she 'maintained an attitude of constant fury at the way men behaved, both at an international and a personal level – and she warned her husband that he would have to be "careful" in the way he spoke of women'. Graves was happy to oblige, and his biographer has no difficulty in relating this compliance to the poet's lingering Dick-trauma (if one might so put it): 'Her unquiet nature and propensity to criticise was something that Graves was no doubt unconsciously seeking out.'

Graves himself has described his early married life with Nancy in *Goodbye to All That*: he glumly records there that 'although my love for Nancy made me respect her views', it often seemed a bit unfair that he should be included in her tirades against men:

> . . . male stupidity and callousness became such an obsession with her that she began to include me in her universal condemnation of men. Soon she could not bear a newspaper in the house, for fear of reading some paragraph that would horrify her – about the necessity of keeping up the population; or about women's limited intelligence; or about the shameless, flat-chested modern girl; or anything at all about women written by clergymen.

Graves was by this time a 'mature student' at Oxford University, living on Boars Hill with a Georgian anthology of neighbours: Robert Bridges, John Masefield, Edmund Blunden, and Robert Nichols. He had published one book of verse and was working on another. With Nancy's shrewishness gathering strength, Graves toiled in both life and art to fathom the true 'meaning of lust'. Although he and Nancy had four children between 1919 and 1925 their marriage did not permit much scope for passion.

Seymour-Smith describes the poet's predicament at this point in breezy biographese:

The only eventuality upon which he did not then reckon was that his exploration of the meaning of lust would have, for a considerable period, to be conducted in the absence of the exercise of it.

In Seymour-Smith's diagnosis, Graves would probably have put up with this state of affairs if Nancy had been a truly tyrannical She-Goddess. Her feminism, though, was essentially 'milk-and-water', 'mannered rather than powerful'. Graves, it is made clear, yearned for sharper humiliations, and in 1926 his dreams came true.

Graves had for some time been corresponding with the American poet Laura Riding Gottschalk. Riding was connected with the Fugitive group of poets, and had for a time enjoyed the gentlemanly encouragement of Allen Tate (who, gentleman to the last, spoke of her fifty years later as 'All right from the neck down'; 'Unforgivable terseness,' comments Seymour-Smith). She was quick to accept Graves's suggestion that she might some time visit him in England. She didn't just visit him; she moved in. Riding arrived in England on 2 January 1926, just as Graves and his family were about to set off for Cairo, where Graves had taken a professorial appointment. When the Graves's ship set sail on 9 January, Riding was on it – and already, it appears, one of the family.

A Trinity had been formed, with Robert and Nancy brought closer together (or, simply, made less irritable) by their joint regard for Riding. How all this was accomplished Seymour-Smith does not say, and Graves's own amusing account of his short stay in Egypt (in *Goodbye to All That*) makes no reference to his new friend. At first Riding's compatibility with Graves extended beyond literary criticism (they shared a simple, Gertrude Stein-ish view of this discipline – 'the way to say it is to say it' – and they also believed themselves to be the first on earth 'to take a truly psychological approach to poetry'). They became lovers, with Nancy's approval. At first, Riding managed to keep Graves happy 'on the physical plane . . . without cutting him off from his needed unhappiness (that is, from his natural puritanism and delicacy about sex)'.

Although, as Seymour-Smith confides, Graves's 'erotic performances towards her' were soon 'undermined by his insistence on
her superiority to him', there does seem to have been a stretch of
several months in which Riding, at any rate, was prepared to make
do with simple adoration. The pair launched themselves as a literary
team: they co-authored pamphlets, they set up a printing press, they
wrote letters to the papers. On poetic matters they spoke always
with a single voice, haughty and self-advancing. Riding's repeated
question was, 'When will man grow up . . . become woman?' and
Graves seems to have spent many a long hour trying to come up
with the correct answer:

> Neither Graves nor she desired to undergo a sex change; that was
> not what she meant at the time. What she meant was that she
> would initiate a programme of the education of men – starting
> with Graves.

On returning from Egypt, Graves and Riding set up house in
Hammersmith (Graves's bedroom was Riding's workroom, we
are told) and Nancy and the children were installed in a houseboat
on the Thames nearby. The 'strange Trinity of friendship and love'
seems to have functioned for a time – Nancy genuinely admired the
fierce Riding, she no longer had to cope with Graves's timorous
sexuality, and she was involved in a wonderfully 'modern' arrangement which had already achieved the status of a small scandal:
the Hammersmith set-up was known as Free Love Corner. The
whole thing came under strain, though, with the appearance of
one Geoffrey Phibbs, an Anglo-Irish poetaster of 'unstable' yet
(some thought) 'demonic' character. Phibbs had written to Graves
that 'Laura Riding's work has been getting more important for me
thru the last six months.' Riding was intrigued by the prospect of a
new disciple. She ordered Graves to 'recruit' Phibbs, but to warn
him in advance that if he truly wished to become her devotee he
would have to learn to 'shed' a great deal of his current self. It is a
sad picture, Graves the procurer, but Seymour-Smith does his best
to dignify it:

> Graves carried out his task conscientiously but felt unhappy
> about forcing himself to conceal the contempt he could not help

feeling for Phibbs as soon as he met him. But he indulged in his best hopes and wishes, as unfortunately he always does, and did his best.

Phibbs was recruited; the Trinity became the Four. That is to say, Graves and Nancy became Riding's helpmates as she set about 're-educating' Phibbs. Graves was detailed to instruct Phibbs in the ways Riding should be loved. He seems not to have done too good a job. Phibbs, although he was beguiled by Riding's wordy passion, had no wish to be eaten alive. He kept running away; and when he did, Graves would be dispatched to bring him back. Throughout all this, there was constant Riding-directed debate on how Phibbs might be made to see the light. It was never admitted that Riding was in a state of high infatuation, that Phibbs was terrified, that Graves was jealous. One simply didn't talk that way to Laura Riding. The discussion was all to do with 'instructing' Phibbs on the principles of good and evil, with the search for a 'finality' (one of Riding's favourite, never explained terms), with escape from 'the tyranny of time', of 'the annihilation of matter', and so on. This was a Laura Riding enterprise; no aspect of it could be short on cosmic weight.

The climax of the Phibbs episode has been variously described over the years, and variously distorted. Seymour-Smith has laboured hard and well to set the record straight. In his account, the climax comes when Phibbs announces his determination to make a final break with Riding. This bold move was treated by Riding as a matter of high policy, and she convened a special meeting of the Four. As Graves later recorded: 'The Four talked nearly all night trying to help him [Phibbs] to come to a clear decision, his reasons for staying away being uncertain and contradictory.' Phibbs, though, would not be budged, even though the Trinity kept at him until 9 a.m. the following morning. Seymour-Smith records the outcome:

At about 9 a.m. Phibbs repeated that he wanted no more of Riding, that he preferred Nancy and would go with her. Riding drank Lysol, but it had no effect. While Graves, Nancy and Phibbs watched, she said, 'Goodbye, chaps!' and jumped from the window. Graves and Nancy were horrified. Phibbs took to his heels without waiting to find out whether she was dead or alive.

Riding had dived from a fourth-floor window. Graves, ever conscious of his rank, jumped after her from the floor below. Nancy shrewdly decided to sit this one out. Riding's spine was broken, Graves escaped unhurt; the Trinity, however, had finally come down to earth, and nothing was quite the same again. Graves nursed Riding back to health, carried a few more messages to Phibbs, and told Nancy that he wanted a real separation. Nancy took up with Phibbs. After a few months, there seems to have been a mutual, exhausted agreement that the comedy was done. In October 1929, Graves and Riding left England and settled in Majorca – where Graves has lived ever since. [Graves died in 1985].

The Phibbs affair has some moments of grand farce: it offers us high minds refusing to recognise low deeds, the bungling, humourless theatricality of intellectuals-at-play. By comparison, the next ten years of Graves's life with Riding were sheer drudgery. The couple resumed their literary and financial partnership, but sexually the 'marriage' was quite dead. The battered Riding had decided that 'bodies have had their day', and of Graves she commented: 'No doubt his mind has its brutal lapses; they are not important, only psychologically interesting.'

Graves's task in Majorca was two-fold. He was to write potboilers for money, and he was to advance Riding's international career as a poet. *Goodbye to All That*, Graves's marvellously lucid, weary memoir of his life up to 1929, had made some money, and he was encouraged to believe that he could finance poetry with prose. (Eventually, he could and did.) He could also finance Riding, who was keen to set up a Majorcan 'community' – a gathering of disciples who would ponder with her the 'fundamental relation which has to be made . . . between the male mind and the female mind'. Applicants would have been well advised to note that 'in this judgement the female mind is the judge, and the male mind the subject of judgement . . .'.

As to her career as a poet, Graves genuinely believed that she had a talent superior to his own. She was a magician, a dispeller of darkness, and – through her – the 'truth' would be 'uncovered'. According to Seymour-Smith, Riding's own belief that her verse would have world-altering significance, if understood, had carried her to 'the very edge of sanity'. Visitors to Majorca during these years would depict Graves as being 'like a small boy dancing attendance on a rich aunt of uncertain temper'. He was treated 'like a dog'.

Yet Graves kept a tough-guy image in the literary world during the thirties. Few of Graves's fellow poets escaped his lash. Dylan Thomas was a 'Welsh demagogic masturbator who failed to pay his bills', Auden (whom Graves often accused of borrowing from Riding) was 'the kind of man who borrowed a flat for the weekend and then left it in a filthy mess'. Notice in each case the voice of the tidy-minded house-husband. The most telling example of feebleness masquerading as high moral strength comes in an exchange Graves had with W.B. Yeats concerning Yeats's *Oxford Book of Modern Verse*. Yeats wrote to Graves asking permission to include four poems in the anthology – and, as a cordial afterthought, suggested that he might visit Graves in Majorca later in the year. Graves wrote back that he was 'rather surprised' by Yeats's request. Surely he and Laura Riding had made their views clear on the subject of anthologies?

> I do not know whether a letter from you to Laura Riding is on the way from some forwarding address. But if so, the answer for both of us, your anthology being what it seems to be (from the indication of those four poems of mine and from the absence of any awareness in you that we do not lend ourselves to any but cooperative activities), would have to be, I think, No.

As to Yeats's proposed visit . . . well, one can imagine the doggy hopefulness with which Graves proposed to Riding that he (they?) should make the following reply:

> We are both very watchful in our relations, whether in literature or in neighbour-ship: never casual, and least of all here in Majorca where we live permanently in hard-working privacy. With the many foreigners who visit the island we have, as a rule, nothing to do – unless they are friends of ours, who come here purposely to see us. Certainly we like to get to know people and especially those with whom there may be something in common; but we

102

are not sure what there might be in common between you and L.R. (someone in a press-cutting a few months ago said that you and she had learned things from each other – but certainly L.R. does not go about 'learning' from people) and between you and me; and we hate the mere literary-name fraternising – but perhaps you feel the same about that.

The Riding–Graves Majorca partnership lasted for ten years, and Seymour-Smith offers no evidence that the balance of power was ever altered. Nor is there any hint that Graves wanted things to change. The end came in 1939, and it was as absurd and messy as might be expected. In April 1939 Riding returned to America (with Graves), partly to gain support for a scheme she had devised that would 'save the world from war' – she was collecting signatories for something called 'The First Protocol of the Covenant of Literal Morality'. At Princeton, she met a dilettante literary figure called Schuyler Jackson, and immediately fell for him. Needless to say, this was not how it was presented. First of all, Riding and Jackson joined forces in a plan to 're-educate' Jackson's wife. They subjected her to lengthy 'inquisitions' and so wore her down that she, quite literally, 'went mad'. Seymour-Smith does not give details of these inquisitions, but the outcome is not in dispute.

Graves disapproved of Jackson, as he had disapproved of Phibbs – on the other hand, Laura had chosen this man. Even when Riding and Jackson locked themselves in a bedroom for two days, Graves waited patiently outside the door. Riding eventually emerged with the pronouncement that bodies had not, after all, 'had their day'.

But the real showdown came when Graves perceived that Riding was gradually 'shedding' her tyrannical White Goddess role: she was becoming soft, submissive, the female to Jackson's somewhat brutish male. As an observer exclaimed later: Riding was 'being treated like dirt and liking it!'. She was also protesting that the coarse Jackson might be a fit helpmate in the various grand schemes that she and Graves had been toiling on back in Majorca. (In addition to the peace protocol, there was a plan to issue a new dictionary – of 'real meanings'.) Seymour-Smith sums up as follows:

He had been supplanted by Schuyler. He did not resent being supplanted as lover – though Riding's lapse into crass vulgarity ill-disguised by high talk shocked him – but he did resent being supplanted as intellectual collaborator by an idiot. He could not accept that Jackson's half-articulate obstinacy, and his roughness, were much more to Riding's liking than his own self-confident literacy.

Martin Seymour-Smith devotes more than two hundred pages of his 500-page biography to Graves's relationship with Riding – thirteen years of the poet's eighty – and there can be little doubt that he has got the balance right. If Graves's early life was a preparation for Riding then his life after the split can easily be seen as a long effort to recover from her and then to find a strong woman to replace her. Shortly after he broke with Riding, Graves married Beryl Hodge (formerly the wife of Alan Hodge, co-author with Graves of *The Long Weekend*), and he enjoyed with her some ten years of equilibrium. He was in his mid-forties when Riding left him and at that point he declared that he had had 'enough trouble' in his life. With Beryl's agreeable, low-key companionship secured, Graves went back to Majorca and, quite simply, did a lot of work. He became a prolific writer of prose – *I, Claudius, King Jesus, Wife to Mr Milton*: each of them intelligent and highly readable, and each nicely calculated to needle orthodox historians and academics.

Much of this middle period he also spent wrangling with agents, waiting for Hollywood producers to call back, soliciting advances from publishers, and so on. Interesting enough, but even a writer as devout as Seymour-Smith finds it hard to inject much vitality into this slice of the life. It was not until the fifties that the old worm began to wriggle once again:

> To love one woman, or to sit
> Always beneath the same tall tree
> Argues a certain lack of wit
> Two steps from imbecility . . .

Graves had already evolved his theory of the White Goddess – the female Muse whose commands the poet must obey. The problem was that Beryl, his wife, was not Goddess material: for one thing, she was too nice to him.

Seymour-Smith is indulgent towards Graves's restlessness, and towards its consequences. He talks solemnly of the poet's 'four

ROBERT GRAVES

post-Riding Muses' (i.e., the four young girls Graves fell chastely but theatrically in love with between 1950 and 1975), and he carefully explains that:

Graves differs from most other men in his feeling that any sort of resistance to romantic love is in itself a kind of sin: a refusal of the Goddess, of what the Goddess means to him. But it is hard for those who know only the public Graves, bent on explaining his devotion to the Goddess (whose genuine manifestations he feels that he must under no circumstances ignore), to realise that although he has the compulsion to fall in love, he also hates to do so. He does not enjoy suffering more than anyone else. Moreover, so far is he from being a Don Juan that his fallings-in-love-with-a-Muse have presented him with the serious problem of reconciling them with his permanent love for his wife. He never convincingly worked this out in intellectual terms . . .

The girls Graves fell in love with in his old age were all fairly ordinary girls – flattered a bit by the poet's ardent protestations, irked a bit by his insistence that they live up to the Muse-like qualities with which he had chosen to invest them. There was never a sexual component – it was the Muse's task to possess Graves and it was his task to obey. Even so, with each girl, Graves was plunged into a very public state of torment; his wife, his friends, the girls, the girls' boyfriends, all were supposed to sympathise with the great man's suffering. Letters poured out from Majorca, urgent meetings were arranged, crisis discussions were demanded. If one of the girls took up with another man, Graves would be outraged – how could a Goddess indulge a 'secret passion' for 'serpents . . . corpse-flesh . . . the sly, the barren and the damned'. Could Margot (or Judith, or Emile) not *see* where her high duty lay?

I don't know if this helps, but this is how I see it. You sought me out and before I said anything about it identified yourself with the Love Goddess, throwing the remark over your shoulder one day . . . You thus securely tied yourself to the most ancient theme in the world (which I wrote about in the *White Goddess*) and faithfully played the part of the Love Goddess and the twins . . .

105

As Randall Jarrell commented, Graves had become his own Laura Riding. Unluckily, he could not see this. If – aside from a handful of fond Darby and Joan poems to his wife – Graves's love poems seem anonymous and unfocused, not written to anyone who might actually read them with a shock of recognition, then the explanation is on display in the later chapters of Seymour-Smith's biography.

Graves's best gifts as a poet, it seems to me, are for moralistic ballads and quirkily instructive fables: sometimes (as in the excellent 'Welsh Incident') he can be rather funny. The matter of love, though – or Love, as he would put it – brings out the regimental in him: we are very rarely allowed to hear the poet's vulnerable human voice. Indeed, there is often a smug distancing in Graves's habit of address: the antique diction, the mythological backcloths, the school-masterly delight in paradox and aphorism. There is always something off-puttingly 'expert' in Graves's tone when he discourses on this topic:

> Lovers in the act dispense
> With such meum-teum sense
> As might warningly reveal
> What they must not pick or steal,
> And their nostrum is to say:
> 'I and you are both away.'
>
> After when they disentwine
> You from me and yours from mine,
> Neither can be certain who
> Was that mine whose I was you.
> To the act again they go
> More completely not to know.

For some, Seymour-Smith's tale might contribute the edge of poignancy that Graves's text so magisterially shuns. For others, knowing about Graves's life will make such fluent and authoritative postures ('To the act again they go. . . .') seem all the more irritating and evasive.

And yet Graves has evidently cooperated in the telling of the tale, no doubt because he could trust Seymour-Smith to go along with his Goddess delusions. For much of the time, we are forced to keep a straight face because we know that the facts could not be offered differently. There is a similar obligation in other chapters of the book, and all along we have to bear in mind that this is the Graves version of the Graves biography. Thus, when Graves is interviewed by the police after Riding's suicidal leap, we learn that he 'maintained an insolently aristocratic manner in face of the policemen's persistent questions'. Since the book is not footnoted, we assume that Seymour-Smith did not interview the policemen. Should we therefore conjecture the following exchange between Graves and his biographer: 'What was your manner when questioned?' 'It was insolently aristocratic, as a matter of fact'?

There are some fifty instances of this sort, and several others where Seymour-Smith goes in for straightforward mind-reading: 'He was aware etc., etc., . . . but he hid this from himself', 'She could not forgive him for it, although she would never admit it – even to herself.' And on the matter of the Laura Riding saga, the biographer's source is a mystery, even to himself:

> I suppose I am grateful for a large bundle of material relating to Laura Riding – it includes photocopies of letters to and from her written over a period of forty years – but I do not know whom to thank. It arrived anonymously. I have made use of whatever was relevant to Graves, but not of the rest. Clearly it had been assembled by an assiduous collector with access to many files. Certainly it did not come from anyone I know well.

Finally, the book's irregularities and mysteries have a sad charm that is somehow in keeping with the blundering, gullible, assiduous lives it mainly chronicles. And there is something touching – something almost Gravesian – in Seymour-Smith's now bold, now nervous efforts to make the best sense of his subject's bullied personality.

1983

MARTIN SEYMOUR-SMITH
Robert Graves: His Life and Work
New York: Holt, Rinehart & Winston

Roy Fuller

The run-up to the election of Oxford's new Poetry Professor has aroused a good deal of mirthful interest. There was the candidature of Barry MacSweeney, unknown pop poet from the North, and in his wake a clutch of joke nominees, each more elaborately hopeless than the last. There was Yevtushenko, backed with foam-lipped enthusiasm by poetry-loving Thomson House and similarly denounced by poetry-loving Kingsley Amis. There was the Ladbroke's favourite, Enid Starkie, friend of Oxford, canvasser extraordinary, touchingly untroubled by the principle she herself helped to erect: that the Professor ought to be a poet. And so on. It was a colourful crew, and the posher gossip columns responded with grateful, daily vigour. Meanwhile the election was being won by Roy Fuller. His single, dreary claim to notice was that he was a better poet than the others.

Pleased as he is to have won the professorship, Fuller is probably even more pleased to have won it in the way he did, discreetly and with the minimum of personal embarrassment. To have been examined in newsworthiness, and found sadly wanting, is an achievement he will surely prize. It fits in with the self-deprecating habits of his verse and of his social conduct. When Fuller talks about his life, he talks with a fond ironical disappointment – rather like a father whose favourite son has let him down. His modesty is genuine, indeed obsessive, but it is also formal and humorous; he tries to avoid the personal pronoun. 'If one is a reserved character who sees what a BF he is, one can't be a personality poet,' he confesses, quite ungloomily, and with more than a trace of scorn for the legions of boastful, glamorous BFs who lack this elementary self-awareness. Fuller the self-effacing poet and companion has surprised many with the astringency of his critical pronouncements. Hard on his own pretensions, he is free to be at least ungenerous to those of his contemporaries.

'Maintaining standards' is not for Fuller a mere catchphrase. A sense of holding out against impending chaos runs through much of his poetry and shapes most of his cultural attitudes; it is a kind of egalitarian aestheticism, rich in idealism and defeat. He was one of a handful of young poets whose criteria, of objectivity, intelligence, social concern and so on, were formed in the thirties but whose reputations had to be made in the forties, a decade in which – especially towards its end – 'standards' simply didn't operate. 'A period of deplorable critical standards and of slapdash poetical practice,' he has called it. Guarding against this kind of breakdown (and he would regard the Black Mountaineers and the Liverpool poets as currently ominous symptoms) is the critic's minimal, but solemn, mission. The Oxford students who clamoured for the vibrant Yevtushenko probably won't listen when Fuller tells them that the Russian often writes 'the sort of poetry one looked down one's nose at in 1935 – choral declamations from some party hack', but if they do they will at least find themselves involved in a more rewarding debate than the one Kingsley Amis has provoked. And they will find it hard – at any rate, one hopes they'll find it hard – to sneer at a poet who will also tell them: 'I seem to have been resigned most of my poetic life to the virtues of keeping one's powder dry rather than trying to fire the big guns.' Fuller has always preferred the 'austere miss' to the 'romantic woolly hit'.

Roy Fuller dates the beginning of his 'poetic life' from a meeting with John Davenport in 1930. Davenport introduced him to the youthful work of Auden and Spender, and from then on Fuller was a Thirties poet. He had already contributed a poem (in 1928) to the celebrated Poets' Corner of the *Sunday Referee* – where the souls of Dylan Thomas and Pamela Hansford Johnson first snugly intertwined – and he had composed unpublished volumes in the manner of Humbert Wolfe. He had also begun to discover Pound and Eliot and to realise that modern poetry contained more than his school librarian had dreamed of. This new work, though, from poets of about his own generation, chimed in more excitingly with his awakening political enthusiasms.

Fuller was eighteen at the time, articled to a solicitor in Blackpool and he felt depressingly remote from the real centres of literary activity. Looking back, he admits to a certain resentment of those who organised his education. He attended a genteel unambitious private school in Blackpool (his novel, *The Ruined Boys*, is based on it) and the question of his going on from there to university was simply never raised – pupils became solicitors, chartered accountants, or, more usually, they went into their fathers' businesses. Fuller's own father, who worked his way up to become a director of a rubber-proofing firm and prospered supplying groundsheets to the army in the 1914–18 War, had died young, when Fuller was eight years old. It was therefore a toss-up between law and accountancy, and Fuller still doesn't know why he chose the career which he has turned out to be notably good at (he is now solicitor to a large building society and a member of the Law Society's working party on conveyancing). At the age of sixteen he was articled, he passed his finals at twenty-one, and at twenty-two he was managing a local branch office.

By this time, he was writing like Auden and was deeply caught up in the activities of a local group of left-wing intellectuals, members of the CP, ILP and SPGB. For him this was the one brief period when poetry seemed dramatically and usefully bound up with day-to-day political affairs. Unable subsequently to recapture this kind of excitement, he has never stopped wondering what happened to it, and never stopped insisting that poetry *ought* to have this relevance. A frequent persona in his poetry ever since has been that of the artist whose neurosis prevents him from turning to social account the insights which it gives him access to, whose dreams of grand remedial activity are mocked by a crippling alienation from the 'unteachable mass'.

After moving from Blackpool, in 1935, to Ashford, Kent, Fuller's political activities began to peter out. He remained, and remains today, 'absolutely sympathetic to Marxist ideas. I don't think I really changed my fundamental belief in the materialist conception of history, but I must have become doubtful about any role I could play practically and also dubious about any simple party allegiances.' His deepening conviction during the second half of the thirties (he was, he says, 'too timid' for Spain) was that 'history had caught up with one so it didn't matter too much what one did', that 'one was entering into a period of Caesarism, that civilization would end'. In 1941, he was called up and 'opted for the Navy, influenced by a friend, and thinking woollily that any hostilities in which I might be involved would be conducted at a genteel distance'. He was posted to Africa as a radar mechanic in 1942, spent most of 1943 in Nairobi – 'idling time away or repairing radar sets' – and returned to England in 1944 to a commission and a desk at the Admiralty. Apart from a bout of malaria, nothing very hazardous had happened to him.

He had, though, written two books which rank with the very best work of the period – *The Middle of a War* and *A Lost Season*. The subjects of Fuller's war poems are the familiar ones – transit camp boredom, awed response to foreign climes, separation from loved ones, ludicrousness of army life, pervading sense of doom and so on – but in attempting to break away from Auden's generalising idiom into something more sharply autobiographical, he struck an original and moving vein. His style in these poems, though it runs easily to the loose and rhetorical, works as a kind of bridge between two epochs: the public, admonitory manner of the Thirties attempting to accommodate the personal suffering it had so fluently predicted. It is a style that works unevenly, but at its best it generates a curiously formal species of despair which, in its stiff, bleak, rather stilted way, can be very powerful.

Since the war, Fuller has been prolific in both verse and prose and until an illness last year obliged him to adopt more relaxed habits, he would regularly rise in the early hours and work at his writing until it was time for a full day of legal chores. Five books of verse, several novels (one of which, *My Child, My Sister*, he regards as 'better than any book of poems I've written'), detective stories, children's books, reviews and articles: an impressive output for a spare-time writer. He has also paid the full penalties of middle-aged eminence in terms of committee work, prize panels and the like. It would be untrue to say that none of his writing during this busy period bears signs of haste, but there has been no serious default from standards of intelligence and honesty, from what he himself has called 'the criterion of success in poetry: brain power allied at least to a dogged alertness and integrity'. And his latest book, *New Poems* – most of which was written in a very short period under stress of illness and its attendant fears – was much more direct and deeply felt, it seemed to me – though this is not the kind of praise Fuller really savours – than almost anything he had written since the war. Now, victimised by an 'officious gland', he is easing up a bit and looks forward to the ruminative labours of his new office. He is going to use the professorship to work out his ideas about poetry, 'from a practitioner's point of view', in more detail than he has yet had the chance to. Oxford is lucky to have given him this chance.

1968

Alun Lewis

It is forty years since Alun Lewis died, but his ranking as a modern poet still seems insecure. He routinely gets bundled in with the Poets of World War Two (along with Keith Douglas and Sidney Keyes) but he is by no means an automatic choice for non-specialised anthologies – not in the way that Douglas now is, for example, although Douglas's posthumous repute got off to a much slower start.

The reason may be that it is hard to decide on a Lewis poem that 'works' all the way through. There is an unfinished look to almost everything he did – half a dozen haunting lines, a couple of inspired stanzas, and then the thing seems to wobble into awkwardness or over-emphasis. In *Raider's Dawn*, the tilt is towards wildness and excess, abetted by Lawrentian self-inflation; in *Ha! Ha! Among the Trumpets*, there is an almost opposite tendency, an overmellifluous rhetoric of general wisdom.

There are those who believe that Lewis's future as a writer would have been in prose, and it is certainly true that stories like 'The Last Inspection' and 'The Orange Grove' have a consistency and self-assurance that cannot easily be located in the verse. But Lewis's ambition was for poetry, and I think his sensibility was too; it was, however, a reflective sensibility and maybe it could only have found its best expression if his war-nerves had been allowed to heal.

Alun Lewis was no warrior. His background was in education and socialist good works. Born in a South Wales mining town, he was not from a mining family – his parents were both teachers – but many of his boyhood friends had fathers who toiled underground. Lewis was both of the miners and above them – the 'above' meaning that he felt a peculiar obligation to care for their plight and to speak out on their behalf.

The Depression (plus a high-minded literary mother) shaped the essentials of Lewis's almost feverish sense of duty. From early on, though, he had trouble reconciling his dreamy, introverted personality with the ruder requirements of public service. And the war brought this conflict to a head. On the one hand, Lewis wanted to serve, to fight in what he saw as a just cause, and he wanted also to experience some intense kinship with his fellow soldiers. On the other hand, he viewed the war as a kind of high romantic quest, an assignation with self-testing perils, and perhaps with death. He would not kill, he said at the outbreak of war, and he was ready to 'be killed, instead'.

In army camps in England, Lewis was torn between an educationalist zeal to improve the hearts and minds of the soldiers placed under his command (Lewis took a commission with misgivings and later rather regretted having done so) and the alienated stance of the romantic bard. He organised debating societies, lectures on world affairs, he wanted to start a weekly magazine; at the same time, though, he was writing poems like 'All Day It Has Rained' and 'After Dunkirk' in which the fastidious author is painfully distanced from his unaware and cultureless comrades:

[Nightmare rides upon the headlines . . .]
But leisurely my fellow soldiers stroll among the trees.
The cheapest dance-song utters all they feel.

In India, where Lewis was posted in 1943, the same conflict is at work, but with more subtlety and depth. Lewis was both appalled and thrilled by India. The humanitarian individualist was shocked by poverty and backwardness on a scale that simply paralysed goodwill; the fated poet was stirred by the sufferer's benign acceptance of his lot. All the old radical decencies were made to seem puny and irrelevant; the questing self (or, some might say, the selfish quest) could move forward into mysticism and obsession.

For nearly three years, Lewis had been in the Army without making any sort of contact with the enemy – the longer he waited, the more excited and exalted he became: the Indian jungle, he knew, would be his battlefield and he began to see its lush, intoxicating silences as promising some final spiritual showdown: 'a showdown with fate', he called it. At last within fighting distance of the foe, Lewis was about to set off on a patrol:

> Alun was in an excited mood. After shaving and washing, he left the hut carrying his revolver (loaded arms had to be carried at all times) and made for the officers' latrines on the hillside. Shortly after, a shot was heard. Tudor [Lewis's batman] ran towards it and saw him lying about five yards down the slope. The revolver was in his hand; he had been shot in the right temple.

The official Army verdict was Accidental Death, but there was no one in Lewis's regiment who did not believe that it was suicide.

Until now, the details of Lewis's last months in India have been blurred and uncertain. In his writings, there was his persistent representation of Death as the healer of all wounds, the resolver of all conflict, and this has been enough to persuade most readers that his own death was probably no accident. But what was the true source of his agitation? Was it the prospect of finally having to choose between killing or being killed, was it the strain of separation from his wife Gweno, whom he had married shortly before embarkation, was it to do with his uneasy relations with his senior officers?

All of these circumstantial explanations have been ventured, at one time or another, but John Pikoulis's biography supplies a new, and probably crucial, ingredient. A few months before his death, Lewis fell in love with Freda Ackroyd, a married woman he had met on leave in Madras. For two months, he and Freda exchanged passionate letters and then they spent a week together in Bombay. Back home in Wales, Gweno was puzzled by a new eroticism in Lewis's poems, and indeed scolded him for it, but he could not bring himself to explain what had happened. As for Freda, she had already detected in him something blind and futureless. Immediately after his break with her (not a formal break, but they both seem to have known that the romance could not continue) Lewis was back with his regiment and on the brink of facing his long-awaited showdown at the front. Freda herself is in no doubt that he killed himself.

This is the first full-length biography of Lewis, and it must be said that in order to make it so, Pikoulis has had to stretch the material somewhat. There are leisurely paraphrases of short stories, lengthy quotations from the poems, and a good deal of unnecessary literary-critical waffle. Also, the tone is cloyingly over-fond at times:

Alun loved his sister. She was for him a type of beauty and sensitivity and he would often put a hand on her shoulder. Filling her with pride and happiness.

Gushy stuff like this sits uneasily alongside Pikoulis's occasional lapses into trendy colloquialese: 'At least he told it like it was . . .', 'something of a loner, but sociable with it'. Still, he has done the work and the Freda Ackroyd revelations alone require that we should not be too churlish about his manner of delivery.

1984

JOHN PIKOULIS
Alun Lewis: A Life
Bridgend: Poetry Wales Press

Richard Wilbur

Framed in her phoenix fire-screen, Edna Ward
Bends to the tray of Canton, pouring tea
For frightened Mrs Plath; then, turning toward
The pale, slumped daughter, and my wife, and me
Asks if we would prefer it weak or strong.

Weak or strong, pale or reddish-black, academic or barbarian,
neo-Augustan or psycho-apocalyptic . . .? Such other oppositions
may or may not have been in Richard Wilbur's mind as he watched
his hostess pour the tea, but with this poem – written perhaps some
twenty-five years after the event it describes – he almost certainly
expects one or two of them to be in ours.

In 'Cottage Street, 1953', Wilbur recalls meeting the twenty-
year-old Sylvia Plath at a tea-party hosted by his mother-in-law.
Plath, it seems, had recently made one of her suicide attempts:
the encounter with a well-adjusted literary celebrity like Richard
Wilbur was meant to persuade her that successful poets need not
be insane. In the poem, Wilbur pretends that he is not too irked
by the role he has been given: 'It is my office to exemplify / The
published poet in his happiness / Thus cheering Sylvia, who had
wished to die.' All the same, he is embarrassed, feeling himself
likely to come across as a somewhat 'stupid lifeguard'. How can
someone like him really help someone like her: a 'girl / who, far
from shore, has been immensely drowned / And stares through
water now with eyes of pearl'? Faced with Plath's 'large refusal',
what effective comfort can be offered by Wilbur's 'genteel chat', or
indeed by the sort of orderly, life-recommending verses that have
won him the recognition she so pitiably seems to crave?

The poem ends, as so many genteel Wilbur poems try to, with a

117

ringingly emotive punch-line. Plath, he concludes, was 'condemned to live' for a further ten years after their awkward tea-time meeting but was eventually allowed – after much 'study' – 'To state at last her brilliant negative / In poems free and helpless and unjust'. Free, helpless and unjust – the opposites, really, of what Wilbur would look or aim for in a poem. His taste from the beginning was for the shaped, the celebratory, the equable. Looking back on his meeting with Sylvia Plath, he is not simply resavouring some long-ago social discomfiture, nor does he greatly wish to perform a decent elegiac chore. There is a mechanical feel to those lines about a girl 'immensely drowned' – in 1953, did Wilbur really think of Plath as doomed, or indeed think much of her at all? Is such distancing deliberate: does Wilbur mean us here to find him over-smooth, as maybe Plath did when she read him?

Of course with a real smoothie it is hard to tell, but the chances surely are that what Wilbur wants to measure in this poem is the distance between Sylvia Plath's kind of poetry and his own. For all his modesty, which seems genuine, he knows very well that the decline of his reputation since the mid-sixties has been in large part a consequence of Plath's posthumous appeal. 'Unjust' is his last word on Plath's poetry; it could also be applied to the way in which his own glamour was eclipsed by hers.

With Plath's death in 1963, the shift of taste that had begun with Lowell's *Life Studies*, W.D. Snodgrass's *Heart's Needle* and – we are perhaps now ready to concede – the more gifted of the Beats, did for a time draw strength from making mock of campus wits. A generation of university-based, neo-classical, Europe-admiring Americans found themselves shunted to the sidelines; soon they were thought to be *too* dazzling, insufficiently distraught. Some of these, like Wilbur, were in their early forties, with two or three highly praised books behind them, and could look forward to exercising their skills as tenured scholar-poets; they were embarked on 'careers' which would be garlanded from time to time with grants, prizes, ambassadorial tours of foreign lands. In 1962, Wilbur gave a reading in London at the American Embassy, and Clive James was in the audience, agape at this poet who seemed then to be the

> epitome of cool. It was all there: the Ivy League hair-cut, the candy-stripe jacket, the full burnished image of the Amherst

phi beta. Riding his audience like the Silver Surfer, he took European Culture out of his pocket and laid it right on us. We were stoned. It was the Kennedy era and somehow it seemed plausible that the traditional high culture of Europe should be represented by an American who looked like a jet-jockey and that the State Department should pay the hotel bills.

Such poets had grown used to being thought of as exemplary, as embodying qualities of cultivation and humane subtlety that had been imperilled by the war: affirmative conservatives, they believed in the graceful potency of what had gone before, pre-1939. Writing in the early-fifties, they could believe that chaos had been averted; now was the time to put civilization back in order. Poets who lived through the war, who fought in it (as Wilbur did; he was an infantryman in Italy and France), necessarily found it hard not to celebrate the peace. For Wilbur in 1953, the most terrible world-horrors seemed safely in the past. For Plath (aged thirteen in 1945), and for others of her generation, the war still had to be imagined, fed upon, internalised – perhaps re-lived.

By the time Wilbur met Sylvia Plath, he had published *The Beautiful Changes* (1947) and *Ceremony* (1950). In neither book does Wilbur's war experience much show itself; indeed, when writing directly about war this naturally elegant poet can be pretty crude. But the memory of war is always there. Wilbur is recognisably a post-war poet in his hunger for the orderly, the difficult-to-interrupt, and in the sense he gives of a talent grateful simply to be functioning again. There is gratitude also in these early poems for a world restored: a world where things in nature can be pondered without haste, and in which books, paintings, sculptures can be rediscovered and straightforwardly enjoyed: 'What wholly blameless fun/To stand and look at pictures.' This playtime lightness can in itself be rather moving. Much of the time, what the poet 'wants to say' is very simple indeed, something like: Look what the imagination can contrive when it is genuinely free;

You know those windless summer evenings, swollen to stasis
by too-substantial melodies, rich as a
running-down record, ground round
to full quiet. Even the leaves
have thick tongues.

And if the first crickets quicken then,
other inhabitants, at window or door
or rising from table, feel in the lungs
a slim false-freshness, by this
trick of the ear.

Chanters of miracles took for a simple sign
the Latin cicada, because of his long waiting
and sweet change in daylight, and his singing
all his life, pinched on the ash leaf,
heedless of ants.

Others made morals; all were puzzled and joyed
by this gratuitous song.

There is a gratuitous melody too in the performances of those acrobats, jugglers and architects whom Wilbur celebrates so warmly in his early work. As a poet he would wish to be like them and make his skill seem perilous, a hard-to-bring-off act of balance. At first his zestful mood and the delighted quickness of his eye and ear made a virtue out of a seeming paucity of subject matter. Wilbur's youthful poems 'took off' into abstraction from something sharply seen or heard: the flight seemed irresistible.

Later on, though, we would begin to see why he was being drawn more and more to translation as a means of energising his technical adroitness and his brilliant way with words. He had begun to scratch around for things to take off *from*. The movement in each poem from observation to speculation no longer seemed entirely effortless. 'Seed Leaves', one of several weekending nature poems to be found in *Walking to Sleep* (1969), is fairly typical in its too-ponderous declaration of intent:

> Here something stubborn comes.
> Dislodging the earth crumbs
> And making crusty rubble.
> It comes up bending double,
> And looks like a green staple.
> It could be a seedling maple,
> Or artichoke, or bean.
> That remains to be seen.

120

OK, get on with it, we are inclined to murmur here. In middle to late Wilbur there is an almost constant sense of skills that have become habitual, enabling the poet to drone on rather prettily, to keep talking so long as the rhyme supplies hold out.

Maybe his post-1963 pigeon-holing did have its influence. During the seventies, Wilbur was idly talked of as an out-of-touch academic dandy. This being so, he may well have felt tempted to make a point of not being lured out of his library – except, of course, at weekends, to inspect the seedlings. For whatever reason, there was a long dull stretch of his career during which he became all too easy to neglect. This was unjust, certainly, because his poems were never unintelligent or ill-made, but before shedding tears on his behalf we should perhaps consult a (fairly recent, it seems) poem like 'Icarium Mare'. Poets who do not have the tumbling Icarus high on their list of unmentionables are surely immune to the ups and downs of critical opinion:

> We have heard of the undimmed air
> Of the True Earth above us, and how here,
> Shut in our sea-like atmosphere,
> We grope like muddled fish. Perhaps from there,
>
> That fierce lucidity,
> Came Icarus' body tumbling, flayed and trenched
> By waxen runnels, to be quenched
> Near Samos riding in the actual sea,
>
> Where Aristarchus first
> Rounded the sun in thought; near Patmos, too,
> Where John's bejeweled inward view
> Described an angel in the solar burst.

There are so many irritating details here (accidental repetitions, ugly rhymes, hideous archaisms, arch inversions and so on) that it seems superfluous to take issue with the pleased-with-itself tone in which the whole thing is served up. The poem goes on for a further five stanzas and does not improve.

It is this side of Richard Wilbur that has perhaps blurred our sense of how sparkling and likeable his poems used to be. They are still likeable, from time to time – see, for example, 'The Ride', 'Leaving' or 'The Catch' – but we tend to like them now, when they don't try to sparkle. Wilbur seems to have accepted some time ago that in choosing to be a poet of the 'shallows' (as he puts it in his Sylvia Plath poem) he has under-extended his considerable talent. In 'The Writer', he tells of his daughter writing a story in an upstairs room: 'From her shut door a commotion of typewriter-keys/Like a chain hauled over a gunwale.' The poet is almost alarmed by her intensity, and we cannot help remembering that 1953 tea-party when he reflects:

> Young as she is, the stuff
> Of her life is a great cargo, and some of it heavy:
> I wish her a lucky passage.

Wilbur knows this life/cargo business to be an empty literary flourish and he scolds himself for it, as his furious young daughter surely would. Trying again, he remembers that two years earlier a bird had been trapped in his daughter's room and had battered itself almost senseless in its efforts to find the 'right window' to escape through. Is this comparison more apt? Well, yes, but our real interest is in fathoming the extent of Wilbur's self-reproach when he remembers

> how our spirits
> Rose when, suddenly sure,
>
> It lifted off from a chair-back,
> Beating a smooth course for the right window
> And clearing the sill of the world.
>
> It is always a matter, my darling,
> Of life or death, as I had forgotten. I wish
> What I wished you before, but harder.

1989

RICHARD WILBUR
New and Collected Poems
Faber

Philip Larkin: 1. The Collected Poems

Philip Larkin, we are told, left instructions in his will that certain of his writings had to be destroyed, unread. His executors obeyed: the word is that several of the poet's notebooks, or journals, are now ashes. Did Larkin expect to be so obeyed? Or did he imagine that perhaps someone, somehow, might take a peek at the material before it reached the flames? And if such a thought did cross his mind, why didn't he destroy the stuff himself? He must have known that, by not doing so, he was bequeathing at least the possibility of a dilemma. But then some of his most moving poems contrive a subtle, unsettlable dispute between revelation and concealment. There is a wanting-to-be-known that can desolate or undermine our self-sufficiency.

And now, it seems, there are things about Philip Larkin that we'll never know. So what? Well, put it like this, the loss can be made to sound not at all what Larkin, as we know him from the poems, would have wholly wished. But then again, who knows? After all, those now-incinerated notebooks might have been full of household accounts or noughts and crosses: the instruction to destroy them a librarian's last, bleakest joke. Throw these away and you are doomed to imagine that my life was not really as boring as I always used to say it was. Having something to hide is generally reckoned to be better than having nothing to show, he might have thought.

There are no explicit instructions in Larkin's will concerning the publication or re-publication of his poems. He seems not to have minded the idea of having his most early work exhumed. Nor did he leave any advice about what ought to happen to the various unfinished pieces he would leave behind. We can assume, therefore, that he must have envisaged a *Collected Poems* rather like the one we've now been given: a volume that adds something like eighty poems to his lifetime's known tally. This is a hefty addition, since the poems we already know him by and most admire total a mere eighty-five. I'm thinking here of the poems collected in *The Less Deceived*, *The Whitsun Weddings* and *High Windows*. So his 'output' has been almost doubled. (I say 'almost' because *The North Ship*, reprinted 'with considerable hesitation' in 1966 and offered more as a curiosity than to be admired, adds another thirty titles to the list.) What it all boils down to, or up to, is that Larkin the thrifty now has a *Collected Poems* of substantial bulk.

Ought we to think, though, as he generally did not, that adding means increase? Kilograms aside, the plumpened Larkin oeuvre does not carry a great deal of extra weight. On the contrary, a poet whom we value for his sparingness, for not out-putting work that he wasn't 'pretty sure' amounted to the best that he could do, is now to be seen as somewhat cluttered with botch-ups, immaturities and fragments. It's as if this most bachelor of poets had suddenly acquired a slightly messy family life.

Apparently, it could have been messier. Anthony Thwaite has decided not to include various squibs and limericks (these will appear later on in Larkin's *Letters*), and has also ruled against certain of Larkin's unfinished pieces; he mentions an 'attempt at a long poem called "The Duration" . . . which takes up fifteen pages of drafts between April and June 1969; and what was apparently his final struggle with a substantial poem, "Letters to my Mind", drafted in October and November 1979'. I am not sure that these items don't sound to be more interesting than some of the bits and pieces Thwaite has chosen to include. But then, ought we to have any 'fragments' at all in an edition of this sort? And if we do have them, ought they not to be herded off into a section of their own? This was Eliot's method, and it might have been Larkin's if he'd had the choice and if – a big if – he had thought as highly of his own 'The Dance' fragment as Eliot did of *Sweeney Agonistes*.

Was there not a case, in Larkin's case, for two *Collected* volumes: the first a one-volume reprint of the three grown-up, finished books plus the handful of poems he completed after publishing *High Windows* (these, of course, would include the marvellous 'Aubade'); the second, a mop-up of juvenilia, fragments, occasional light verse, even limericks and squibs? Thwaite's edition does divide itself in two, with mature Larkin at the front of the book and learner

Larkin at the rear, but it makes no other formal separation between the poems Larkin passed for press and those which, for one reason or another, he hadn't wished to see in print.

I find this a bit disconcerting. The beauty of Larkin's three grown-up books, or one of their beauties, is that you can open them at any page and find something that only Larkin could have written. And even his most light-weight pieces are consummately 'finished' – there is nothing slovenly or make-weight or derivative. With this *Collected Poems*, there is an almost fifty-fifty chance that 'any page' will reveal lines which you'd swear could not possibly have sprung from Larkin's pen.

> I declare
> Two lineages electrify the air
> That will like pennons from a mast
> Fly over sleep and life and death
> Till sun is powerless to decoy
> A single seed above the earth:
> Lineage of sorrow; lineage of joy . . .

The next line does not, alas, read: 'Going well so far, eh?' In fact, there are about fifty similarly exalted lines to go before the thing finally deflates:

> Joy has no cause
> Though cut to pieces with a knife,
> Cannot keep silence. What else could magnetise
> Our drudging, hypocritical, ecstatic life?

This poem, entitled 'Many famous feet have trod', was written in October 1946, and thus earns its place among the 'mature' work. 1946 is the year in which Anthony Thwaite believes Larkin's 'distinctive voice' can first be heard. So it can, in the poems 'Going' and 'Wedding Wind', which we already know. In the other 1946 poems printed here, we have to strain to pick it up, in odd lines, now and then; and in 'Many famous feet . . .' I'm afraid I can hear no trace of it at all. Larkin used to chuckle that he of all people had once written a never-published volume called *In the Grip of Light*. I'm inclined to think that the chuckle

125

was intended to cover those 'pennons from a mast', that 'lineage of joy'.

1946 was in fact the year in which Larkin read Thomas Hardy's 'Thoughts of Phena' and experienced a literary conversion, 'complete and permanent'. Hardy rescued him from Yeats, just as Yeats – three years earlier – had captured him from Auden. Under the Hardy regime, he was indeed able to find his own distinctive voice, but the Yeats and Auden periods offer almost nothing in the way of even potential Larkinesque. To peruse the eighty or so pages of juvenilia that are reprinted here is to discover scant line-by-line poetic 'promise'. Anthony Thwaite finds Larkin's Auden poems 'astonishing and precocious' and they are, to be sure, pretty good going for a kid of seventeen. But they are also fairly stiff and dull, and, because of their enslavement to the icy Master, we have no way of guessing what their author might or might not do should he ever manage to break free: it could be everything or nothing. Larkin himself, writing of these poems at the time, said: 'As for their literary interest, I think that almost any single line by Auden would be worth more than the whole lot put together.' Now there we *do* hear the later man's distinctive voice, and that was in 1941.

The sheer bulk of Larkin's juvenilia might seem irksome when presented as part of a *Collected Poems*, but biographically the bulk does matter quite a lot. This juvenilia period, 1938–46, would be later looked back on as a lost idyll of aliveness and fertility. By the age of twenty-four Larkin had written two books of poems – *The North Ship* and *In the Grip of Light* – and two novels – *Jill* and *A Girl in Winter*. Three of these books were published, but none of them had made much of a splash. In 1947 and 1948 he seems to have written almost nothing, and when the poetry does start up again in 1949 it is a poetry of failure, loss, rejection. In 'On Being Twenty-six', the poet regrets the flagging of his 'pristine drive', the withdrawal of 'Talent, felicity', and is bitter about having now to settle for something 'dingier' and 'second best':

> Fabric of fallen minarets is trash.
>   And in the ash
>
> Of what has pleased and passed
>   Is now no more
> Than struts of greed, a last

> Charred smile, a clawed
> Crustacean hatred, blackened pride – of such
> I once made much.

Thus burnt-out, and 'clay-thick with misery', the poet falls silent yet again. There is nothing between May 1949 and January 1950. In this month, Larkin's first really spectacular development takes place. In 'At Grass' the theme is still to do with 'what has pleased and passed', but the subject is thoroughly *out there*: retired racehorses perhaps plagued by memories of erstwhile triumphs. In the next few months, we have 'If, My Darling', 'Wants', 'No Road' and 'Absences'. Within a year, the clay-thick self-pity of 1949 has become lighter, wiser, more sardonic:

> Always too eager for the future, we
> Pick up bad habits of expectancy.
> Something is always approaching; every day
> *Till then* we say.

It's an extraordinary falling-into-place, and the month-by-month dating of the poems gives the whole business a certain narrative excitement: although we will have to wait for Andrew Motion's biography to tell us what happened, or didn't happen, in 1947–8.

Throughout the book, the precise dating of the poems (meticulously recorded in the poet's worksheets) can evoke a sort of mini-tale: we learn, for instance, that January is a strong month for Larkin poems but that July is almost always a complete write-off, that 'Home is so sad' was composed on New Year's Eve, that the anti-marriage poem 'Self's the Man' immediately follows 'The Whitsun Weddings' and was completed on Guy Fawkes Day, and that in one month (January 1954) Larkin wrote 'Reasons for Attendance', 'I remember, I remember', 'For Sidney Bechet', 'Born Yesterday' and 'Poetry of Departures'.

Although I have grumbled about Thwaite not separating the unfinished pieces from the finished, there is undeniably a drama in observing that straight after finishing the expansive 'Dockery and Son' (just in time, one guesses, for it to be included in the *Whitsun Weddings* book), Larkin spent over a year grappling with a longish narrative poem, to be called 'The Dance'. The wish, evidently, was to build on the 'Dockery' model, to combine narrative relaxation

127

with verse-strictness, but Larkin seems to have discovered that relaxation, for him, usually means a drift towards light verse, or over-surly self-parody – not at all what he wanted for this essentially angry and distressed love poem:

> In the slug
> And snarl of music, under cover of
> A few permitted movements, you suggest
> A whole consenting language, that my chest
> Quickens and tightens at, descrying love –
> Something acutely local, me
> As I am now, and you as you are now,
> And now; something acutely transitory
> The slightest impulse could deflect to how
> We act eternally.
> Why not snatch it? Your fingers tighten, tug,
> Then slacken altogether. I am caught
> By some shoptalking shit who leads me off
> To supper and his bearded wife, to stand
> Bemused and coffee-holding while the band
> Restarts off-stage, and they in tempo scoff
> Small things I couldn't look at, rent
> By wondering who has got you now . . .

The very awkwardness reminds us how many of Larkin's best effects depend upon him sounding both superior *and* vulnerable, unloving and in need of love. It's a difficult balancing-act, breathtaking when it works; when it doesn't, he can veer uneasily between the boorish and the sentimental. 'The Dance' was, it seems, en route to failure, and Larkin was probably right not to persist with it, but there is a memorable painfulness in watching him trying to wrench this exposed and ambitious poem into shape.

Since 'Aubade' in 1977, Larkin published only four poems – two rather charming birthday poems (one for Gavin Ewart, the other for Charles Causley), a poem about a dead hedgehog, and a couple of stanzas specially written for a *Poetry Review* special number on poetry and drink. After his death in 1985, a handful of unpublished poems was found. The strongest of these are desperately miserable, indeed inconsolable, as if Larkin had grown weary of trying to fathom 'whatever it is that is doing the damage'. The last poem of any weight was written in 1979 and it isn't easy to read, if you care at all about what happened to this awesome yet companionable poet. But unhappily it does help to explain the six-year silence:

> Love again: wanking at ten past three
> (Surely he's taken her home by now?),
> The bedroom hot as a bakery,
> The drink gone dead, without showing how?
> To meet tomorrow, and afterwards,
> And the usual pain, like dysentery.
>
> Someone else feeling her breasts and cunt,
> Someone else drowned in that lash-wide stare,
> And me supposed to be ignorant,
> Or find it funny, or not to care,
> Even . . . but why put it into words?
> Isolate rather this element
>
> That spreads through other lives like a tree
> And sways them on in a sort of sense
> And say why it never worked for me.
> Something to do with violence
> A long way back, and wrong rewards,
> And arrogant eternity.

1988

PHILIP LARKIN
Collected Poems, edited by Anthony Thwaite
Faber and Marvell Press

Philip Larkin: 2. The Selected Letters

There is a story that when William F. Buckley Jr. sent a copy of his essays to Norman Mailer, he pencilled a welcoming 'Hi, Norman!' in the Index, next to Mailer's name. A similar tactic might happily have been ventured by the publishers of Philip Larkin's *Letters*: the book's back pages are going to be well-thumbed. 'Hi, Craig', see p. 752, you 'mad sod'; 'Hi, John', see p. 563, you 'arse-faced trendy'; 'Hi, David', see p. 266, you 'deaf cunt', and so on. Less succinct salutations will be discovered by the likes of Donald Davie ('droning out his tosh'), Ted Hughes ('boring old monolith, no good at all – not a single solitary bit of good'), and Anthony Powell, a.k.a. 'the horse-faced dwarf'. There is even a 'Hi, Ian': he calls me 'the Kerensky of poetry'. Not too bad, I thought at first. Alas, though, the book's editor advises me that Larkin almost certainly meant to say Dzerchinsky, or somebody – some murderer – like that. He had probably misread a communication from Robert ('the great terror') Conquest.

Anyway, it is already pretty clear that one of the chief excitements of this publication will be in finding out who has been dumped on, and how badly. Few well-known names escape the Larkin lash and although Anthony Thwaite seems in this area to have been abundantly forthcoming, we can surmise that he must have done *some* toning down. After all, this is merely a Selected Letters and there are over three hundred [. . .]'s sprinkled throughout.

Apart from Thwaite himself, the few who are spared include figures like Vernon Watkins, Gavin Ewart, Barbara Pym: allies who are genuinely liked and admired but who are nonetheless junior to Larkin in talent and repute. The really big hates tend to be reserved for sizeable poetic rivals. Ted Hughes is a recurrent, near-obsessive target, with S. Heaney advancing on the rails. Even

John Betjeman is given a few slap-downs here and there. All in all, I think it is true to say that Larkin has not a kind word for any contemporary writer who might be thought of as a threat to his pre-eminence. Kingsley Amis seems to be the exception but actually isn't, quite: in this complicated case, the kind words are often double-edged. And as Larkin got older, he became increasingly disposed to downgrade the literary heroes of his youth. Auden, once worshipped, becomes a 'cosmopolitan lisping no-good'; Yeats turns into 'old gyre-and-grumble'. Only Lawrence, Larkin's earliest 'touchstone against the false', survives more or less intact.

It would be easy enough, then, to argue that – fun and games aside – the really important revelation of these letters is that Larkin, the above-it-all curmudgeon and recluse, the arch-self-deprecator, was in truth nursing a champ-sized fixation on matters of literary rank – a fixation perhaps Maileresque in its immensity and scope. The settings, we might say, are different, drabber, Hull not Brooklyn, and so on, but the ache for supremacy is much the same. Mailer, in his *Advertisements for Myself*, set out to annihilate the opposition, rather as Larkin seems to here. The American made a show of his megalomania; he overplayed it, with a grin. Larkin, being English, being Larkin, chose a public stance that was meant to disguise the ferocity of his ambition.

This sounds plausible, and could be backed up with some fairly unappealing extracts from these once-private letters. Larkin *was* surprisingly alert to questions of literary-world status and to the encroachments of his rivals. No attempt to account for his lifelong unhappiness can now possibly pretend that he was not. But his ambition, as its largely dismal narrative unwinds, seems anything but Maileresque. There is no zest in it, no Tarzan-calls, no muscle-flexing self-delusion, no . . . well, no ambition, really, as somebody like Mailer would define it. The yearned-for bays are withered; they may even turn out to be made of plastic – *withered plastic*, if this boy's luck runs true to form. Larkin knew himself to be the champ – but he knew also that he was a smalltime, local sort of champ. He was unlikely to make it in the heavyweight division, nor was he a serious contender for world titles. He was at best perhaps a bantam-weight or – ho ho ho – a cruiser. But then, God bugger me blue, what did *that* make all the other craps and shags – the Wains, Hugheses, Davies, *Holloways*, for Christ's sake? At least he, Larkin, didn't show up for readings in a *leather jacket*.

'You've become what I dreamed of becoming,' Larkin wrote to Kingsley Amis at a point quite late on in their careers, seeming to mean by this that Amis was an esteemed, successful novelist and that he himself was a mere poet. But there were other ways in which he envied Amis – or rather there were other ways in which he measured himself against what Amis seemed to represent.

In a very early letter – not to Amis – Larkin finds himself brooding, as he often does, on 'ways of life', and he ends up contrasting two types of literary artist: there is the 'ivory tower cunt . . . who denies all human relationships, either through disgust, shyness, or weakness, or inability to deal with them', and there is 'the solid man with plenty of roots in everyday living by which his spiritual and mental existence is nourished'. Although Larkin would surely have guffawed later on had Amis proposed himself as an example of the second type, he knew that he, Larkin, had grown into a pretty fair example of the first. What was it that had made him stay put, miss out, cave in, while his comrade voyaged out to grasp the goodies?

'After comparing lives with you for years/I see how I've been losing', Larkin wrote, in a poem which was not published in his lifetime but which he tinkered with for two decades. The addressee may not have been Amis but one's guess is that it was. Even after the pair of them have become grand figures, Larkin still has the Amis model on his mind. When the *Oxford Book of Twentieth-Century Verse* clocks up sales of 85,000, this is 'chickenfeed compared with *Lucky Jim*'. On the other hand, Larkin is delighted to find that his entries in the *Oxford Dictionary of Quotations* outnumber Amis's by five to one ('Poor Kingsley only has one, and that "More will mean worse". I haven't searched beyond that').

Twenty years' worth of the Amis–Larkin correspondence has gone missing, so it is not easy to track their rivalry in detail. From what there is, though, we get the sense that Amis's worldly success had some significant bearing on Larkin's precocious sourness, his posture of exclusion and defeat, the sense even that without the Amis irritation Larkin may not so readily have found *his* subject, his unlucky Jim. At the beginning of their friendship, Larkin took it for granted that he was the more serious, the more loftily destined of the two. On the face of it, in 1941, the two were neck and neck, a couple of randy bachelor types who didn't give a bugger, partners in pornography, swapping smut, comparing readings on their ever-active masturbation charts, and all the rest of it. Each of them was working on a novel, and although we don't know what Amis thought of his own work at this time (or, come to that, of Larkin's) we are in no doubt of Larkin's intensity of purpose.

'I so badly want to write novels' he wrote (again, though, not to Amis), novels that would be 'a mix of Lawrence, Thomas Hardy and George Eliot'. In order to achieve this aim, he is already shaping up to distance himself from enfeebling human attachments: 'I find that once I "give in" to another person . . . there is a slackening and dulling of the peculiar artistic fibres . . .' As early as 1943, he is looking forward to a 'lonely bachelorhood interspersed with buggery and strictly monetary fornication'. At this stage, such resolutions are for art's sake and are anyway half-joking. Amis's readiness to get sexually involved is to be envied in some ways but it also suggests a failure of essential seriousness. On the very few occasions when Larkin does address Amis solemnly, as writer to writer, the tone is close to condescending: 'You know that the putting down of good words about good things is the mainspring of my endeavours.'

By the age of twenty-five, Larkin had published two novels and one book of poems, with another book of poems ready, as he thought, for publication. Amis had managed but one volume of his verse; none of his fiction had appeared. Six years later, Larkin had one further publication to his credit – the privately-printed *XX Poems* – and Amis had come out with *Lucky Jim*, a novel that had its comic roots in the ribald world which he and Larkin had once shared and which (so Larkin may have thought) they had invented. Its spectacular success, coming when it did, must have been hard for Larkin to endure. Or maybe he didn't give a toss.

It is unusual for a writer's letters – all foreground and virtually no background – to come out in advance of a biography, and the Amis connection is just one of several areas on which conjecture is rather teasingly encouraged. More familiar, perhaps, than the idea of Larkin-the-careerist is the idea of Larkin-the-depressive, but here too we have too many gaps in the life-story, too many possible crisis-points, too many relationships that are insufficiently explained. Even so, as a chronicle of ever-deepening wretchedness, this book has weight enough. From 1945, when he takes his first job as a librarian in Leicester (having already written his two novels), until his death forty years later, the pattern of complaint remains more or less the same: the job is boring, the writing is going badly or not going at all, the relationship he is in – if there is one – is dreary, futureless and guilt-inducing, the world – and England in particular – is going to pot, thanks usually to lefties, foreigners and niggers.

Pornography, cricket, jazz, gin, Mrs Thatcher and the occasional spring day provide relief but even these oases are eventually discovered to be tainted. Pornography is all very well but where – in real life – do you get to see 'schoolgirls suck each other off while you whip them'? Test matches have to be avoided because there are 'too many fucking niggers about', too many 'Caribbean germs'. Even good jazz gets boring in late middle age and the trouble with spring is that you're *supposed* to like it. Gin, he was advised, is killing him. Only Mrs Thatcher (along with D.H. Lawrence) fails in the end to disappoint, but Larkin lashes himself for having disappointed *her*: he refuses the offered Laureateship because, he says, he has become 'a turned-off tap'. 'A Laureate can fall silent but he cannot be dumb from the start.'

Larkin stopped writing altogether in 1977, the year his mother died, and in his last years the routine misery takes on a sharper, more urgently self-loathing edge, as if the one thing that had made the rest just about possible to bear had, by withdrawing, left him exposed – to the world, and to himself – as an imposter, a grotesque: 'In the old days, depression wasn't too bad because I could write about it. Now writing has left me, and only depression remains.' 'So now we face 1982, sixteen stone six, gargantuanly paunched, helplessly addicted to alcohol, tired of livin' and scared of dyin', world-famous unable-to-write poet.'

Now and then, Larkin's misery sounds clinical, there from the start, as when he writes that 'Depression hangs over me as if I were Iceland' or (in 1949) that he feels as if he has been 'doctored in some way, and my central core dripped on with acid'. At other times, of course, it comes across as Larkinesque, the act he opted for because it was so easy to perform, so 'true to life'. What might have made a difference? In 1944, he wrote:

You see, my trouble is that I simply can't understand anybody doing anything but write, paint, compose music – I can understand their doing things as a means to these ends, but I can't see what a man is up to who is satisfied to follow a profession in the normal way. If I hadn't the continual knowledge that 'when all this bloody work is through for today I can start work again' or 'this half-hour is simply ghastly, but one day it will have been digested sufficiently to be written about' – if I didn't think that, I don't know what I should do. And all the people who don't think it, what do they do? What are they striving for?

The great novel never happened and perhaps Larkin recognised – and hated to recognise – how little of the true novelist's generosity, or curiosity, of spirit he could actually muster or sustain. But he was proud of what he did write, even though it was in the nature of his gift that its appearances would be intermittent, and it is unlikely that he was all that tormented by his failure to write fiction. He may have wanted to *be* Kingsley Amis (now and then) but it seems doubtful that he would have wanted to swap oeuvres.

The love of a good woman? Larkin's misogyny was well entrenched by his early twenties – all women are stupid, he would say, they make scenes, they cling, they are forever parading their 'emotional haberdashery', they want babies, and so on – but who knows how things might have turned out if he had been luckier in his liaisons? Or, he would no doubt have retorted, more courageous, better-looking, or more ready to fork out for endless boring dinners (with no money back when it's all over)? In the early-fifties, there was one affair (described by the editor as 'passionate') which seems to have made more than the usual impact. Patsy Strang, a married woman, actually has Larkin addressing her as 'sugarbush' and 'honeybear'.

The episode is short-lived but the recollection of it somehow hangs over all subsequent involvements. When it ended Larkin wrote to her:

You are the sort of person one can't help feeling (in a carping sort of way) *ought* to come one's way *once* in one's life – without really expecting she will – and since you did, I feel I mustn't raise a howl when circumstances withdraw you, however much I miss you – it would be ungrateful to fortune, if you see what I mean . . . do you? At least, that's what I try to feel! But oh dear, oh dear! You were so wonderful!

There is no other moment quite like this in the book. To turn the screw, Patsy Strang died – of alcoholic poisoning – in 1977, two months before old Mrs Larkin died. This was, of course, the year of Larkin's 'retirement' from writing poetry, and the year too in which he finally completed the poem 'Aubade': 'the good not done, the love not given, time/torn off unused.'

1992

ANTHONY THWAITE (Editor)
Selected Letters of Philip Larkin, 1940–1985
Faber

Philip Larkin: 3. The Biography

A couple of weeks ago, there was a write-up in the *Independent* about a rap performer name of Ice Cube, author of 'A Bitch is a Bitch' and 'Now I Gotta Wet'cha'. Ice Cube, we were told, is notorious for his misogyny and racism and for whipping up his fans into ecstasies of loathing: he has them 'grooving to a litany of hate'. Only one of Ice Cube's lines was quoted – 'You can't trust no bitch. Who can I trust? Me' – but the reviewer did attempt to pinpoint his subject's characteristic manner of address. He called Ice Cube's language 'incessantly Larkinesque'.

Larkinesque? Did this mean that Ice Cube, for all his appearance of commercialised aggression, was secretly a somewhat poignant type of artist, wry, subtle, elegiac; that his dignified, distressful lyrics were likely to linger in the memory for decades? It seems not. In this context, 'Larkinesque' signified 'foulmouthed'. And the *Independent*'s readers were supposed to know this. Oh, Larkinesque, they'd think as one, *that* means Cube uses the word 'fuck' a lot.

And who can blame them if they do so think? After all, in the week before the Ice Cube notice, these same readers were treated to a daily dose of Philip Larkin's more repulsive aperçus: sexual intercourse is like having someone else blow your nose, women are stupid, kids should be sent away to orphanages more or less at birth, and all the rest of it. At the bottom of one page, in a little box, we would get the *Independent*'s 'Daily Poem' – usually some workmanlike concoction without a flicker of inspiration or originality – and on another, similarly boxed, there would be the ugly mug of Philip Larkin, together with a line or two of his off-the-cuff plain-speaking. What a busy newspaper: encouraging *les jeunes* and les no-hopers even as it chips away at the repute of the best poet we have had since Auden.

A few years ago, 'Larkinesque' suggested qualities both lovable and glum. Nowadays, it means four-letter words and hateful views. As Larkin once predicted, his 'Lake Isle of Innisfree' has turned out to be not 'Church Going' or 'The Whitsun Weddings' but 'This Be The Verse': 'They fuck you up, your mum and dad'. 'I fully expect to hear it recited by a thousand Girl Guides before I die,' he said. A thousand Ice Cube fans, more like; or can we look forward to the formation of a new rap ensemble, name of Larkinesque?

How did this come about? Many would say that last year's *Selected Letters* are to blame. Without meaning to, the edition showed Larkin to be a fairly unpleasant piece of work, mean-spirited and – yes – foul-mouthed, and there was not enough in the way of biographical context for his would-be defenders to get hold of. The *Letters*, amusing as they sometimes were, gave us a mouthpiece not a man. But even so, the widespread outrage seemed excessive. It was not as if the living Larkin had gone out of his way to make us want to be his chums. Unlike John Betjeman or Stevie Smith, two poets he admired, he did not set out to be 'much loved' – although he did like to be much mentioned. There was a vein of coarseness on display from the beginning. Larkin turned it to advantage in his work, setting it off against an equally strong vein of tender sentiment, but we always believed him when he said that 'self's the man'.

We knew too that this poet's personality, his off-colour ribaldry and slang, had been shaped in the 'come-off-it' postwar years and nurtured in dreary provincial towns, in seedy digs and gas-lit libraries. We had no proof, but we rather suspected that Larkin collected hardish porn, had it in for blacks and queers, was careful with his money and, when it came to relationships, too morbidly obsessed with his own failings to be much of a lover or a friend. Plenty of this we were able to pick up from the poems but these were usually so well judged, as dramas or confessions, that we could speak also of a Larkinesque 'persona' – a self-projection that might in part be a disguise.

When Larkin died in 1985, at sixty-three, the obituaries were full of warmth; there was much talk of our 'nation's loss'. He was known to have gone a bit funny in his final years, falling in love with Mrs Thatcher and giving out with some reactionary comment, but all this was reckoned to be amiably bufferish, a bit of a self-parody, and somehow valuably English in its concern for old-style ways.

Only a few people knew that there was nothing at all funny about the way Larkin had gone funny, that his conservatism was tinged with the same vehemence that marked his ever-deepening self-hatred and despair. There was also a drink problem, a port-for-breakfast kind of drink problem. Since the death of his mother in 1977, he had stopped writing poetry, or stopped expecting to write poetry, and when he did take up his pen it was either from duty or from rage – and it was not always easy to tell which was which.

When Larkin's *Collected Poems* appeared in 1988, Anthony Thwaite – the book's editor – was criticised for certain policy decisions, but nobody complained that he had left out late, unpublished pieces like 'Prison for strikers/Bring back the cat/Kick out the niggers/What about that'. Some readers, though, did wonder about his inclusion of a startling poem called 'Love Again', which he had discovered among Larkin's papers:

> Love again: wanking at ten-past three
> (Surely he's taken her home by now?),
> The bedroom's hot as a bakery,
> The drink gone dead . . .
>
> Someone else feeling her breasts and cunt,
> Someone else drowned in that lash-wide stare,
> And me supposed to be ignorant,
> Or find it funny, or not to care,
> Even . . . but why put it into words?

It might seem at first that this poem should not have come as a surprise, that it was just another bit of grumbling about girls. And yet it did. None of Larkin's earlier unburdenings had had anything like the same unmerciful ferocity, the same screaming-point force of attack. There is no attempt here to mitigate the central emotion of the poem, no 'Well, what do you expect?', not even much of a late bid for plangency, for general wisdom – indeed, on this score, it is the failure of his attempt to open the thing out that does the clinching:

> Isolate rather this element
>
> That spreads through other lives like a tree
> And sways them on in a sort of sense
> And say why it never worked for me.

Something to do with violence
A long way back, and wrong rewards,
And arrogant eternity.

If Larkin had lived, he probably would not have published 'Love Again'. On the other hand, one's guess is that he rather badly wanted us to see it. We knew he was 'fucked up' because he'd told us so, in poem after poem, but the Larkin we admired *was* 'supposed to find it funny or not to care' or at any rate to have the gift of transmuting daily glooms into great haunting statements about love and death – ours as well as his. In 'Love Again' the unhappiness strictly belongs to him: our share in it is that of the pitying spectator.

Andrew Motion knew Larkin during the years of 'Love Again' and although his biography begins at the beginning, and has many interesting revelations about the poet's early years, there is nearly always a sense that he is working backwards from that poem, or from what he had learned from that poem about the essential hopelessness of his subject's predicament. Motion has said that he wrote this biography 'with love'. He loves the poems, certainly, and leads us through them, one by one, with easy reverence, but his feelings about their author often seem to be equivocal. He wants to love Larkin but much of the time the best he can muster is a sort of muffled, reluctant pity-cum-contempt. Much of the time also there is simple bewilderment: why *did* Larkin get so little sense of achievement out of what he had achieved?

A sense of achievement is not the same as a need to be acknowledged as the tops. Larkin from the start believed, or said he did, in his own 'genius', but even as an adolescent he seems to have spent more time worrying about how to make it as a writer than he did enjoying the satisfactions of a job well done – or, come to that, making sure the job *was* well done. He was constantly checking his age against the ages of his rivals, both alive and dead, his progress against theirs, and when he first met Kingsley Amis he was appalled to find himself 'for the first time in the presence of a talent greater than my own'.

And this Amis rivalry was all-important later on. Larkin fancied himself as a novelist and when he finally conceded that fiction was beyond him, or beneath him, he also had to concede that, unlike Amis, he would never be able to 'live as a writer': the toad work would squat on him for keeps. And this meant that other puerile fantasies had to be relinquished: the villa in the South of France, the quilted smoking-jackets, the under-age groupies, and so on. The young Larkin had a somewhat raffish, Maughamesque notion of how writers lived, and he would dress the part: bow ties, cerise trousers, poncy kerchiefs, lashings of Brylcreem – the stuff, verily, of fiction.

When Larkin abandoned fiction for verse, out came the cycle clips. Poems may be wonderful but being a poet was for him a bit like being, well, himself – the self he hoped Art would help him to escape. As a novelist, he might have got rid of his stammer, his thick specs; he might have become better-looking and mastered his awkwardness with girls. As a poet he would be condemned to relive or to perpetuate his grotty adolescence. It would be introspection all the way. No routes would open into the thrilling, despicable, exterior 'real world'. Poetry would ensure that he stayed where he was, stayed who he was.

We have now seen enough of Larkin's early unpublished poems to be certain that, had he not stayed where he was, he might have grown up to be a cut-price Yeats or Auden. Immobility became his subject, and the Hardy influence intruded just in time. And it is the Hardy biography that often comes to mind as we scrutinise Larkin's dull, complicated life. There is the selfishness, the stinginess, the petty vanities. There is the clenched and murky wistfulness about sex, the near-sentimental veneration of animals and landscapes, the yearning for romantic absolutes. Remorse is a powerful emotion in both poets. Larkin spent most of his life complaining about his mother's trivial-minded possessiveness but when she died he knew exactly how to feel.

Larkin once predicted of himself: 'I believe when I am old I shall bitterly regret having wasted my life, which I may have done. This is because I shall never attain the absolute – in other words the *continual* ecstasy – because it doesn't exist. Therefore in addition to being afraid of death, I shall feel cheated and angry.' This is the kind of talk that gets poetry a bad name. In Larkin's case, a whole lifetime was spent avoiding not just the 'continual ecstasy' that 'doesn't exist' but also the non-continual fragments of near-ecstasy that actually did come his way, the sort of ecstasy that costs money, wastes time and is productive of much personal inconvenience. One of the last poems he wrote was about a hedgehog he had accidentally killed. 'We should be careful of each other', he wrote, 'We should be kind/While there is still time.' To which we might feel like responding, as to some of Hardy's similar laments: perhaps there was still time.

'We should be careful of each other' assumes an ambiguous import when we explore, with Motion's guidance, Larkin's dealings with 'his' women. It turns out that far from being cut off from the world of sexual entanglements, he was up to his neck in them, to the point sometimes of near-strangulation. The strongest part of Motion's book comes with his coverage of the final years, when Larkin had at first two, then three women who felt themselves to have a claim on him. There was the long-serving Monica, his mostly absentee companion for more than thirty years. There was Maeve, a Roman Catholic with strong views about pre-marital sex, who kept Larkin at bay for seventeen years before finally submitting. And then, five years before he died and about five minutes after Maeve's capitulation, there was Betty, his 'loaf-haired' secretary at the Hull University Library. Maeve knew nothing of Betty (nor did she know, until after Larkin's death, about his porno mags; the revelation made her feel unclean). Monica and Maeve knew about each other, but Larkin assiduously kept the two apart, and mostly in the dark: he was always telling the one that he had stopped caring for the other. For a long stretch, then, of his adult life, Larkin was able to see himself as under siege, his dismal bachelorhood a citadel. Much of his anguish, in the later stages, was to do with his fear that the invaders might simply pack up and go away. The crunch came when Monica's ill-health required Larkin to allow her to move in with him.

Andrew Motion skilfully prepares the ground for all this complication. He has at least one eyebrow raised but decently tries to see things from the Larkin point of view. And in the book as a whole, he is in no doubt that sex is the narrative mainspring. Early on, Larkin's sex-life was as we had imagined it: all in the mind. He had no luck at school, and not much luck at Oxford, where the bluestockings he ineptly groped would cry: 'I'd really rather not, thank you.' There was a fleeting homosexual liaison – 'a few messy encounters', recalls the favoured swain, one Philip Brown, a co-student at St John's – and after that a period of ambivalent dream-jottings in which Larkin recorded visions of male-membered girls. This was followed by a sado-masochistic interlude, during which he wrote fiction about schoolgirl swishings at St Bride's.

Real women began to enter his life in 1943, when he started work as a librarian – work, as Motion shows, which he took far more seriously than he let on. By this time, though, he had already devised his Philosophy of Sex. His parents' marriage – the father a bookish, imperious Nazi-fancier, the mother a vacuous slow-drip complainer – had instilled in him a determination to stay unattached. Their union, he said, had 'left me with two convictions: that human beings should not live together and that children should be taken from their parents at an early age'. When he was twenty-one, and stepping out with his first girl (a schoolgirl, Ruth Bowman, whom he had been helping with her literary research), he was telling his male friends: 'I *don't* want to take a girl out and spend circa £5 when I can toss myself off in five minutes, free, and have the rest of the evening for myself.' When he did briefly get himself engaged to Ruth, he made it clear that 'marriage would not automatically follow'. Poor Ruth has described one of their typically lacklustre dates: the young poet had fallen strangely silent, she recalls, and when she asked him what the matter was, he'd said: 'I've just thought what it would be like to be old and have no one to look after me.'

And this rather set the tone for the relationships that followed. One affair, with Patsy Strang, does seem to have carried a romantic-erotic charge, but this was perhaps because Strang was safely married and anyway a bit of a bohemian; she was also quite well off. Even so, one of the few touching letters in the Thwaite selection from the *Letters* was the one Larkin wrote to Strang when she ended their affair:

> You are the sort of person one can't help feeling (in a carping sort of way) *ought* to come one's way *once* in one's life – without really expecting she will – and since you did, I feel I mustn't raise a howl when circumstances withdraw you, however much I miss you – it would be ungrateful to fortune, if you see what I mean . . . do you? At least, that's what I try to feel! But oh dear, oh dear! You were so wonderful!

Motion, in his printing, unaccountably lops off 'You were so wonderful!' so that the letter feebly ends: 'Oh dear, oh dear! . . .'

143

This seems unfairly dampening when one considers how rarely Larkin let himself catch fire.

A question is raised here about the relationship between Andrew Motion's biography and Anthony Thwaite's *Selected Letters*. Most people found it odd that the *Letters* preceded the *Life* and after reading Motion they may find it odder still. It seems that, whenever possible, Motion avoids quoting from letters which are already available in Thwaite. Thus, in a few instances, he appears to deny himself evidence which is more powerful or telling than his own. For example, the letters Larkin wrote to his friend Jim Sutton seem to have been shared out between Motion and Thwaite. There are about two hundred letters in existence, Thwaite has said. Of these, Thwaite prints over seventy and Motion cites about one hundred and twenty. Forty of the letters to Sutton that appear in Thwaite are not referred to in Motion and some that Motion does quote from sound more interesting and important than one or two of those picked out by Thwaite. Now and again, in order to get a full picture of Larkin's response to this or that event, we are obliged to turn from Motion to Thwaite and back again. You may not want to know the full extent of Larkin's worship of D.H. Lawrence or about his early interest in the visual arts, but if you do, don't throw away your Thwaite. Are the two books meant to dovetail in this way or is it just that a biographer instinctively prefers new material to old – six months old, in this case? Either way, it seems a bit rough on the reader. Larkin would have thought so, to be sure. One remembers his response to the break-up of the marriage of two friends: 'I suppose I shall have to start seeing them both now – take double the time. Arrgh!'

Andrew Motion has taken five years to write this book and his industry can be applauded. He has dug up many gems – an autobiographical fragment, pocket diaries, not-known-of early drafts – and he has persuaded people to talk to him who had good reason to refuse. Maeve Brennan's testimony is surely something of a coup, although she may not be delighted to read here that Larkin used to get excited by her hairy arms ('PAL to author' is the source). We don't get as many letters *to* Larkin as we would have wished, so that it is not always clear what *he* is having to put up with, but presumably Motion's witnesses drew the line at this more intimate kind of exposure.

As a biographer, Motion is painstaking and intelligent and he has some valuable insights but for my taste he is too solemnly intrusive: he likes explaining things and is forever teasing out supposed internal conflicts, in case we can't see them for ourselves. The teacher in him is often at war with the narrator and, in the early sections of the book, where he is guessing, he slips easily into an inert biographese: 'It was a tentative step towards the high mountain of art', 'By the summer of 1938 the fountain of creativity was jetting up poems as well as stories'. 'Fountain? Mountain?' we can hear his subject growl, 'make up your mind.'

1993

ANDREW MOTION
Philip Larkin: A Writer's Life
Faber

James Merrill

Twenty-five years ago James Merrill and his friend David Jackson began taking dictation from The Other World. It was a kind of parlour game – the two chums would set up their Ouija board and smilingly invite smart-talking spirits down (or is it out?) to play. The spirits, luckily, turned out to be chaps rather like themselves – droll, aesthetic types with a taste for whimsical speculation and a fast ear for silly puns. Merrill began taking notes of some of their exchanges and indeed incorporated one or two fragments of spirit speech into his poems. His transcriptions, it seems, were not entirely word for word, and he permitted himself a certain amount of creative editing.

Such airy interventions did not sit oddly in James Merrill's work. Even though (with *Water Street* in 1962) he had toughened and colloquialised his verse line and eliminated much of the wan artifice that marked his very early work, there was still – in his usual persona – a strain of yearning otherworldliness, a delicate discomfiture which was neither neurotic nor ideological. His was a poetry of, and for, the few – the few kindred spirits, one might say.

It seems to have been in the early seventies that Merrill recognised the larger possibilities of his Ouija evenings: the 'openings' they offered him into a limitless new realm of subject matter – or, rather, of subjects without matter. He could, with a little help from his teacup, summon a cast of unchallengeable wits and seers – he could quiz them and cajole them, he could submit to their rebukes, he could be instructed by them in morality and art, he could invest them with comic otherworldly personalities, he could dream up post-mortal ranks and stations. He could even, if the mood took him, resurrect and chat for hours with his favourite dead friends.

There would be opportunities also for the poet to play around

146

with theology and science, to dabble in history and myth, to invent comically unsuitable reincarnations for the recently departed, as well as strange 'earlier lives' for the still-with-us. Best of all, Merrill – the poet and auditor – could himself remain entirely sane throughout all this; altogether this-worldly in his ironies, his wry asides, his mock-bafflement, his amused deference to intelligences more spacious and untrammelled than his own. He had discovered, in other words – and, come to think of it, in others' words – a way to launch a modern epic, a vast catch-all enterprise on the scale of Pound's *Cantos*. The advantage of Merrill's epic, though, would be that he could always deflate it from within – the heavens he listened in on could always be brought down to earth.

Well, after some eight years of truly awesome labour, Merrill here offers us the finished work. Three parts of it have, of course, already appeared in book form – *The Book of Ephraim*, published as *Divine Comedies* in 1976, *Mirabell: Books of Number* in 1978 and *Scripts for the Pageant* in 1980. The whole poem – incorporating these three books and adding a new 'coda', *The Higher Keys* – is to be known as *The Changing Light at Sandover*.

All in all, it is a sprawling, daunting work, running to over 500 pages: that's to say, some 20,000 lines – about twice the length of *Paradise Lost*. Harold Bloom has said of *The Book of Ephraim*: 'I don't know that [it], at least after some dozen readings, can be over-praised.' A neat way of disarming reviewers who have only had time to read the work 'some once', or at the very best 'some twice'. Evidently, we should be cautious about anything resembling a final judgement on this thoroughly original verse monster.

Even so, something must be said, however unreliably impressionistic. It seems clear that Merrill's epic has not been constructed to any Miltonic grand design: it has simply unfolded, year by year. One doubts that the poet quite knew where it would lead him when he first started out. It could be that Merrill was egged on by his admirers to keep extending the work's Larger Importance. At any rate, it is hard for the new reader not to detect a gradual drift from sprightly wit to leaden wisdom, from inspiration to sheer effort. At the beginning, with *Ephraim*, we have a nice idea, rather brilliantly executed. As the work progresses, it becomes bloated with its own epic pretensions. The longueurs get longer, the speculation more solemn or emptily fanciful, the human presences more numb, the comedy more strenuously 'gay'. Since Merrill is a clever man, and a real poet, he never quite gets bogged down – indeed, there are some strong lyric parentheses throughout the later books – but he does move perilously close at times to mere garrulity. A quotation from one of his more prostrate fans, Charles Berger, might unwittingly hint at something of this sort:

> When *Divine Comedies* appeared in 1976, including the book-length *Ephraim*, readers could still praise Merrill's superb artistry while evading the content of his vision. This is no longer possible. For *Mirabell* and *Scripts* raise so many profound questions about sacred poetry and the relation of the individual to the cosmos, that evading their doctrines would also entail ignoring the wisdom literature of Merrill's greatest predecessors – poets such as Dante, Homer, Milton, Blake.

What can this mean (it is printed on the dust jacket of *The Changing Light at Sandover*)? We will never know, but in the meantime it is hard to warm to a text which attracts such bovine homage.

Ephraim, the first book of Merrill's sequence, does indeed permit us to evade 'the content of his vision', and is all the better for doing so. The book has a vivid central ghost, Ephraim himself, who is far more than a device for instructing us on 'the relation of the individual to the cosmos'; he is a memorable fictional character in his own right. And there is a fine balance in the book between supernatural high-jinks and earthbound woes. The trouble begins precisely when Merrill starts using the poem to raise 'profound questions' and to make sure that we are unable to 'evade' them.

In the later books there are, to be sure, several stretches in which the old balance is recaptured, and Ephraim does make welcome reappearances, but as we read on, the first volume comes more and more to seem a triumph of correct scale. It offers a cosmology that is touchingly miniature and incongruously social. Once this scale gets abandoned, Merrill feels free to indulge himself, to ramble and inflate. Here again, he is ready to disarm us with talk of '. . . this net of loose talk tightening to verse/ And verse once more revolving between two poles/ Gassy expansion and succinct collapse', but this kind of easy charm is, surely, far too easy.

In all four books, the Ouija board's messages are presented in upper-case type – like a computer printout, as someone has observed. In *Ephraim*, this seems an originality to be savoured.

JAMES MERRILL

In the later books, though, there is a growing oppressiveness as we encounter yet another five-page slab of not entirely lucid capitals. After a time, the snatches of humble upper and lower case typography (used for the human voices) seem to beckon like oases. When Merrill is writing as Merrill – setting a scene, fondly reminiscing, or offering some wry rejoinder to the gods – there is an immediate access of sharpness and weight in the actual writing. Although he seems content to let the spirit world bore us to distraction, he is careful never to let the character J.M. surrender our esteem. And in this, it must be said, he does largely succeed.

A selection from Merrill's first nine books is now gathered together in one volume – somewhat coyly titled *From the First Nine* – and it offers an opportunity to remark once more the strength of his lyric and short-narrative gift during the decade 1962–72, and also to note continuities between those earlier volumes (particularly *Nights and Days* and *Braving the Elements*) and the several haunting earthly sections which are embedded in his epic.

1983

JAMES MERRILL
The Changing Light at Sandover and *From the First Nine: Poems 1946–76*
New York: Atheneum

149

Wallace Stevens

Although it is fairly commonplace nowadays for Wallace Stevens to be ranked as one of the major modern poets, it is rare to hear him or his works spoken of with great affection. He is admired, and often imitated, and the Ph.D. industry in America would not be the same without him, but not even his most ardent fans seem able to get close to the personality behind the poems. And this was precisely how Stevens wanted it to be. In his lifetime, he made sure that other people were kept at arm's length and, although he cared little for posterity, it would have pleased him to know that his invisibility was built to last. He had no wish for a readership that would warm to *him* via his poems. Of Robert Frost, he once said: 'His work is full (or said to be full) of humanity.' Using the Stevens lexicon, there could have been no more withering indictment.

From the beginning Stevens's aloofness was a source of irritation to his critics, and in some quarters remains so to this day. He did not publish his first book, *Harmonium*, until he was forty-five (in 1923), although he had been writing and publishing in magazines for over twenty years. 'A book of poems,' he used to say, 'is a damned serious affair.' There was in this an implied disdain for the hustling of his contemporaries and one or two of them took it amiss: after all, they would say, it was easy for Stevens to take his time – he was Vice-President of an insurance company, he lived in a big house in Connecticut, he had no exposure to the rigours of the committed literary life, he took no risks. Nobody then knew that the 'fat cat' Wallace Stevens had been told by his doctor that he would probably die in his forties. The problem was high blood-pressure: another routine anti-Stevens line was that he was 'thin-blooded' and 'complacent'.

Admittedly it did not help that *Harmonium* was a somewhat

150

dandified affair, cryptic, unyielding and yet 'gaudy'. It was full of seemingly show-off dictionary words like 'fubbed' and 'princox', 'girandoles' and 'carked', and it exhibited a modish Francophilia – this was much-mocked because Stevens had never been to Europe and took all his holidays in Florida. There was also a vein of conceited playfulness on show, in titles like 'The Paltry Nude Starts on a Spring Voyage' or 'The Bird with the Coppery, Keen Claws' and a weird jungle-exoticism, a 'dreaming of tigers/in red weather' that seemed to derive more from the travel brochure than from any intense personal imaginings. The manner throughout was urbane, and the tone ranged from the chuckling-oblique to the mellifluous-sublime. There are lines in Stevens that are silly or boring but almost none that are incompetent. 'No one else,' wrote one critic of the day, 'monocled and gloved, can cut so faultless a figure standing in his box at the circus of life.' But even when Stevens seemed to be taking himself most solemnly there was thought to be a sinister contentedness in his celebration of the hedonistic here-and-now in 'Sunday Morning' or in the jaunty and ingenious annotations of 'Thirteen Ways of Looking at a Blackbird'.

Harmonium was a commercial failure, even by the standards of poetry publishing: it sold fewer than a hundred copies. For the next five or six years, Stevens gave up writing poetry and concentrated on consolidating his career in business. When he did start publishing again he was careful to do so in limited editions (150 copies) from small presses. It was not until 1936 that he reappeared in the market-place, when Knopf brought out his second volume, *Ideas of Order*, the book that is usually taken to signal his move away from dandy-aestheticism into the 'philosophical' mode for which he is now (probably) best known. Stevens was approaching sixty, and would live for another twenty years, years in which he published four more books and became a revered and prize-laden American poet. Remarkably, for such a late starter, his *Collected Poems* runs to over 500 pages and the newly re-issued *Opus Posthumous* carries another twenty or so late poems together with a sheaf of 'juvenilia' (in Stevens's case, work written in his twenties and thirties). The parsimonious connoisseur had discovered the necessity of eloquence.

Remarkable, yes, but looked at more closely, Stevens's new productivity could hardly have been otherwise: it was an irresistible function of those theories which he seems to have finally settled on in the mid-thirties and not much changed thereafter, theories which held the writing of poetry to be inseparable from the continuance of life – his own life, but also any human life that would seek to be worth living. It was this claim for poetry that became the subject of his poems, as it had to: 'After one has abandoned a belief in God,' he wrote, 'poetry is that essence which takes its place in life's redemption.' It was not that we should all be writing poetry: what matters is that we cultivate to the full our human 'ways of seeing': 'The sea is loveliest far in the abstract when the imagination can feed upon the idea of it. The thing itself is dirty, wobbly and wet.'

The imagination was godless, but had the power to be godlike: not godlike in the sense of issuing commandments or of telling us how we ought to deal with one another, but in its processes, in the activity of its own compositions ('the poem of the act of the mind') and in its continuous enrichment of the perceptible, created world. It was this process of enrichment that Stevens came to describe as the Supreme Fiction, although he was always careful to call his poems 'notes towards' that Fiction. We might think of them as notes towards some supreme, though finally elusive, Consolation.

In the thirties and the war years, there were those who saw the whole notion as a Supreme Self-Indulgence and were angered by Stevens's rapt aloofness from the common struggles. Asked in a questionnaire: 'As a poet what distinguishes you, do you think, from an ordinary man?', Stevens replied: 'Inability to see much point to the life of an ordinary man.' His critics were not appeased by the poet's willingness to add: 'The chances are an ordinary man himself sees very little point to it.'

Postwar, it was easier for readers to digest Stevens's talk about the supremacy of the Imagination and, having digested it, some critics were able to look back to the poems of *Harmonium* and detect in them, behind the gaudiness, that sense of near-intolerable loss, or lack, which breathes through everything that Stevens wrote. Stevens was a natural believer but he had the spiritual aristocrat's contempt for beliefs that were lazily or sentimentally espoused. *Harmonium* pulls faces at middle-class America and its inherited Religion, but behind the mockery there is a blank: no longer believing, what do I believe? Re-read thus, a poem like 'Sunday Morning' can seem less than fully committed to its own majestic cadences, and we are drawn also to shift a near-desolate piece like 'The Snow Man' somewhat closer to the centre of the stage. Here the poet is merely 'the listener, who listens in the snow,/And, nothing himself, beholds/Nothing that is not there and the nothing that is'.

Harmonium is the book we keep going back to, not only because most of Stevens's anthology pieces are in it, but because it is a book full of doubts and disguises. Throughout his long middle or late period, Stevens knew what he believed and his poetry became an enactment of that sure belief – each individual poem being not so much an intolerable struggle with words and meanings as a massively impressive demonstration of the imagination-at-work. Sometimes to read these poems is like listening in on some private, exquisitely well-mannered act of worship.

Like other sorts of worshipper, Stevens was not afraid of monotony, or repetition, or of an obscurity which even the most finely tuned eavesdropper will find hard to clarify. His critics have continued to complain, with some justice, that he had little or no interest in the dramatic, the social, the autobiographical, that there is nothing 'vulnerable' in his work. And it is surely because we know all this that we are likely to respond so readily to the unexpectedly heartfelt final act in Stevens's 'non-drama': the poems he wrote at the very end of his life, poems in which he was obliged to face the Fact which had all along both mocked and energised his Fictions:

> It makes so little difference, at so much more
> Than seventy, where one looks, one has been there before.

> Woodsmoke rises through trees, is caught in an upper flow
> Of air and whirled away. But it has often been so.

From another poet, this might sound merely defeated. From Stevens, who had 'been there before' so often and with such an enraptured vitality of mind, it comes across as near-heroic. And this final surge of poignancy can make us all the more alert to what was heroic in Stevens's monotonies and repetitions:

> The man-hero is not the exceptional monster,
> But he that of repetition is most master.

1990

WALLACE STEVENS
Opus Posthumous, edited by Milton J. Bates
Faber

Seamus Heaney

'About the only *enmity* I have is towards pride.' Seamus Heaney said this in an interview and, since we know him to be the most over-interviewed of living poets, perhaps he shouldn't be forced to say it again here. Put in its context, though, this too-worthy sounding protestation has much to reveal about the disposition of Heaney's work so far, and can even be read as a riposte to those critics who complain that, for all its verbal richness and its moral courage, his work is strangely without 'personality'.

In the interview, Heaney was talking about his Catholicism, about how his sensibility had been 'formed by the dolorous murmurings of the rosary, and the generally Marian quality of devotion' afforded by the Roman Church – a Church which Heaney, even in his twenties, continued to go to for Confession and which 'permeated' the whole life of his Northern Ireland childhood. Thanks to this Church, its doctrines and its rituals, Heaney's sensibility was from the start centred towards what he calls a 'feminine presence'. It was this presence that induced in him his 'only enmity':

> A religion that has a feminine component and a notion of the mother in the transcendental world is better than a religion that just has a father, a man, in it. I also – just in my nature and temperament, I suppose – believed in humility and in bowing down, and in 'we' rather than 'I'. I hate a *moi* situation, an egotism, a presumption, a *hubris*, and I'm used to bowing down to the mother as a way of saying that. About the only *enmity* I have is towards pride.

When people complain about the absence of 'personality' in

154

Heaney's work, they are at some level complaining also that the 'moi situation' has been skirted or suppressed, and that as a result his poems lack the sort of sharply individual human tone that Larkin has, or Frost, or Lowell. I have heard it said that Heaney's work is 'teachable but not memorable', that lines of his don't linger in the mind, and it certainly seems to be true that admirers of his do tend to remember images or situations or stylistic brilliances rather than cries from the heart or haunting melodies. He has written few 'inter-personal' poems that are any good, and he is better at addressing the dead than he is at confiding in the living.

Of course, when Heaney started writing – in the late-sixties – there was 'moi-poetry' aplenty to be haunted by, and we can now see that the literary-historical moment was precisely right for the eventual, if not imminent appearance of a poet for whom none of all that held any magnetism. A new Auden, a new Stevens might have seemed to be the answer, and shortly there were indeed new Audens, new Stevenses to choose from. But neither intellectualism nor playfulness nor mere perfection of technique would be enough to reclaim glamour for the impersonal, or anti-personal. The only real challenge to the over-intimate would have to come from a poetry that risked its opposite: the too-theatrical. A poetry to be listened in on would be most effectively displaced by a poetry that dared to resurrect some of the art's discredited rhetorical/theatrical presumptions. (These, it should be said, had by the early-seventies been 'discredited' not just by the aching whisperers of Confessionalism but also by cute performance stars and by sloganisers of the 'Left'.)

In terms of the desirable 'next step' for British poetry, Seamus Heaney had some obvious natural advantages. After all, confessional poetry was unlikely to seduce a Catholic. And, for the wishing-to-be-humble, there was not much allure either in the mock-humilities of Larkinesque. Even so, Heaney did not at first seem to offer much of a challenge to anything, or anyone – he was too much like Ted Hughes, minus the Lawrentian, black-magical ingredients, and he was a shade too youthfully delighted with the plopping, slopping, thwacking sounds of spade on soil, or milk in pail, etc. (Donnish critics have always loved this onomatopoeic side of Heaney, though: maybe because it gives them the chance to exhibit their own 'sensibilities' – 'You'll notice how the "thwa –" of "thwack" is shyly answered by the "plu –" of "plump"'.)

And yet, if one looks back now at Heaney's first two books, *Death of a Naturalist* and *Door Into the Dark*, it becomes evident that he had already there begun a sort of rebellion against the '*moi*', against the autobiographical 'I', the nervously wracked victim 'me'. The voice he spoke in, or rather the voice in which his poems spoke, already had a tinge of bardic anonymity, a suggestion that the self had indeed been humbled, but momentously: Seamus Heaney the man was being elected, so it seemed to him, into the role of Seamus Heaney, poet.

If this makes him sound like George Barker, it absolutely shouldn't. What is attractive about Heaney's response to his vocation is that he is never entirely happy that it is *he* who has been chosen: a childhood spent wondering how to avoid the priesthood had perhaps ill-prepared him for such singularity. And it is the marvelling near-reluctance with which he acknowledges his own election that silences, or ought to silence, any post-Movement tendency to scoff.

Like Dylan Thomas, like Graves, Heaney assumed the noble vestments, but he did so with an engaging awkwardness, a persuasive lack of flourish. One of the fascinations of Heaney's work, read from the beginning until now, is in observing how he shifts this way and that to find a genuinely comfortable *fit*, a non-fake, non-proud way of living in the sacred robes he knows he has the obligation and the right to wear. He can neither fling them off nor swap them for the more workaday gear which, in certain moods, he might feel more 'at home in'. But there is always a touch of 'Why me?' in his sometimes effortful transcending of the 'me', and this has given him a rare sturdiness of posture – rare, that is, for the 'chosen' sort of poet he's become. Indeed, it could be said that one of Heaney's principal achievements is that he has re-dignified the bardic stance.

There are those who would say that he has been helped in this by having something to be bardic *about*, by having arrived on-stage at a place and time when it was possible for him to say:

> To forge a poem is one thing, to forge the uncreated conscience
> of the race . . . is quite another and places daunting pressure and
> responsibilities on anyone who would risk the name of poet.

Certainly, it is hard to think of how an English poet could get away with saying this; but with Heaney 'getting away with it' does not arise. A Heaney without the Troubles that erupted just as he was finishing his second book would maybe have been all vocation and no job: archaeological, etymological, nostalgic, literary-grandiose and 'good on nature'. He might even have fallen victim to some Irish version of the thin-spined Californian-meditative which showed faint signs of enticing him around the time of his third volume, *Wintering Out*. From his first two books, it's hard to tell. These were much concerned with the *discovery* of his vocation, with measuring the distances between his sort of digging and that of the farm folk he'd grown up with, and with registering a sense of awe at the mysteries which seemed to lie ahead. When he has spoken of this period he has usually portrayed himself as almost-passive: the poems were already *in* him, he would say, and his task was to uncover them, to excavate, or even just to make himself available to their arrivals. He was also reading a lot of modern poetry, late in the day and in something of a hurry, it might seem, as if to seek directions, signs. The dark behind *The Door into the Dark* was, simply, dark.

The Troubles did erupt, though. Heaney wintered out the first few months, tinkering with place-names and imperilled Irish crafts, but he sensed from the start – from 1969 – that the bard's moment had almost certainly arrived, that from now on 'the problems of poetry' had changed 'from being simply a matter of achieving the satisfactory verbal icon to being a search for images and symbols adequate to our predicament'. Again, it is 'our' predicament, not his, although as a liberal, bloodshed-hating Northern Ireland Catholic with strong ties to the British, both personal and cultural, he could hardly have felt all that 'representative'. The 'we' at this point could so easily have surrendered to the '*moi*', and Heaney could respectably have withdrawn to the margins of his maddened tribe. He could even have done this without handing in his robes.

But he didn't, and his poetry since then has been a moving drama of discomfiture, of trying to reconcile the 'magic' aspects of his calling with, so to speak, the 'duties' of the tribal bard. He has never been confident that the two can be reconciled and whenever he has had to make the choice he has almost always chosen to safeguard the 'mystery' of his vocation. There have been wobbly moments, as in the second part of *North*, where he has tried to confront the 'Irish thing' in ordinary speech, as Seamus Heaney, but all in all he has held honourably fast to the objective he set himself at the beginning of the seventies: 'to discover a field of force in which, without abandoning fidelity to the processes and experiences of poetry . . . it would be possible to encompass the perspectives of a humane reason and at the same time grant the religious intensity of the violence its deplorable authenticity and complexity'. These words must have been arrived at with some anguish, and much care. It is not easy, perhaps not even possible, to speak of 'deplorable authenticity' without seeming to favour the 'authenticity' aspect of that formulation.

Heaney has looked for his 'field of force' in some out-of-the-way places, as remote sometimes from the present tense as he could reach: not in order to seek comfort from the past – unless there is comfort in knowing that history is comfortless – but to bring back 'befitting emblems of adversity'. Befitting they have been, and delivered with a curt or stoic shrug, as if to say: 'What can I say?':

> I am Hamlet the Dane,
> skull-handler, parablist,
> smeller of rot
>
> in the state, infused
> with its poisons,
> pinioned by ghosts
> and affections,
>
> murders and pieties,
> coming to consciousness,
> by jumping in graves,
> dithering, blathering.

It was with his fifth book, *Field Work*, that Heaney found a voice that is neither bleakly antiquarian nor awkwardly portentous. By this time the Troubles really had become *his* troubles. Friends and relatives of his were being killed: the *'moi'* could no longer be prevented from intruding some of its own nervous cadences. In poems like 'The Strand at Lough Beg' and 'A Postcard from North Antrim', Heaney sounds that 'heartbreak' note which Robert Lowell used to talk about. Maybe Lowell talked to *him* about it. *Field Work* has an elegy in memory of Lowell ('the master elegist'),

158

and the two poets saw each other often during the mid-seventies. In this book, even the 'love-poems' (a genre Heaney says he hates the sound of) are unaffectedly meant to be listened to by the beloved – and thus listened in to by the rest of us. But it's Heaney's Irish elegies that hurt the most:

> Across that strand of yours the cattle graze
> Up to their bellies in an early mist
> And now they turn their unbewildered gaze
> To where we work our way through squeaking sedge
> Drowning in dew. Like a dull blade with its edge
> Honed bright, Lough Beg half shines under the haze.
> I turn because the sweeping of your feet
> Has stopped behind me, to find you on your knees
> With blood and roadside muck in your hair and eyes,
> Then kneel in front of you in brimming grass
> And gather up cold handfuls of the dew
> To wash you, cousin. I dab you clean with moss
> Fine as the drizzle out of a low cloud.
> I lift you under the arms and lay you flat.
> With rushes that shoot green again, I plait
> Green scapulars to wear over your shroud.

Field Work, to my mind, is the book of Heaney's which we ought to keep in mind (how can we not?) when there are grumbles about 'anonymity' or 'suppression of the self'. His '*moi*' poems are all the stronger, all the more hard-won, it seems to me, not because they go against his notion of a tribal role but because – at their best – they don't: it's just that, in these poems, the 'I' lurks behind the 'we', and vice versa. And the elegy is, of course, the perfect form for such lurking, or entwining: an intimacy meant to be made public.

In *Station Island* (1984), Heaney returned to pondering the 'poet's role', but with a new despondency. He enlists the assistance of other artists, from Dante to James Joyce, and yearns guiltily for the 'clumps' and 'clunks' and 'clogs' of his most youthful verses. Not so guiltily, though, that he cannot welcome some jeering Joycean advice: 'Keep at a tangent./When they make the circle wide, it's time to swim/out on your own'. After all, what had those grand elegies in *Field Work* actually *done*, except perhaps to 'saccharine' with literature the suffering of those they claimed to mourn? The Dantesque apparitions contrived by Heaney in *Station Island* are accusatory, and our instinct (also contrived by Heaney?) is to spring to the defence of the accused, to tell him to 'Let go, let fly, forget/You've listened long enough. Now strike your note'. In the 'Sweeney' versions and translations which appeared in this country at the same time as *Station Island* the central fantasy is one of flight – of elevation *and* liberation.

Heaney's new book, *The Haw Lantern*, does strike one or two new notes, but it is slight and low-powered, by his standards. It shows signs not so much of high vocation as of obedient professionalism: a Phi Beta Kappa poem for Harvard, a poem for William Golding on his seventy-fifth birthday, a poem for Amnesty International, Irish Section, on Human Rights Day, 1985. And there are signs too that Heaney has set himself to learn from the oblique, clandestine parables and allegories which poets of Eastern Europe use to fox the censors. I am not sure that he has a light enough touch for modes like these (and in any case does their 'lightness' not thrive on necessity?) but perhaps for the moment they offer a relaxing middle path between the druid and the '*moi*'. A sense of exercise prevails throughout the book, except in the group of sonnets written in memory of the poet's mother, who died in 1984. These are touchingly uneven: fondly anecdotal, with some strongly sentimental moments, but sometimes almost breathtakingly ill-made:

> She'd manage something hampered and askew
> Every time, as if she might betray
> The hampered and inadequate by too
> Well-adjusted a vocabulary.

Or is Heaney himself attempting to avoid a similar betrayal? Certainly, throughout the sequence, there is a reluctance to reach for anything that might be thought of as poetic grandeur.

'Silence' and 'emptiness' are what these sonnets register, and one senses that silence and emptiness are at the emotional centre of this book. Weariness, also. Dutifully, mechanically almost, Heaney continues to be full of words, and full of worries about what to do with them. But he has been tired of such worries for some time: those robes, it seems, will never fit. In a poem called 'From the Frontier of Writing' he describes being stopped at an army road-block where 'everything is pure interrogation'. When he is eventually let through, he feels 'a little emptier, a little spent/as always by that quiver in the self,/subjugated, yes, and obedient'. The same kind of thing happens, he says, at the 'frontier of writing': the writer is interrogated, guns are aimed at him, data about him get checked out, he could easily be shot. If all goes well, though, he's allowed to cross the frontier, 'arraigned yet freed'. Seamus Heaney has been arraigned often enough, by himself and by others' expectations of him. Why is it so hard to think of him as ever being 'freed' – he who has dared to 'risk the name of poet'?

1987

SEAMUS HEANEY
The Haw Lantern
Faber

Andrew Motion

Andrew Motion is a lyric poet who wants to write non-lyric poems: he wants to tell stories, he wants to be chatty and discursive, he wants to move around in the world non-intensely, like a wise grown-up. Or, put it another way, Andrew Motion is a narrative poet who would rather be writing from the heart, whose long poems hunger to be short, whose 'adult sensibility' is useful to him chiefly as a means of making sense out of his half-remembered childhood.

There are indeed two ways of looking at this gifted poet. You can take your choice. Either way, you are left with a body of work which often gets its forcefulness from not quite knowing what sort of work it wants to be. Motion is an anthologist and editor of other people's verse: wondering about 'sorts of poetry' or 'what comes next?' is how he earns his keep. Maybe he worries too much about these things, or maybe his strength is that he's prepared to test himself in genres other than the ones which come to him most naturally. Certainly, there is a tension in his poetry – call it a tension between personality and practice – and to wish for it to be 'resolved' is perhaps to wish for something rather less intriguing than what's already on display.

In Motion's *Dangerous Play*, a selection of his Poems 1974–84, the most powerful piece of writing is in prose: a memoir of the poet's childhood. In it Motion tells of his mother's death after a long illness: she lay 'more or less comatose' for three years after a riding accident, then gradually recovered her speech 'before dying without leaving hospital almost exactly ten years after the accident'. Throughout these ten years, Motion's father visited his sick wife 'nearly every day, unstinting and saintly in his devotion to her'. Motion himself was sixteen when the accident happened:

he adored his mother and when he writes of her, alive and well, we like her too. The terrible ten years, and their conclusion, seem to cast a huge shadow over Motion's verse: a sense of the precarious is close to the heart of almost everything he writes, and so too is a regard for loyalty, for holding on. However relaxed he tries to be as an impersonal narrator, however many other voices he assumes – either in dramatic monologues or in the italicised snippets of dialogue he's keen on – there is almost always, line by line, an air of treading carefully, a feeling of anticipated loss.

This can make for a faint numbness in the actual language of the poems, even as we admire and understand what's going on. Motion's adjectives (and he does seem to feel a little lost without them) are not exactly the obvious ones, but at the same time they don't run any risks: moss, after all, is furry and the chances are that hedges *will* be scraggy, and so on. But rather this, perhaps, than to be told that someone's 'Sunday paper blows free/its awkward panicking wings/flap on the lawn'. All in all, Motion has probably been wise to keep his verbal inventiveness in check.

Treading carefully also comes into what he writes about: it is sometimes his subject – and when it is most evidently so, the impact is not easy to resist. His uncolourful speech seems just the right colour for what is being said. Motion has shown this in, say, the lyric sections of his long story-poem, 'Independence', and in 'Anniversaries', a group of short poems addressed directly to his mother: poems of bereavement in which keeping steady, holding on, is both the subject and the method.

Elsewhere in Motion's work there can be an uncomfortable tugging between the teller and the tale, and too often we find the poet trying to redeem a piece from prosiness by jacking up the resonance of its concluding lines. At best, though, the 'story-line' in Motion's story-poems does usefully inhibit his tendency to droop. And the stories are usually worth telling, even though their subject matter can, in outline, be made to sound off-puttingly exotic: they are quite often stories of Empire and the wars that have been fought in its defence.

In other words, they speak of the sort of Englishness his parents took for granted. Looked at in this way, they too can be read as poems of bereavement: Motion writes of these past epochs with a modest but persuasive intimacy – as if, by imagining himself back into his parents' youth, he has been able to re-connect with what he's lost. None of this, one ought to say, is on the surface, and there is maybe a presumption in calling it essential. And yet Motion is interested in ideas about fiction, ideas about what we use it for:

> Florrie sat on a grass-grown crumbling stack of peat with the boy by her side, and as soon as she whispered *Come on. We've done it before*, I made him imagine his father garotting the stag, slitting the stomach and sliding his hands inside for warmth. He was never myself, this boy, but I know if I tell you his story you'll think we are one and the same: both of us hiding in fictions which say what we cannot admit to ourselves.

There is not much hiding going on in Andrew Motion's latest book, although the verse-story genre is still prominent – most notably with a rambling, or ambling, memoir of his schooldays that is readable enough but too often makes you wonder why it has to be in verse:

> A fool, that was the thing to be,
> a Holy Fool – perhaps for life,
> perhaps for a term, or a week –
> but always living inside the law,
> as long as the law allowed me time
> to please myself with my own devices.

There is also a likeable fantasy about a dancing hippo, in which the oddly endowed beast seems to be presented as a sort of artist-type: '*I know it was useless, of course, the dancing./I know. Like Everything else we do. But God above/it was beautiful. God!* – or something like that.' This sort of amusing magazine-poem now comes to Motion with more ease, more genuine light-fistedness, than in the past, but it still leaves a more than slight sense of 'So what . . .?'

The real strength of *Natural Causes*, though, is in its most directly personal poems. Motion has learned from his narrative excursions how to enrich the short lyric with some inexplicit jolts of drama – as in 'Hare Lip', a strange, rather fearsome poem about fear. And throughout the book the sense of anticipated loss is even sharper: Motion the bereaved child is now a husband and a father. Having once lost everything, or so it seemed, he now – for a second time – has everything to lose. In the title poem, 'Natural Causes', and in 'Hare Lip' and 'Firing Practice', there is a resignation tinged with panic that reminds us of Philip Larkin, but with no attempt at any Larkinesque self-mockery:

> . . . soon you will die,
> and not only you but this person
> you love, her children, everyone else;
> . . . no one prepared you for this –
>
> no matter how early
> you realised nothing connected
> with anything, ever . . .

These poems are hard to quote from because another thing Motion has learned from Philip Larkin is how to handle extremely complex sentences in verse that comes across as ordinary speech. The last five and a half stanzas of 'Firing Practice' seem modelled on Larkin's cunning use of syntax at the end of 'Mr Bleaney': to use that as a model without floundering demands considerable skill.

But then to admit Larkin as an influence at all is to risk, as a poet, some serious loss of personal identity. The last poem in *Natural Causes* is in fact an elegy for Larkin: it's a mixture of reported Larkinisms, quotations and echoes from the poems, and some modest first-person recollection. The whole thing is delicately done: the weighing of homage and grief is judged most conscientiously. But then 'conscientious' is another word, like 'cautious', that has often come to mind when reading Motion. In this new book, there are several signs that he might soon be asking us to think again.

1987

ANDREW MOTION
Natural Causes
Chatto and Windus

PART III
SOME NOVELS

John Updike's Couples

Couples is set in what John Updike has oddly called 'an ideal community, a Utopia'. Oddly, that is, unless by ideal Updike simply meant hard to swallow. Or perhaps he meant ideal for the scrutinising novelist who likes to keep things neat. *Couples* is a very neat novel. There are ten couples in it, they live in Tarbox, a prosperous commuter town some twenty miles south of Boston, and their lives are hungrily interpenetrated. No one else in the town really matters, nothing that goes on outside the town really impinges. The couples are tribal, a 'magic circle', they have 'made a church of one another' and they go to worship every day. They spend their evenings and weekends 'growing old and awful in each other's houses', meeting up for suppers, parties, garden sports, for love affairs, abortions, showdowns. 'The men had stopped having careers and the women had stopped having babies. Liquor and love were left.' The novel charts their bleakly un-Utopian entanglements with fervent care and detail.

And there are a number of ways in which the effort might have been worthwhile. As an exercise in social anthropology, perhaps – Updike has spoken of his couples as being like Polynesians, exemplars of communal living. Can people live in the modern world, apparently holding down fairly responsible positions in the running of it, but at the same time keep themselves so totally outside it? Updike never really answers this question, but he keeps on posing it – and not always, one decides, quite knowingly. The couples' separation from the larger world outside is underscored throughout, and seems to be offered as something essentially culpable in the kind of life they lead in Tarbox – newscasts and headlines about world upheavals whisper ironically around the margins of the narrative, and one of the novel's big scenes

169

is a party which the couples fail to cancel after getting word of John Kennedy's assassination – but we are never sufficiently convinced to blame them for it.

For one thing, Updike can never resist a smart, aphoristic bout of dialogue; the book's dinner parties ring with conversation which, though hollow and inconsequential, does bear evidence of at any rate more worldly know-how than could readily have been gained within the confines of the magic circle. There is, we all know, a yawning gap between what people care about at dinner parties and what they really care about, but the one thing the couples *are* supposed to deem important is the dinner party. And what about their jobs? 'One of their unspoken rules was that professions were not criticised; one's job was a pact with the meaningless world beyond the couples.' So much for their jobs. So much, indeed, for anything about these people which does not conveniently ramify within the circle – within, that is, the fiction that has been invented for them.

Updike wants us to believe that there's nothing else to tell, but this is so demonstrably not true that we are finally left powerless to judge his characters as he would like us to. And this is bound to be a major setback for the novel; if the book is to work we need above all to be convinced of the weird strength of these people's inter-dependence: 'I hate it, this way we live', 'He told me he gets frightened if he doesn't see us over the weekend', 'I guess I'm past asking myself if I like them or not. They're mine.' The couples, then, are just as puzzled as we are, and we are often urged to see them as futilely huddling together in defence against the futile void beyond. Here again, though, we don't feel we know enough to make the full, censorious or pitying, response that seems to be required of us.

And this, in the end, is simply a failure of characterisation. We can't be expected to sustain much interest in the plight of, say, Frank Appleby who is equipped with the identikit habit of forever quoting Shakespeare, or Albert Smith, who winds up every sentence with a phrase of French. Pitiable fragments of a lost cultural tradition? No doubt, but since these absurd traits are just about the only means we have of distinguishing Frank and Albert from their co-couples (and they are not minor characters, exactly, since a whole rather tedious section of the novel is taken up with an account of their wife-swapping pranks) the small symbolic gem

170

seems ludicrously over-priced. Other couples are similarly rigged for instant recognition: the Jew, the Catholic, the homosexual, the oriental.

Outside the two characters on whom the novel chiefly centres, only the demonic Freddy Thorne emerges from the ruck with any clarity. He occupies (the blurb tells us) a priestly role in the tribe; certainly he is the mocking scourge, the nagging oracle, and casts himself as the couples' 'humaniser'. Updike cuts him down to size by revealing that his scandalous conversation is a cover for his impotence, but Thorne, by that stage in the book, has done his job – of allying himself with the spectator, with the judicial non-participant, with us. He therefore works for us in two ways: as judge and as victim. He has everyone's number, but we have his: he is the most powerful and the most pitiable of the couples, the most aloof and the most cruelly shackled. In this sense he succeeds where the potent couples fail: he is of the world outside and yet convincingly imprisoned in the Tarbox setup.

Prominent among Freddy's priestly duties is that of arranging the tribe's rituals. One of the innumerable games which the snug couples use to pad out their flagging parties is called 'Wonderful'. The idea is that contestants must name the most wonderful thing they can think of. Piet Hanema, the novel's central character, comes up with the following:

His mind skimmed the world, cities and fields and steeples and seas, mud and money, cut timbers, sweet shavings, blue hymnals, and the fuzz on a rose. Ass. His mind plunged unresisted into the truth: nothing matters but ass. Nothing is so good.

Piet, we perceive, is not as simple as he thinks he is. A man who can think such beautiful thoughts, and in such silkily alliterative cadences, has more than just ass on his high mind. Like earlier Updike heroes, Piet has the church at his back, and before him, in the distance, dim intimations of sublime apotheosis. Assisting him in his quest, he has the lush music of Prose Style. If he seeks 'ass' it is because he doesn't know where else he might seek God. The most tensely sinful moments in the lives of Updike's heroes are attended by the ringing of church bells. 'There is no way from us to God . . . the god who stood at the end of some human way . . . would not be God.' This assertion of Karl Barth's, though the sense of it hangs over much of Updike's fiction, expresses a despair and contentment which his heroes find it impossible to settle for. Piet Hanema is a regular churchgoer, he dreams long, guilty dreams, he soliloquises with great stylistic prettiness (can critics continue pretending that Updike's grotesque verbosity and self-indulgence are somehow marginal to what he's really up to?) and yet he is the randiest adulterer in town.

And not, of course, just randy. He cuckolds three husbands but is ever seeking from his women some deeper, richer, more blindingly wicked species of beatitude. The old taboos, on adultery, on wife-swapping, on 'bad language', and so on, don't mean much any more – though the couples maintain token security measures when the adultery is one-sided. The thrill of transgression must be sought in – as it were – other areas. Hence, in his relationship with the stately Foxy Whitman, Piet discovers two rich veins of sinfulness: copulation with a married woman of advanced pregnancy and – more or less in consequence – the thrills of being 'blown' (i.e., oral copulation). The hero of *Rabbit Run* found that being blown was the far limit of his flight from the shackles of convention (on the night of his delight his wife was giving birth to his child, a child who later dies as a result of Rabbit going back to his mistress for more). Similarly, Piet and Foxy achieve, through their adventurousness, a delinquency which even delinquent Tarbox would be shocked at, and Piet's religious sensibility is nourished anew by keen infusions of both guilt and bliss. Updike gets it both ways too: on the one hand there are the transcendental gropings of his style and on the other the fierce system of punishment that shapes his plot. The style elevates the hero, but events will crush him: the centaur cannot win.

This could, of course, have come across as an interesting conflict. In fact, Piet's inner life is so cruelly burdened with Updike's pretentious prose that we can never be sure that it is really his, or that his confusions are not merely the confusions of his author. He is too deeply sunk in literary confectionery for us to, say, even think of blaming him for being literary. There are moments of sharpness and subtlety in his dealings with Foxy, and with his ungenerous wife, Angela, but it is significant that he is most convincing when we have no access to his soul.

And this almost amounts to a fair verdict on Updike's writing; it can be arrestingly tight and incisive when it keeps within the

172

JOHN UPDIKE'S COUPLES

limits of a dramatic situation (there are detachable lumps of *Couples* which he might have done better to publish as short stories) and appallingly mannered and confused as soon as those limits – the limits of authorial impartiality – are 'transcended'. In spite of some good moments, in spite of a laboriously ornate backcloth and in spite of all that 'ass', the real hero of *Couples* is vocabulary:

> Mouths, it came to Piet, are noble. They move in the brain's court. We set our genitals mating down below like peasants, but when the mouth condescends, mouth and body marry. To eat another is sacred. *I love thee, Elizabeth, thy petaled rankness, thy priceless casket of nothing lined with slippery buds.* Thus on the Sunday morning, beneath the hanging clangor of bells.

1968

JOHN UPDIKE
Couples
Deutsch

Norman Mailer's Ancient Evenings

His bushy hair is white and cropped more conservatively than in the past . . . his eyes are clear and surprisingly blue. He moves with the grace of the boxer he has sometimes pretended to be . . . his ample waist looks solid rather than soft . . . He is remarkably fit for a man of sixty, which is what he became last Jan 31.

> *Time* on Norman Mailer, April 1983

His hair showed the silver of a virile maturity, while the lines on his face had not yet become a myriad of wrinkles, terraces and webs, but exhibited, instead, that look of character supported by triumph which comes to powerful men when they are sixty and still strong.

This second identikit is from *Ancient Evenings*, and it describes the novel's central character Menenhetet, a figure for whom Norman Mailer exhibits a warm and virile admiration as well as a certain wistful fellow-feeling. Mailer, *Time* tells us, has had six wives; Menenhetet, Mailer tells us, has had four lives. According to *Time*, Mailer's alimony payments regularly remind him of the earlier Mailers he has been; according to Mailer, Menenhetet is obligation-free: even though the 180-year-old Egyptian can recall, in much detail, all his previous lives' great triumphs and disasters, nobody is serving him with any writs. *Ancient Evenings* is set in ancient Egypt (1290–1100 BC) but an element of its otherworldliness does seem to spout, near-plaintively, from Brooklyn Heights (1972–82 AD).

174

This is Norman Mailer's Big Book, he has often said. The hugeness of its 'sight-unseen' publisher's advance would, he promised, be more than matched by the hugeness of the book's ambition, scope, imaginative daring. Publication Day was awaited, in New York, as if some vast, breathtaking revelation were at hand. Well, 'here it is at last' (*New York Times*), and there can be no doubt that it captures the spirit of its own promotion. The whole book bubbles with a desperate giganticism – indeed, is often pretty well deranged by it.

'Why ancient Egypt?' has been the question most often put to Mailer in pre-publication interviews. His answers have sounded bumbling or evasive. 'I wasn't sure I could really write about America any more', 'These were people where everything I'd learned wasn't much help in understanding them', 'I want people to realise, my God, there are utterly different points of view that can be as interesting as our own.' Worthy purposes, and there are a few stretches early on in *Ancient Evenings* when Mailer is respectful and tentative in the manner implied by such solemn declarations of intent: the early scenes at the court of Ramses IX, for example, and the first dabblings in ancient Egyptian telepathy (his own invention, it would seem, but plausible). This delicate approach, though, is at best intermittent and after some hundred pages it gets thoroughly abandoned. The remaining six hundred suggest that, for Mailer, ancient Egypt offered not mysteries but opportunities – and fairly cheap opportunities, at that.

There is, for example, the opportunity to seem to have been grappling with mysteries: those elaborate mosaics of religious metaphor, those fearsomely exact death rites, the intricately mapped country of the dead. Except in rare flashes, though, all Mailer has done here is to 'write up' (i.e. Mailerishly empurple) the available texts and histories – from the *Book of the Dead* to the *Journal of Egyptian Archaeology*. Since Egyptologists are for ever disagreeing, there is much scope here for swaggering creative licence. As it turns out, however, Mailer's history lessons are slower and stodgier than anything you might find in, say, *The Splendour that was Egypt*. 'My story must be long like the length of a snake,' says one of Mailer's raconteurs, as if he too had signed a big book contract with Little, Brown. And then there are all the lulling schoolroom exchanges:

'May I ask any question?'
I was fearful, but I looked back into Her eyes and nodded calmly.
'You will not think it is a silly question?'
'Never.'
'Very well then,' She said, 'Who is this Horus?'
'Oh, He is a great God,' I told Her.
'Is He the Only One? Is He the First?'
'I would say He is the Son of Ra and the Beloved of Ra.'
'So He is the same as the Pharaoh?'
'Yes,' I said, 'the Pharaoh is the Son of Ra and the Beloved of Ra. So the Pharaoh is Horus.'
'He is the God Horus?' She asked.
'Yes.'
'Then the Pharaoh is the Falcon of the Heavens?' She asked.
'Yes.'

But for Mailer ancient Egypt offers more than just the opportunity to spin out his material. One key attraction for him was surely that the Pharaonic religious beliefs were so earth-centred and non-ethical. The ancient Egyptians held the firm and vivid conviction that Immortality was *fixable*, that the Gods could be 'got to', rather like American politicians. Indeed, this was one of the frailties that they most admired in Them. As one historian put it, 'the ancient Egyptian felt a warmer affection for his Gods if they suffered from the same weaknesses as himself.' For the Big Novelist what could be more alluring? If Gods are men, and if men can, now and then, be Gods, then how simple it becomes to invest one's weary fictioneering ploys with what can be made to look like Cosmic Weight. 'The earth moved' takes on a new freshness, a lively literalness, in ancient Egypt.

Similarly, the ancient Egyptian version of the after-life lends itself admirably to the Big Novelist's need for upmarket novelty locations. The Egyptian's 'earnest desire was that the next world should resemble the pleasant land of Egypt as much as possible. He wished to continue all the bodily activities which he was accustomed to perform when alive' (J.E.M. White, *Ancient Egypt*). Thus when Mailer locates his first bout of gay fellatio in some shadowy corner of the Land of the Dead (a long-gone incumbent is spiritedly welcoming his newly-enrolled grandson) the whole effect is . . .

176

well, so much more spooky and *theological* than if he had set it in the men's room at the Barbizon Plaza. The same might be said of any one of Mailer's repeated forays into grand-scale celestial-style pornography, into an other-world where all phalluses are seen as massive shafts, where all bottoms are bottomless, all orifices aureate:

> Now, feeling her wet breast by one hand, and the crevice of her hips by the other, recollecting the view of the open thighs as He saw them in the light of a flame in a censer of oil, the Gods gleaming in the wet flesh of her hair, He knew a second pleasure, and His life stirred inside her belly and began to grow long as the Nile and dark as the Duad. The great force of the phallus of his ancestor, Usermare, covered his own phallus like the cloak of a God. At that instant His Secret Name must have opened the door for He had an instant when the Gods went in and out of him a second time and the Boat of Ra flew past as he came forth. The Two-Lands shivered beneath . . .

Self-aggrandisement was no sin in ancient Egypt. In fact, the more splendidly boastful one's passage into the next world, the more secure one's hold on the eternal goodies. Mailer's main characters spend many a page locked into formal bouts of boasting – they brag about their virility, their wealth, their courage, their magical powers, their proximity to the great god Horus, their powerful sense of containing the vast Nile waters in their loins, the black Nile silt within their bowels. In pharaoh-land, nobody objects to an eloquent self-advertiser. They know not the word 'hyperbole' – no more than doth N. Mailer.

Several times, during the Nile-long course of *Ancient Evenings*, one gets the image not of a writer writing a book but of a child contentedly playing with his toys: dressing them up, giving them funny voices, making them perform sudden, improbable acts of violence, and so on. When Mailer wishes his hero to be humiliated by a brutal Pharaoh, for example, he makes his Pharaoh-toy bugger the hero-toy – just like that. Of course, this being a big American novel, the hero-toy strangely enjoys it – but even so, the nursery-image is never quite dispelled. This is certainly true of Mailer's lengthy battle-scenes. He pumps these full of every imaginable type of carnage, from straightforwardly sadistic body-slicing to nervously thrilled cannibalism, but for all the lip-smacking effort he puts into his descriptions, we don't ever quite believe that the violated limbs aren't made of lead, or plastic, nor that at any moment Mummy (well, Mother) won't come in and tell naughty Norman that it's time for tea.

The 'story' of *Ancient Evenings* is really a collection of stories, most of them well known, and all of them bloated and distorted by Mailer's infantile megalomania. Structurally, the novel is made to seem more ingenious than it really is by having all its principals a. believe in reincarnation, and b. possess some sort of telepathic gift. These two (non-historical) relaxants enable minds to flit in and out of other minds, live sensibilities to respond to dead events. There are fun-and-games to be had here, of course, and it is entirely in line with almost everything else in the book that Mailer should use the telepathy device mainly to keep us up to date on who is thinking of doing 'it' to whom. (Nobody, it should be said, is ever not thinking of doing it to someone.)

As a structural aid, however, the real usefulness of each device is to help set up the book's central dialogue: between Menenhetet and his current Pharaoh, Ramses IX. Ramses IX wants to know how things really were during the reign of the notorious Ramses II, the Pharaoh of Menenhetet's first life – some hundred and fifty years earlier. Ramses II was the last of the truly formidable Pharaohs, and Ramses IX knows that he is but a pale shadow of that bygone warrior, builder, fertiliser and, according to Norman Mailer, homosexual rapist. How pale a shadow, though? Menenhetet spends the bulk of the novel recounting the 'true story' of the Battle of Kadesh, of Ramses II's controversial marriage to a Hittite princess, of his countless sexual misdemeanours (not too much is related on the subject of Ramses II's architectural exploits – at Karnac, Abydos and Abu Simbel). At various times, Menenhetet had been Ramses II's chief charioteer, his harem-master, and the lover of the best-looking of his several wives, so he has fair claim to be something of an expert. He remembers and tells all, prompted intelligently by the telepathic Ramses IX – being a Pharaoh, his telepathic skills are of a higher order than anybody else's: he can actually read the minds of the long dead.

This, then, is the set-up which enables Mailer to stage a braggart first-person narrative of the declining years of the Egyptian

Empire. Menenhetet, like Mailer, has no problem about length:
Ramses IX

> laughed with true merriment: 'I want you to tell me,' he said, 'of
> my ancestor, Ramses the Second . . . I want to know what took
> place at the Battle of Kadesh, and all that followed upon it.'
> 'To tell you might take every moment that is left in
> this night.'
> 'I am awake until morning.'

To get around any problems of courtly decorum, Mailer has the
dialogue take place on the Day of the Pig, the one day of the year
on which the mouth was required to be at its most foul. And to
avoid the likely tedium of a two-voice exchange, he also arranges
for an audience (a man, a woman and a child) to supply interludes
of turbulent sexual telepathy. The air of contrivance, though, is
always evident, and the suspense level usually flickers just above
the zero mark. Again, it is a matter of excess, of Mailer never
knowing when to stop, nor – it seems – much caring. '"Why, as
slowly as you wish," said the Pharaoh, and inclined His hand most
graciously.' No doubt we are meant to be similarly gracious.

And perhaps we would be, or would try to be, if there were
any evidence that Mailer himself was taking the thing seriously.
Throughout the book, there are hints of other ways in which the
subject, or some aspects of the subject, might have been pursued.
The character Menenhetet, for example, has possibilities which
Mailer simply fails to follow through. It seems that he is based
on a historical figure called Menna who appears in Ramses II's
numerous self-glorifying accounts of the Battle of Kadesh. He
was the charioteer who, for all his usual valour, cracked in the heat
of battle. In Mailer, Menenhetet (or Menna) claims that Ramses
has falsified the record in order to inflate his own history-book
reputation. In Menenhetet's account, Ramses would not have
made it without his charioteer's help. For a few pages here
Mailer seems to be inviting us to ponder the rather large matter
of how (and by whom) most history gets written. The trouble
is that Menenhetet's account is far more luridly windbag than
anything even Ramses seems to have been able to come up with.
Instead of the common soldier's sober and precise corrections of
the Pharaoh's bombast, we get what amounts to a macho punch-up

between Norman Mailer and the Pyramid Texts. Few of Mailer's nastier embellishments would be easy to translate into hieroglyphs. In the end, Ramses's famous graffiti are made to seem prissy and insipid when confronted with the bold-stroke phallo-graphics of New York.

Ramses II, of course, was not just a famous warrior, architect and fornicator. He is also well known as a busy persecutor of the Jews. Some name him as the Pharaoh of the Book of Exodus. On this topic, *Ancient Evenings* is at its most peculiar. Mailer makes only one reference to the Jews. After the Battle of Kadesh, Ramses II exiles his charioteer to the gold quarries of Nubia. There Menenhetet meets one Nefesh-Besher who tells him that 'in the same season that Usermare' – Ramses II – 'marched to Kadesh, Moses arrived in Pithom dressed as an Egyptian officer and told the Hebrews he would take them to a land in the East they could conquer.' Nefesh-Besher had been unable to go with Moses (his wife was out of town that night) and was later packed off to the quarries as a punishment for having been linked with Moses's plot. When Menenhetet meets him, he is dying.

> When I asked him if he hated Moses, he shook his head. Not at all. Moses had passed on a great secret. It was how, on your last breath, you could put yourself into the belly of your wife.
> Here he was. This Nefesh-Besher, this Ukhu-As – dying – yet he spoke of living. And not at all in the way some speak of continuing one's name through the respect of one's descendants. No, he told me, the child you make in your last moments of life can become a new body for yourself.

And this is how Menenhetet (alone, it seems, among Egyptians) learns the secret of reincarnation, the secret on which the whole of *Ancient Evenings* is based. Three times he has contrived to die in the act of impregnation: each time, needless to say, described for us in detail. And where does the trick come from? It comes from the leader of the Jews. What, then, are we meant to make of this? A sly Jewish boast? A retort to those (like me) who would wonder how a Jewish writer can manage to eliminate the Jews (apart from this one mention) from a 'biography' of Ramses II and his immediate successors? Or is it a self-insuring way of signalling – to those who care to pick it up – that the whole book can be read as a kind of wild anti-pharaonic spoof?

1983

NORMAN MAILER
Ancient Evenings
Macmillan

Philip Roth's Portnoy's Complaint

In *Letting Go*, Philip Roth painstakingly documented the predicament of two Jewish boys whose emotional lives were crippled, though in quite different ways, by the suffocations of parental love: both heroes yearned to 'let go', to cut loose into some kind of independent manhood, but neither could sustain a life that was not stoppered at both ends by massive blocks of guilt. A common enough predicament? Oh sure, was Philip Roth's implied riposte, but for a Jewish boy it's twice as common. In *Portnoy's Complaint*, Roth pushes his attack on Momma several stages further, and with more devastating acrimony, but the basic allegation remains more or less the same: that the stifling solicitude, the network of impossible demands and unanswerable recriminations, the sheer emotional gluttony, that go into constructing a Jewish childhood are no preparation for an integrated adulthood. The only thing a Jewish childhood engenders, as Roth sees it, is a Jewish child.

'These two are the outstanding producers and packagers of guilt in our time,' whines Alexander Portnoy of his parents. Paul Herz and Gabe Wallach, in *Letting Go*, took much the same view of theirs. The chief difference between the two books is that Portnoy plays the predicament for laughs. In *Letting Go*, there were moments when the book's minute, rather studied naturalism seemed to be breaking up into caricature; the parents, particularly the fathers, came close at times to looking like joke Jewish stereotypes. *Portnoy's Complaint* not only makes no effort to avoid such stereotypes; it embraces them enthusiastically, indeed inflates them to more farcical, more cruel dimensions. 'I am the son in the Jewish joke,' says Portnoy, '*only it ain't no joke!*'

Alexander Portnoy, age thirty-three (b. 1933), is New York's Assistant Commissioner for Human Opportunity – a Lindsay appointment; he is champion of the down-trodden, widely noted for his work in exposing the television quiz racket and for other humane deeds. His mother is proud of him. How is it then that we discover him stretched (where he lies throughout the book) on the couch of one Dr O. Spielvogel, author of *The Puzzled Penis*? Portnoy is suffering, it transpires, from a disorder which medical science will shortly document as 'Portnoy's Complaint', a disorder in which 'strongly felt ethical and altruistic impulses are perpetually warring with extreme sexual longings, often of a perverse nature. Many of the symptoms can be traced to the bonds obtaining in the mother–child relationship.'

The book comprises a transcript of Portnoy's account, to his analyst, of how he caught this interesting malady, of the excesses of lust and shame to which it has driven him, of the troubles he has had disguising it from the admiring world and, worst of all, from the two fond, rapacious monsters who gave it to him in the first place – mum and dad.

On the face of it, Portnoy's condition does not seem as peculiar as he thinks it is. After all, what's so special about sexual longings warring against ethical impulses, what disorder *can't* be traced back to the mother–child relationship? In Portnoy's case we would have to concede that his adolescent masturbation practices were probably above average in frequency and ingenuity, and that in his maturity he is more deviant than most – though surely it was a stroke of fortune rather than a symptom of disease that he met the athletic mannequin he calls the Monkey, a girl of unusually experimental willingness? Portnoy is always more appalled by his behaviour than we are, and he knows it. And this, of course, is his real problem: (a) why does he do these dirty things and (b) why does he think they're dirty? The book works on two levels of self-laceration, and Momma is thus doubly open to attack. The only way Portnoy knows of escaping her is to plunge deeper into the very delinquencies which will bind him closer to her. He cannot enjoy sex without transgression, and he needs Momma to provide that sweet spice.

Roth's device of placing his hero on the analyst's couch, of letting him groan on without pause, might sound like a recipe for self-indulgence, and indeed it is often difficult to accept Portnoy as more than a neat excuse for Roth to exorcise, without penalty, some of his own anti-semitic impulses. But by and large the author's wit and skill keep the *Complaint* alive as fiction: in other words, we do finally accept the cartoon Jewish props, the brandished sex adventures, the absurdly scanty view of Portnoy's professional labours, and so on, as issuing from the comically obsessed personality of the character rather than from any lack of industry or insight on Roth's part. At this level, as a comic *tour de force*, as the Jewish joke to end all Jewish jokes, the book is brilliantly successful. The main triumph is a triumph of idiom, of an ear superbly tuned to the pace and emphases, the stoic moan, of Jewish-American speech rhythms, but there is also a real comic inventiveness at work: an inventiveness which is all the more spectacular for having to operate within such narrow bounds.

The liveliest parts of the book are those which focus on Portnoy's claustrophobic childhood: there is a marvellously funny section called 'Whacking Off' in which the young Portnoy, groggy with lust, sustains a tough regime of almost hourly masturbation, nearly – but never quite – under his mother's nose. The boy's task is here complicated by the fact that access to the bathroom (where on one unusually memorable occasion the hot Portnoy fits his sister's brassière to the doorknob and receives a bonus shot of stimulation when his mother tries the door) is restricted by the rival needs of Portnoy Senior, who is suffering from almost terminal constipation. Portnoy's first steps towards the real thing are similarly rich in rueful farce; there are some particularly hilarious forays into the forbidden territory of the Goy, where the most dizzying guilts lurk.

It is when we get on to Portnoy's adult escapades (though we don't actually 'get on' to them in the conventional sense, since the narrative is made up of an intricately discontinuous set of flashbacks) that the comic energy begins to flag. Fellatio with the Monkey does not present the same practical difficulties as whacking off in Momma's bathroom and even when Roth contrives to have the two lovers pick up an Italian whore and perpetrate some rare triangular achievements, one has a strong sense that the real spark has disappeared, that Roth has not really known what to do with his delinquent hero now he is 'grown up' except commit him to more and yet more acts of darkness. Tedium is near to hand at such points. And the final chapter of the book, when Portnoy visits Israel and finds himself unable to summon an erection, seems tagged on, a witty afterthought. Or maybe it's a bid for some more solemnly

PHILIP ROTH'S PORTNOY'S COMPLAINT

generalised parable of the 'Jewish experience' than the book has really been disposed to work for? Could it be that Philip Roth suddenly got that guilty feeling?

1969

PHILIP ROTH
Portnoy's Complaint
Cape

Terry Southern's Candy

Candy was first published in 1958 by the Olympia Press in Paris and it has since appeared, and been a best-seller, in America and elsewhere. No English publisher, however, has been prepared to risk handling it, and over the years the book has gradually come to be regarded as a kind of test case for our literary censorship: if *Candy* can get away with it, the battle really will be won. Well, here it is at last. Do we then applaud the bold publisher Bernard Geis, arrange funds for his defence, call in the expert witnesses? I'm afraid we do nothing of the sort. This 'English edition' is a grotesque travesty of the original. Without a word of acknowledgment or explanation, the book has literally been cut to death. Key scenes are gutted to the point of meaninglessness, characters are watered down to near-anonymity, passages of dialogue are reduced to a few flickering non-sequiturs. The whole thing bears about the same relation to the original as Lamb's *Tales* do to Shakespeare.

It's impossible here to document the carve-up in real detail, though students of Grundyism may well find that a useful exercise one day. But take a few typical examples. The foul-mouthed Aunt Livia (and the whole point of this character is that she is foul-mouthed, sexually rapacious, the American matriarch in heat) consults the menu in a smart restaurant and declares: 'I'm in the mood for cock and plenty of it. About ten pounds please, thick and fast.' In the Geis edition, this becomes: 'I'm in the mood for love.' In *both* editions, Aunt Livia's husband is shocked by what she has said and remonstrates: 'Now, Liv, this won't do.' Dr Krankeit, a psychiatrist who believes that masturbation is the panacea for neuroses, is similarly muzzled. We are meant to see Krankeit as a comically obsessed figure; a symptom of his mania is that terms

186

like 'jack off' and 'wrench off' have become the all-purpose pivots of his whole vocabulary. Thus, he'll say, 'I wonder if you could drop back this afternoon. I've got some work here I'd like to wrench off.' In Geis we find him cured of his obsession: 'I've got some work here I'd like to get rid of.' Similarly, 'You've an ocean of drowned impulses to jack off' becomes 'You've an ocean of drowned impulses to liberate' (even though two lines earlier Krankeit is allowed by Geis to say: 'It's the damned shell you're imprisoned in that I'm trying to wrench off').

There are cuts of this kind by the score. Not only are they done ham-fistedly, so that they frequently make nonsense of the context they're removed from, but they are mystifyingly inconsistent: 'tight quim' is acceptable but 'huge member' isn't, for example. The main objection, though, is that even judged by the most extreme standards of legal caution many of the cuts are quite unnecessary. One can see that there may well be risks involved in, say, the scene in which Candy is humped (literally) by a hunchback or even in the novel's brilliant closing sequence where she is vanquished, with adroit simultaneity, both by her father and by a Buddha's broken nose. The loss of these scenes and others like them does mortal damage to the book, but at least we can concede that it would have needed a brave man to publish them intact. That the publisher of *Valley of the Dolls* and *The Exhibitionist* should baulk at lines like 'as he strove through the final ineffable seconds of his ecstasy' is inexplicable.

Candy, then, is still unobtainable in this country and, as a result of this expurgated publication, it is unlikely to appear for many years. One of the reasons why English publishers, in spite of the recent *Last Exit to Brooklyn* verdict, are still likely to be nervous of the book is that it would be difficult to make out on its behalf the kind of utilitarian defence that was successful with *Last Exit* and *Lady Chatterley's Lover*. It was possible in those cases to pretend that Lawrence had composed a hymn to marriage and that Hubert Selby is a social worker; to plead, in other words, that their books really belonged to, and had a useful role to play within, the court's scheme of morality. 'Don't be fooled by the vocabulary, these books are on your side,' was the dominating argument. With *Candy* (as with *Fanny Hill* – though here, of course, it was contended that the book was useful as 'history') this wouldn't work. For one thing, it makes us laugh about sex and this is both indefensible and undefendable:

judges who have only recently clambered over the 'sex is a holy mystery' hurdle are likely to feel cheated if literary critics now start telling them that it is funny too. Not only that, but the novel refuses to lend itself to any acceptable civilising interpretations. *Candy* is a satire, certainly, but any accurate account of its satirical objectives would involve more than a small measure of contempt for the court that sits in judgement on it. There would be little profit in revealing reformist guns that are aimed, point-blank, at the Bench.

And not just at the Bench. *Candy* laughingly assaults the full gamut of our inhibitions. There is not much subtlety in its methods; it is loose, mechanically episodic, often anxious to wrench the last possible drop of merriment from exhausted situations, and the mock-pornographic idiom, however stylishly employed, is apt to become tedious. At its best, though, the book is witty and incisive: an inspired joke at the expense of both pornography and its pursuers.

The heroine is descended from Candide; simple-hearted, optimistic and compassionate, she is the dumb flower of a principled and abstract education in the liberal verities. She is also spectacularly beautiful. Her adventures are in a male world which, although it seems to her dazzlingly rich in highmindedness and selfless dedication, is in fact centred with a kind of manic energy on but one paramount objective. Whatever the mask – philosopher, physician, mystic or messenger-boy – lust is the violent motor. 'They are all after one thing,' as the saying goes. And Candy's spiritual promiscuity makes her everybody's fall-girl. In scene after scene we find the 'darling girl' trading in her 'fabulous lamb-pit' for two paragraphs of soulful rhetoric: 'Candy leaned back in resignation, her heart too big to deprive him of this if it meant so much.'

In a society ravaged by neurosis and hypocrisy, Candy is the dream-fount of generosity – of pity, sexual pleasure, maternal solicitude, child-like adulation. She is the candy that babies cry for. 'Give me your true warmth,' howls Uncle Jack. '"All my true warmth," breathed Candy, "oh how you need my warmth, my baby."' And she is gift-wrapped: always 'pine-fragrant', hygienic, clad in a 'sweet blouse' and freshly laundered underthings. Her longed-for prize is invariably vaunted as delectable confectionery: 'pink honeypot', 'sweet pudding pie', 'honey cloister' and so on. She is the 'pink-sugar' fantasy of admass, the consumer's Grail.

TERRY SOUTHERN'S CANDY

Everyone in the book, even the pitiable hunchback, has his sales pitch (the authors are particularly sharp on crank psychiatrists and wayout divines) and Candy, who wields the greatest sales pitch of all, falls for every one of them. Her spirituality is victimised and abused, but her body reaps the final victory. All but one or two of her suitors end up on their knees – blubbering, grateful infants. And this, the authors imply, is where America, god-fearing, ad-enslaved, over-analysed America, belongs. 'Good grief,' as Candy might exclaim, 'the book has a message after all!' Had it been delivered with a straight face we might have been allowed to read it.

1968

TERRY SOUTHERN and MASON HOFFENBERG
Candy
Bernard Geis

Martin Amis's Money

'Dollar bills, pound notes, they're suicide notes. *Money* is a suicide note.' So says John Self, the hero of *Money: A Suicide Note*, and what he means is that money is destroying *him*. Self-destruction (along with several of its hyphenated pals: indulgence, interest, loathing) has become Self's hobby, what he does in his spare time, and what he spends his money on. But it's money's fault that this is what he spends his money on. It's money's fault that he hasn't got anything better to do with his spare time. 'The yobs are winning,' said a character in Martin Amis's *Success*, and one could almost take this as the 'burden' of his work so far. In earlier books, there have been yobs aplenty, and from the beginning Amis has scrutinised the species with some ardour. With John Self, though, he shifts the enemy to centre-stage, so that this time he can give him a real going-over.

When the book opens, Self has just arrived in New York to direct a big-money feature film, called *Good Money*. Back home in London, he has won a small reputation for his scandalous TV commercials (extolling the pleasures of junk food, tobacco, porno mags etc), and he has even collected an Italian prize for a short documentary called *Dean Street*. He is one of the new men, the uneducated media slicksters who took over in the sixties, a practitioner and a product of junk culture. If he hears you say that you're going to Stratford to see the two gentlemen of Verona, he'll think you're getting a prize too. Self makes lots of money but he 'pisses it away' – on rubbish food, rubbish booze and rubbish sex. He needs money very badly, but he can't control it. 'I love giving money away,' he confides in us. 'If you were here now, I'd probably slip you some cash.' 'Oh, money, I love you. You're so democratic. You even things out for me and my kind.'

190

Although he has a spare-time problem, Self likes things that are fast. He doesn't quite know why, except that this happens to be the momentum of the moment: get rich quick, if you're not quick you're dead.

The future's futures have never looked so rocky. Don't put money on it. Take my advice and stick to the present. It's the real stuff, the only stuff, it's all there is, the present, the panting present.

Thus, the things he is hooked on are short-term and money-based – like jumboburgers and pornography. And although Self is fat and ugly and in terrible physical condition, he's a fast talker – he can always 'gimmick' a quick deal and (by using his head) foreshorten a yob punch-up. He's thirty-five, mid-Atlantic and of shallow parentage: his father has recently invoiced him for the cost of his upbringing. His grandfather was an inept though dedicated counterfeiter – he *made* money.

Self has an English girlfriend, Selina. She's in it for the money, too. He loves her 'brothelly know-how and her top-dollar underwear' and he gives her money if she dresses up like the girls in the wank-mags he's addicted to. 'While making love, we often talk about money. I like it. I like that dirty talk.' He knows he loves Selina: the 'thrilling proof, so rich in pornography' is that she does 'all this not for passion, not for comfort, far less for love . . . she does all this for *money*. *I love her corruption.*' Loving her as he does, though, Self is susceptible to bouts of torment; it is Selina who haunts him 'during the black hours, when I am weak and scared'. To prevent this happening, he keeps on giving her more money.

For a new man, one of the new princes of our culture, John Self gets weak and scared quite often – and never more so than when he is in the USA, the money-capital, the source, the shrine. This time, he arrives jet-lagged, drunk and gorged on airline hospitality (he loves airline food and has plans for opening an airline-food restaurant in London) and also anguished by the thought of Selina's near-proven infidelity. In other words, a wreck. And from this point on, it's downhill all the way. The junk life Self leads in London can here be magnified tenfold, and he plunges into it face first: 'I gave her all my face, and it's a face that can usually face them down, wide and grey, full of adolescent archaeology and cheap food and junk money, the face of a fat snake, bearing all the signs of its sins.'

The big-money film deal gives Self the chance to exercise self-interest, but here there is a razor-thin separation between art and life. The movie stars he has to deal with are all freaks – money-freaks, naturally, but also ego-freaks, self-freaks. To humour them, Self must self-abase somewhat, because of money. But then, because of money, he has become quite good at this, over the years. The film's chief money-man, Fielding Goodney, is a freak also: but he's a freak of physical well-being, the kind of manufactured self that Self would pay big money for if selves could actually be bought and sold. Perhaps they can. 'He turned and I felt the rush of his health and colour – his Californian, peanut-butter body-tone.' Fielding's eyes are 'supercandid corn-flower blue', he has a 'high droll forehead'; he is both athlete and operator, his money is both old and new. He, too, is a self-indulger, but he is in control, undamaged; he has style. Self dreams of going out to California to get a full-scale body transplant: if he does, he will ask them to fix him up with a Fielding.

Self knows what he sees in Fielding: but what does Fielding see in him? It was Fielding who hired him, and it is Fielding who now supplies him with fat bundles of cash, first-class air tickets, high-tab dinners, chauffeur-driven limos, and so on. Fielding *is* money. No matter that he also seems to be going out of his way to abet Self's self-destruction – he humiliates him on the tennis court, takes him for a walk in Harlem, gets him low-grade drunk in high-grade restaurants: the point is that Fielding does these things with style, and Self, who has no style, is hypnotised. At one point, Self asks Fielding if he does much reading. Fielding says he does, and that he likes the sound and the fury. Self is baffled by this enigmatic answer, but he lets it pass.

As soon as John Self arrives in New York, he starts getting anonymous telephone calls; well, not quite anonymous: '"Just call me Frank".' Frank also says, '"I'm the guy whose life you fucked up,"' and he regularly taunts Self for his drunkenness and gluttony. He berates him, too, for his attitudes to women: at one point, he sends him a present – it's a doll-sized plastic woman with an open mouth. Frank claims to be an aggregate of all those whom Self has treated brutishly since childhood. Somehow he knows all Self's moves – rather better than Self does, very often, since

192

Self's memory is blurred and sometimes cancelled out by drink. Frank knows how many porno palaces he has visited, how many massage-parlour handjobs he has purchased, how many bottles and burgers he has hogged. Is there a connection between Frank the Phone and the tall, red-haired lady in a veil who seems to be following him round town? If there is, Self can't ever quite muster the mental energy to work it out.

Nor does he have the wits to figure out the role of Doris Arthur, the feminist scriptwriter hired by Fielding to work on *Good Money*. At first, Self treats her just like any other chick. He makes a lunge and is frostily rebuffed. Fielding tells him that this was because she is a lesbian, and this effectively disposes of Self's interest in her. Why is it, though, that Doris Arthur's script, when it eventually arrives, seems calculated to kill off the film? Each of Self's big stars has an obsession: Lorne Guyland, erstwhile sex-symbol, has insisted that he gets the girls and wins the fights, and that he be portrayed as a world-famous connoisseur of art; Butch Beausoleil won't be seen doing any housework – not even wiping fingerprints off doorknobs; Spunk Davis, health-freak and charity worker, has demanded a no-decadence clause in his contract; Caduta Massi has a thing about fertility and wants the script to supply her with some extra offspring. In Doris Arthur's finished screenplay, Lorne is senile, a sexual flop and totally illiterate; Butch spends most of her time swabbing toilets and ironing G-strings; Spunk, quite wrecked by his intake of junk food, is discovered, in close-up, goosing waifs down at the local orphanage; Caduta is barren – her big scene requires her to wander across a limitless grey desert, mocked by the distant sound of children's laughter. 'Someone's fucking me *around*,' cries Self. But who? And why? Thirty-five pages earlier, Doris herself had told him who and why but he had been too drunk to take it in. All he knows is that *Good Money* has gone bad.

At moments like this, it is Self's habit to turn to the reader. He has been chatting to us from the start, with lines like 'I'd better give you the low-down on Selina – and quick' or 'Memory's a funny thing, isn't it? You don't agree? I don't agree either.' And he usually seems fairly confident that we'll be on his side: 'I'm touched by your sympathy (and want much, much more of it. I want sympathy, even though I find it so very hard to behave sympathetically).' But then we have access to Self's inner self.

We know about those quiet moments in the whore-house when he is hit by a wavelet of revulsion: 'You know, I suspect I'm not cut out for brothels. I can't help getting engaged on the human scale, minimal though this is, fight it though I do, I just can't get off the scale.' (It should perhaps be said that, behaviour-wise, he doesn't do *too* badly in this instance, ending up with 'one of those handjobs where you go straight from limpness to orgasm, skipping the hard-on stage'.)

We know too about his crying jags, his entreaties that we might help him to 'make sense of things':

> I mean *look* at my private culture. Look at the state of it. It really isn't very nice in here. And that is why I long to burst out of the world of money and into – into what? Into the world of thought and fascination. How do I get there? Tell me, please. I'll never make it by myself. I just don't know the way.

Well, between him and us, we're not quite sure that this is so. After all, whose eloquence *is* this? Self's powerful soliloquies reveal an imaginative self rich (yes, rich) in metaphor, irony and farcical good humour – a literary self which, as the outer Self would put it, has somehow gimmicked a smart tie-up between low slang and high figurative artifice. Sometimes the tie-up comes out sounding like Holden Caulfield done over by Micky Spillane, but at its best it's not like anybody else: an urban-apocalyptic high fever somehow kept steady, helped across the road, by those old redoubtables – wit, worldly wisdom, and an eye for social detail.

> I strode through meat-eating genies of subway breath. I heard the ragged hoot of sirens, the whistles of twowheelers and skateboarders, pogoists, gocarters, windsurfers. I saw the barrelling cars and cabs, shoved on by the power of their horns. I felt all the contention, the democracy, all the italics in the air.

New York is bright red; London is dark grey:

> As I zipped myself up, a pigeon clockworked past on the pavement eating a chip. A *chip*. Like horseflies and other creatures who direct and star in their own tiny films, the pigeon lived in fast motion. It naturally preferred fast food.

194

City life was happening everywhere . . . Flies get dizzy spells and bees have booze problems. Robin redbreasts hit the deck with psychosomatic ulcers and cholesterol overload. In the alleys, dogs are coughing their hearts out on snout and dope. The stooped flowers in their sodden beds endure backpinch and rug-loss, what with all the stress about. Even the microbes, the spores of the middle air, are finding all this a little hard on their nerves.

Self can also come up with softer, more elegiac hues:

I walk more in the streets now. . . . This morning in the sunshine I saw a pale boy, three or four years old or however old kids are these days, wheeled by his father in a hoodless pram. The boy wore thick glasses with thick black rims. Like the pram the specs were cheap. Unhinged, they slipped from the child's pale ears and he groped at this thing on his face, gazing up, appealing to his father, who was thirty-odd, skinny and had long skinny hair, T-shirt, winded denims. The child's face had a gently suffering look you sometimes get among the pale, the small, the hard of seeing: he showed his milky teeth, the expression rapt, expectant, forming a rightful entreaty. The father made his brisk adjustments – not unkindly, no, not at all. The child's pale hand was raised and with its fingertips lightly steadied the darker, busier hand . . . I took this hard, the eyes so old so soon, and coupled to that pale, forbearing thing.

How then might this inner Self break out into real life: is real life really worth the effort? In the novel two possible assistants are on hand. In London, there is a writer called Martin Amis. Self has met him once or twice and found him rather priggish, full of mini-sermons about moral choice. Even so, after the Doris Arthur disaster, he needs a script-doctor in a hurry, and even the puritanical M. Amis can't resist (or so it seems) the mega-bucks. Amis signs up, ingeniously rewrites the script so that each of the stars is mollified, and from time to time treats Self to his musings on the 'moral philosophy of fiction': 'When I create a character and put him through certain ordeals, what am I up to – morally?' What indeed? And can we really blame Self for not rumbling this one? 'The further down the scale he is,' Amis continues, 'the more

195

liberties you can take with him. You can do what the hell you like to him, really. This creates an appetite for punishment. The author is not free of sadistic impulses.' But Self isn't listening. He wants his script; he wants his money.

The reader, of course, now knows something else that poor Self doesn't know. We know that he now has a 'double innocence'. As Amis tries to tell him, the characters in novels are doubly to be pitied: 'They don't know why they're living through what they're living through. They don't even know they're alive.' Not knowing, Self can only listen to so much of this kind of thing. He tries to get Amis to tell him something about *his* private life, but the novelist won't talk. The nearest the two of them get to calling a truce is when they sit down together to watch the Royal Wedding on TV. Self cries his eyes out, but when he is allowed to steal a glance at Amis, he notices that the novelist isn't looking too good, either. He sees 'a grey tear glint in those heavy eyes'. Maybe Martin is a bit like him, after all: 'If I stare into his face I can make out the areas of waste and fatigue, the moonspots and boneshadow you're bound to get if you live in the twentieth century.'

There are those who do not have this wasted look. Lady Di doesn't, nor does Self's other likely helpmate, the American Martina Twain. People like Di and Martina, Self opines:

have a colour. You never see them in the streets, not in the streets plural. That colour, it looks like the sheen of health or sun or gimmicked youth but it is only the colour of money. Money softens the fall of life, as you know. Money breaks the fall. Anyway, Martin hasn't got that colour. And neither have I. And neither have you. Shake.

The thing about this kind of money is that it is old money. It hasn't been scrambled for, and the people who have it usually know what to do with it. 'Money makes you innocent when it's been there all along.' Martina Twain had been a fellow-student of Self's at film school, but he had always considered her out of his league: 'She's class, with a terrific education on her.' Why then does she seem to be taking such an interest in him – this transatlantic female Martin A.? She tries to get him to read books, she takes him to operas and art galleries, she offers him white wine and persuades him to cut down to two packs of cigarettes a day. Self can't make her out: after all, she's a chick, and very good-looking, and yet when he tries to introduce her into his pornographic mind-movie she doesn't seem to fit. 'The thing about Martina is that I can't find a voice to summon her with.' Like Martin Amis, she has a taste for philosophical discussion – and, for all he knows, she too might be trying to alert him to his plight: 'She talked about perception, representation and truth. She talked about the vulnerability of a figure unknowingly watched – the difference between a portrait and an unposed study. The analogous distinction in fiction would be that between the conscious and the reluctant narrator – the sad, the unwitting narrator.' Sad and unwitting, Self tries to make an effort to improve himself for Martina, but the old junk life keeps tugging him back. His libido can't cope with Martina's wholesome sexual bounty. Pornography reclaims him and, thanks to Martin Amis's new script, the film world propels him to the final depths. At the end of it all, he is back in London, broke and broken.

Martin Amis is waiting for him, and even he – the cunning inventor of Self's woes – can't help feeling a bit guilty: 'I remembered Martin, here in my flat, standing over me and saying again and again in a clogged and wretched hush: "I'm so sorry. I'm so sorry."' With that said, Amis hoists himself back on to the title page and plays it cool. The subtlety of these final scenes – the teasing with notions of character, narrative and motivation – can only be done justice to by revealing the book's jigsaw of whodunnits, and I have already come too close to doing that. *Money* really needs to be read twice (at least): the first time for the sheer pleasure of encountering the grotesque and lovable John Self, for the laughs, the plot, the extraordinary urban atmospherics. The second time round (when, as Self would say, you are all laughed out) you can begin to relish the book's marvellously intricate design: the chess motif, the cosmological perspectives, the Othello murmur, the weather vein, and so on. I am already persuaded that *Money* will be thought of for years to come as one of the key books of the decade.

1984

MARTIN AMIS
Money: A Suicide Note
Cape

Julian Barnes's Staring at the Sun

Julian Barnes once trained to be a barrister, and he's been asking questions ever since – questions, mostly, about questions. In *Before She Met Me*, the hero of the book actually suffered from interrogation-mania: try as he might, he couldn't stop himself wondering about the details of his wife's past love-affairs. In *Flaubert's Parrot*, the narrator is a biographer – another snoopy type. In his case, even the answers to his questions are actually questions-in-disguise. In Barnes's books, people don't get worn down by compulsions of the flesh, nor deranged by the pursuit of fame and money: they fall victim to exhaustion of the brain – they become, as Barnes himself might put it, all quizzed out.

But they are not mad. Usually, they know, or think they know, most of the answers. In this sense, Barnes both celebrates and mocks the powers of reason. He shows us Intelligence in overdrive, but he also requires us to wonder if it's chosen the right road. Asking questions is supposed to be a 'good thing', to do with being neither fooled nor squashed. But is it not also an affliction, a disabling distancer-from-life? Wishing to grasp the essence of a genius like Flaubert; doesn't this also mean we'd like to cut him down to size? Is there not more vanity involved in putting a 'good question' than there can ever be in providing a sound answer? And if there *is* a sound answer, can the question really have been all that good?

These are the circles that Barnes's people tend to move in, round and round, and never before more nakedly than in this latest book. There are three hundred question-marks in *Staring at the Sun*; that's about one-and-a-half of the little worriers per page:

> . . . she would occasionally ask questions. The trouble was, how could you know what questions to ask? It seemed to her that

198

you were in a position to ask a really correct question only if you already knew the answer, and what was the point of that?

The victim here is Jean Serjeant, the book's biographee, whose life we follow from her childhood in the early-thirties to her very old old age in 2021. She spends a lifetime asking questions and receiving answers both sound and unsound: in her antiquity, however, we find her knowing plenty and yet still relishing the invincibility of certain riddles and metaphors that had stuck – 'like burrs' – to her imagination when she was a child.

The book opens brilliantly – that is to say, with an image so powerfully lit that it will haunt us for the book's duration. At any rate, this is the author's stratagem, and it's a bold one. If Barnes's power-supply had failed, or even faltered, on this opening page, his whole enterprise would have been seriously imperilled:

This is what happened. On a calm, black night in June, 1941, Sergeant-Pilot Thomas Prosser was poaching over Northern France. His Hurricane 11B was black in its camouflage paint. Inside the cockpit, red light from the instrument panel fell softly on Prosser's hands and face; he glowed like an avenger . . .

There was no prey that night. At 3.46 Prosser set course for base. He crossed the French coast at 18,000 feet. Perhaps disappointment had made him delay his return longer than usual, for as he glanced up the Channel to the east he saw the sun begin to rise. The air was empty and serene as the orange sun extracted itself calmly and steadily from the sticky yellow bar of the horizon. Prosser followed its slow exposure. Out of trained instinct, his head jerked on his neck every three seconds, but it seems unlikely he would have spotted a German fighter had there been one. All he could take in was the sun rising from the sea, stately, inexorable, almost comic.

Finally, when the orange globe sat primly on the shelf of distant waves, Prosser looked away. He became aware of danger again; his black aeroplane in the bright morning air was now as conspicuous as some Arctic predator caught in the wrong fur by a change of season. As he banked and turned, banked and turned, he glimpsed below him a long trail of black smoke. A solitary ship, perhaps in trouble. He descended quickly towards the twinkling, miniature waves, until at last he could make out a tubby merchantman heading west. But the black smoke had stopped, and there seemed nothing wrong: probably she had just been stoking up.

At 8,000 feet Prosser flattened out and set fresh course for base. Halfway across the Channel he allowed himself . . . to think about hot coffee, and the bacon sandwich he would eat after debriefing. Then something happened. The speed of his descent had driven the sun back below the horizon, and as he looked towards the east he saw it rise again: the same sun coming up from the same place across the same sea. Once more, Prosser put aside caution and just watched: the orange globe, the yellow bar, the horizon's shelf, the serene air, and the smooth, weightless lift of the sun as it rose from the waves for the second time that morning. It was an ordinary miracle he would never forget.

Prosser describes this 'ordinary miracle' to the young daughter of the house he lodges in, and Jean Serjeant is at once doomed not to forget it either. She never quite makes up her mind what it is about Prosser's tale that moves her most: is it the twice-risen sun, or is it the heroic image of Prosser in his Hurricane, courageously alone: he who 'put aside caution and just stared'. That life might offer experience which can be 'just stared' at rather than fretfully cross-questioned: this is a notion that Jean treasures for some ninety years but never quite knows what to do with. It is in the fallings-short that we are meant to discover her pathos and resolve.

In the early chapters of the novel, the argument between metaphor and the mundane has both a context and a story to sustain it, and Julian Barnes seems well in charge of both. There are some excellent pre-war atmospherics, and Jean's growing up is studied with an intentness and a care for plausibility that somehow fails to hold up later on. She is portrayed as near-retarded, according to any conventional definition of brain-power, and yet sleeplessly inquisitive. In a way, her mind is too lively for most of what it happens to ingest. There is the golf-club slang of her raffish Uncle Leslie: banal stuff if you can decode it, but to her exotic and mysterious: what is 'The Old Green Heaven', the 'nineteenth hole', and why is Leslie forever nipping off to 'wash behind his ears'? She is similarly exercised when Leslie gets her to play funny games: the Screaming Game, the Shoelace Game. Why shouldn't she report these to her mum? And why is Leslie irritated when she wants to know what happened to the sandwiches Lindbergh didn't eat on his Atlantic flight? 'They're probably in a sandwich museum,' he tells her. 'A sandwich museum. Jean wondered to herself: were there such things? But she knew not to ask any further.' Jean is also baffled by her aunt's collection of animal prints, especially the one that describes the mink as 'excessively tenacious of life'. Nobody can explain to her why this is so.

These early-planted teasers crop up time and again throughout the book, and so too does the image of Prosser staring at the sun. Also recurrent are one or two key phrases from a sex manual Jean studied when she was about to embark on her bound-to-be-unhappy marriage to the local policeman. There are also many descriptions of the sky: Uncle Leslie once told Jean – '"The sky's the limit."' At first, these recurrences lend richness to the tale, and we feel genuinely drawn into the girl's quicky mental world, with its aeroplanes, its sandwiches and its tenacious mink. And the scenes in which she quizzes Prosser about his Hurricane exploits are subtly done, and very touching; it is as if, through him, she graduates from riddle to metaphor, from puzzlement to awe. The climax to this section of the book arrives when Jean goes up to London to have herself fitted for a contraceptive device in preparation for her marriage:

> . . . she stopped thinking about her nether regions. Her eyes were tight shut, like blackout curtains closely drawn: but through them came the red glow of life outside. Black and red, the colour of war: the colour of Tommy Prosser's war. Tommy Prosser in his black Hurricane out in the black night with the hood back and the red glow from the instrument panel softly lighting up his face and hands. Tommy Prosser in his black Hurricane looking out for the red exhausts of returning bombers. Black and red . . .

Prosser stands for metaphor and Michael, Jean's new husband, stands for the mundane. Michael knows nothing of sandwich museums, of tenacious mink, nor does he want to; and he has never seen the sun rise twice. We follow Jean through twenty years of dreary, childless marriage, but at a rapid pace, so that a mere forty pages later she is on her own again, with only a few botched marital embraces to show for her whole early adult life.

She becomes pregnant at forty and leaves Michael: she is finally determined to make for herself 'a first-rate life', and she is still dreaming about Prosser's red and black, still anxious to find out about that mink.

And it is here that the novel changes gear, and Jean turns into someone else, a determined, adventurous type whose only connection with the Jean we've studied in Part One is circumstantial. This new Jean still looks at the sky a lot and thinks of Hurricanes; she is still obsessed with sandwiches and mink. In too many other respects, though, she really is liberated from her former self. She has a son called Gregory, whose upbringing is dealt with as briskly as her marriage was, and it is only when he starts building model aeroplanes (not very well) that we are asked to take much interest in him. The focus at this stage is on the altered Jean. Inconclusively she tries to find out what happened to Prosser; failing here, she decides to visit each of the Seven Wonders of the World. Slides are provided of Jean in China (here experiencing the same kind of translation problems that beset her as a child), Jean at the Pyramids, Jean peering into the Grand Canyon. Yes, she even has her own version of the Seven. In these chapters, she is equipped with a ruminative, wily intelligence which, again, is hard to fit with what she was like before. And it is not enough to have her echo old obsessions. Throughout this middle bit of the book, we can't escape the feeling that, for Mr Barnes, growing up means getting to be a bit like Mr Barnes.

The same kind of niggling rationality afflicts the grown-up Gregory, who suddenly reappears, but as a key figure, about two-thirds of the way through the book. Without any advance warning, he suddenly offloads a witty, worldly, jocularly philosophical treatise on the disadvantages of travelling by air. We pick up the Hurricane connection, to be sure, but then we put it down again. By this stage of the book we are convinced that the novelist has lost interest in the tale he first set out to tell, and that that clever Mr Barnes has begun shoving across at us the assorted sweepings from his study floor. Nice sweepings, in the main, but even so . . .

Things pick up in the last third of the book, although the 'selected essays' feel of things still lingers. We are by now set in the future, with Jean more or less back where she started – wizened and enigmatic where before she was fresh-faced and foolable, she is still clinging to the old mysteries, the old sandwiches and mink. Gregory, now in his sixties, unmarried, unsuccessful and quite glad to be so, pits his questing intelligence against the mighty General Purposes Computer that by now is running everybody's life. He quizzes the machine about God, Death, Heaven, History and finally about Itself: "'Who runs you?" REPEAT. Who runs you? MODIFY. How do you work?'" He gets nowhere and has to content himself with going home to write grittily colloquial essays on theology. One day, as a favour to his mother, he asks the machine why 'the mink is excessively tenacious of life'. No joy. The machine tells him that this is 'NOT REAL QUESTION'. The excessively tenacious Jean reflects:

> But what were real questions . . . Real questions were limited to those questions to which the people you asked already knew the answers. If her father or GPC could answer, that made the enquiry a real question; if not, it was dismissed as being falsely based. How very unfair. Because it was these questions, the ones that weren't real, to which you wanted to know the answers most pressingly. For ninety years, she'd wanted to know about the mink. Her father had failed, so had Michael; and now GPC was ducking it. That was the way it was. Knowledge didn't really advance, it only seemed to. The serious questions always remained unanswered.

And so it's back to Prosser, to the red and black and the twice-risen sun: it's back to miracles, to Art and Nature. For Jean Serjeant, in her hundredth year, it's forward to 'post-mortal phosphorescence'. We leave her not staring, but smiling, at the sun.

Julian Barnes is one of the most intelligent writers we have and, at his best, he writes with an impressive clarity and edge. The inner debate, done in a fractionally elevated version of real speech, is what he's best at, and a book like *Flaubert's Parrot* provided the almost-perfect vehicle for his non-fiction sort of fiction. In *Staring at the Sun*, Barnes shows in the early chapters that he is equipped to handle narrative, but it is as if he gets restless with the simple mechanics of tale-telling, and with characters who are less intelligent than he is. No one ought to blame him for this buoyancy, since he is always fun to read, but maybe next time round the Booker Prize will have to change its rules.

1986

JULIAN BARNES
Staring at the Sun
Cape

PART IV
DOWN GRUB STREET WAY

John Carey and the Intellectuals

When Henry James's play, *Guy Domville*, was booed off the London stage, the embarrassed author remarked that at least *some* of the audience were clapping. These approvers were powerless to out-clamour the 'hoots and jeers and catcalls of the roughs', whose roars were 'like those of a cage of beasts at some infernal zoo', but for James they represented 'the forces of civilization'.

This was one way of describing them. Another would have been to identify them as personal friends of the playwright. Full marks to James, though, for looking on the bright side. A few days later, his face was not so brave:

> I have fallen upon evil days – every sign or symbol of one's being in the least wanted, anywhere or by anyone, having so utterly failed. A new generation that I know not, and mainly prize not, has taken universal possession. The sense of being utterly out of it weighed me down, and I asked myself what the future would be.

This was 1895, and James's way out of his depression was to decide: 'That's right – *be* one of the few', and to direct his art accordingly. He would renounce, he said, 'the childishness of publics', and no longer seek to win over a large audience. Henceforth he would not care if 'scarce a human being will understand a word, or an intention, or an artistic element of any sort' in what he wrote.

There was a strong element of petulance, of 'so *there*', in James's resolution but some would say that this issued from a genuine and significant despair, a despair which should be pondered with sympathy if we wish to fathom not just the personality of Henry James but also the cultural attitudes of some of his almost-immediate successors: Eliot, Joyce, Pound and Co, who seemed similarly indifferent to whether or not their intentions would be understood. Few of our key 'modernist' texts do not partake of James's umbrage, his angered determination to '*be* one of the few'. And yet, like James, these modernists were obsessed with the state of the literary culture: they pronounced on the subject endlessly, and their works can often be read as lamentations over the sorry condition of a world that has no place, no privileged or central place, for works like theirs.

When Victorian literary men mused on the forthcoming challenge of Democracy, they tended to assume that, however rough things got, there would still be aristocrats and peasants: in literary-cultural terms, it would be the task of the intellectual/aristocrat to provide an 'adequate ideal to elevate and guide the multitude', the reader/peasant. The intellectual's prestige in the new order would thus be enhanced rather than diminished. His writings, widely available at last, would be acknowledged as *the* civilizing force. A newly literate multitude would turn with gratitude to its ancient tribal leaders, hailing them as prophets, sages, magicians, witch doctors, druids, take your pick. By this reckoning, maybe Democracy wouldn't be too bad.

A poet who got going in, say, 1910 would have inherited this kind of thinking, would indeed have taken it for granted as the theoretical foundation of his self-esteem. In a utilitarian democracy he would be able to explain his 'function' thus, albeit with shyly downcast eyes. And yet he would also by that date have known that the theory was failing to hold up, or was turning into an impossible ideal. The new literacy had no sooner arrived than it had come under the control and guidance of a new set of tribal chiefs, with Lord Northcliffe and the Editor of *Tit-Bits* at its head. There had rapidly come into being what John Carey describes as 'an alternative culture which by-passed the intellectual and made him redundant'. It was a culture that used itself up as it went along, but its audience could be numbered in millions and the delights it provided were not all that easy to distinguish from those which the old high culture used to have on offer.

This, at any rate, was the consumer's view. The heirs of high culture saw these new vehicles of entertainment as degradations of the human spirit, manipulations of the mass intelligence, for profit. They also saw that, if so directed, the mass-intelligence was likely to turn nasty – books could be banned, homosexuals imprisoned, magazines made to expire from lack of funds. In retaliation, they affected a disdain for the requirements of the mob and began to evoke apocalyptic visions of an imminent 'deluge of barbarism'; they spoke of 'the malodorous rabble', 'the monster with a million worm-like heads'. By this route, it might be argued, literary intellectuals recaptured a notion of their own centrality: unloved by the unwashed, they could become warriors on behalf of an imperilled 'life of the imagination' – or, as John Carey would prefer to have it put, they could figure themselves 'as engaged upon dangerous and energetic pursuits when in fact they [were] merely looking at pictures and reading books'. And if anyone accused them of simply defending the old against the new, they could point to their various experiments and slogans. 'Make it new!' said Ezra Pound, even as he handed out reading lists that stretched back to the middle ages, and beyond.

The relationship between literary intellectuals and mass culture is hardly a novel subject for discussion. Indeed, at the beginning of the century, literary intellectuals seemed to talk of little else. And, thanks to the Leavises and their cohorts, the discussion eventually spread into almost every schoolroom in the land. In my own late-fifties sixth form, it was taken as axiomatic that all advertising was evil, all journalism a threat to the survival of the species, all pop music a sure way of catching something called 'sex in the head' (an ailment we spotty ones already suffered from, and how). We read *Brave New World* so as to learn how things might work out if we did not read *Brave New World*. And Nicholas Monsarratt's *The Cruel Sea* (a current bestseller) was held up for massive ridicule: we asked if we could take this item home with us so that we might the more thoroughly acquaint ourselves with its gross failures of sensibility and moral courage.

And this was pre-TV, pre-Beatles. The actual discussion, such as it was, invariably centred on the 'predicament' of the artist-intellectual, his threatened specialness, his alienation from the main, and mainly dreadful, tendencies of modern life. We were taught to believe that the extreme difficulty of, say, Eliot's *The Waste Land* was a difficulty born not of sulking or snobbism but of a heroic effort of resistance to the vile regiments of the ill-read. It is indeed shaming to recall what little culture-toffs we were encouraged to become – we who had actually read next to nothing.

Perhaps John Carey was once upon a time put through this same post-Leavis mill. Or was it among the mini–Bowras of Oxford that he learned to despise the superior posturings of literary intellectuals? In *Intellectuals and the Masses* critical dictators are treated with the same scorn as wafting aesthetes: what the two groupings have in common is a settled conviction that their culture is *the* culture – it was made by and belongs to them.

A university professor, Carey perhaps feels that he himself has spent too many years cut off from the 'real life' which he repeatedly blames intellectuals for avoiding, or misrepresenting. I remember a seventies essay of his called 'Down with Dons' in which he amusingly derided the idea that university professors should get higher salaries than miners, say, or power-workers; in his view, most dons were lucky to get paid at all. After all, what were they for? What did they do? Who needed them? He feels much the same way about certain novelists and poets. Just as 'the most obnoxious thing about dons is their uppishness', so it can be said that highbrow writers have only their own arrogance to blame if they are ignored or ridiculed by lowbrows. This was the way they themselves fixed it, at the start. Instead of bleating about the death of the old culture, they should have tried to make some useful contribution to the new.

And it is here that Carey risks, and is merrily prepared to risk, getting labelled as some kind of redneck. In his dons essay, he tells a story about living opposite an academic household:

> The father, a philosopher, was a shambling, abstract figure, whom one would glimpse from time to time perambulating the neighbourhood, leering at the milk bottles left on doorsteps and talking to himself. If he had any contact with the outside world, or any control over his numerous children, it certainly wasn't apparent. To make matters worse, the mother was a don too, and the house was regularly left in the children's sole charge. The result was bedlam. The din of recorded music resounded from the place at all hours, and it never seemed to occur to anyone to shut a window or moderate the volume. One summer afternoon, when I was doggedly trying to mark a batch of A-level papers, my patience gave out, and I crossed the street to protest.

Re-reading this now, in the light of Carey's book, I find myself wondering what he would make of such a tale if the complainer had been a drippy poet and the noisemakers opposite a troupe of complex artisans.

In other words, it is as well that the down-with-dons essay was written by a don. Similarly, this polemic against highbrows can the more easily be swallowed, indeed savoured, because it was written by a highbrow. And not just by any old highbrow. It is well known that John Carey reads Milton in the Latin and knows where to find *all* the dirty bits in Ovid. As a reviewer, he is acknowledged to wield one of the sharpest, most entertaining pens in town. Although he berates intellectuals for paying insufficient heed to the details of lives other than their own, he is himself a master of the terminal encapsulation.

It matters little to Carey that this or that artist-intellectual might have been diagnosed by Freud as neurotically excluded from a social mainstream that he yearned to join. So far as this analyst is concerned, there is something obscene and unforgivable in the spectacle of an effete and dandified poseur spouting about the need for a return to 'bloodshed, slavery and the wild ways of the old pagan world' when all he ever *does*, from day to day, is hang around cafés and studios in Paris. Thus, after quoting almost a full page of crazed anti-democratic rhetoric by George Moore, Carey remarks: 'We need to remind ourselves, reading this, that Moore was not (or not merely) a crackpot and a pervert, but the friend and collaborator of W.B. Yeats and a leading figure in the Irish literary renaissance.' It is the 'not merely' that rescues Carey's puritanism from the easy piety which sometimes seems to threaten it, but there is a steeliness there too, perhaps even a mild relish. At moments like these (and there are several in the book) one is tempted to call Carey's humour donnish.

In the end, though, it all comes back to uppishness: the uppishness of other writers, that's to say. When great artists start dipping into their Great Artist box of tricks, Carey is always likely to see red. Indeed, we might easily be left with the impression that he wished the whole lot of them had never chosen to put pen to paper. He intimates at one point that, in spite of all the Nietzschean rubbish he came out with, D.H. Lawrence had some sensuous merit, and Carey has a fondness for James Joyce that enables him to play down that author's mutterings against the 'trolls' and 'rabblement' of Ireland. But it is not clear that he reckons

many of the others – Eliot, Huxley, Woolf and so on – to be
indispensable.

But then the book is not meant to be straight literary criticism.
It is about attitudes not art-works. And on the matter of attitudes,
Carey's testiness can be joyously unreined. He has no patience with
high-flown talk about predicaments and alienation. He is first of all an
educator. His sympathies are with readers rather than with writers and
he believes that, with the advent of mass literacy, a great educational
opportunity was missed. Instead of sneering at Leonard Bast's pretensions, Forster should have been teaching him at nightschool. But that
could never have happened because, however the intellectuals chose to
dress up their disdain, it was actually class-based – it had its roots in a
fear and loathing of the mass, a revulsion which in some cases turned
into mad superman-delusions or fantasies of mass-extermination.
(There is a chapter in the book on Hitler-as-European-intellectual,
student of Nietzsche, colleague of Wyndham Lewis, and so on.)
Carey assembles some damaging material along these lines. Much
of it has already been displayed in John Harrison's 1966 book, *The
Reactionaries*, but not so wittily or angrily as here.

There is an ever-present risk that Carey's generalising bent might
go berserk, so that every bad thing in the world can be traced
back to a few authors of the modernist persuasion. And this
can be disconcerting, since he is also seeking to persuade us that
intellectuals don't matter or that the really sad and funny thing about
them is that they perpetually over-estimate their own importance.
He is on surer ground, and seems happier, when he speaks up
on behalf of writers whom the toffs have, in their arrogance,
misread or under-valued. Authors like Chesterton, Conan Doyle
and, pre-eminently, Arnold Bennett ('the hero of this book') are
not much scrutinised in universities, and this is presumably why
Carey thinks they need defending. And he defends them very well,
evincing a warmth of engagement with the texts which some of his
other, posher subjects might have thanked him for.

To which John Carey might reply that it is Bennett's warmth
of engagement with the lives he writes about that marks him out
from the shrinkings and recoilings of the modernists. Unlike those
self-pampered swells, Bennett sought and gained a large slice of the
new readership; he wrote for it and of it, without uppishness. He
saw no difference between high culture and low culture. The point
of all culture, he believed, is to reveal 'the miraculous interestingness

of the universe'. A writer is an ordinary chap, but lucky: his life is 'one long ecstasy of denying that the world is a dull place'. Not for Bennett the damp souls of housemaids, the lonely men in shirt-sleeves looking out of windows, the constant carping about the drabness of suburbia, the hatefulness of industry, the menace of science, the pathos of book-hungry clerks. This artist–intellectual, Carey says, is one of us. He is inclusive, hospitable, abundant: he 'gives us access to the realities that blaze and coruscate inside dowdy or commonplace bodies'.

There is undeniably a touch of the social worker or the adult-educationist in operation here, and it can lead Carey into some dubious side-sneers of his own, as when – praising Bennett for his attitudes to parenthood – he claims that 'literary intellectuals in the first half of the twentieth century tended to opt for childlessness and child-neglect', and then gives two examples – of neglect. To take childlessness as a symptom of aloofness from the hurly-burly of real living seems pretty stern. Most of the great writers of the eighteenth century were childless – but so what? And we might raise an eyebrow also when, speaking of a sick-bed scene in Bennett, Carey comments: 'What are real are not the pastimes intellectuals value – literature, art, philosophy, but the offices of death-bed and sickroom, where man is reduced to matter.' But then this is Carey's way: he writes all the more lovingly of Bennett because Bennett is routinely patronised by aesthetes. As he once said: a 'common reason for liking particular literary works is precisely the knowledge that other people do not like them'.

1992

JOHN CAREY
The Intellectuals and the Masses:
Pride and Prejudice Among the Literary Intelligentsia 1880–1939
Faber

George Orwell's Essays and Reviews

When George Orwell's *Collected Essays* appeared in 1961, it was felt that their publication was something of an insult to his memory. For over twenty years Orwell had been a professional writer and for most of those years he had been writing 'essays' of one kind or another (sometimes up to four or five a week). Not only had the editor of the so-called collected volume unaccountably dropped one of Orwell's lengthier and best-known pieces – the essay on Kipling – but he had not even begun sifting through the mass of his contributions to the periodicals. A huge task but, it was conjectured, the only way of getting on to really close, conclusive terms with an important author. Orwell's response to the developing events of his momentous epoch had long been seen as, at the very least, valuably representative of the drift into political disillusionment experienced by a whole generation of British left-wing intellectuals, and his copious journalism would surely provide an opportunity of studying this process with an almost week by week exactness. It might also tell us more than the long essays did about his personality.

The job has now been done. Four bulging volumes of essays, book reviews, weekly columns, diaries, letters, broadcasts, all arranged and edited with considerable care. And one's first, awed, response is simply to the *amount* Orwell wrote. How did he manage it? At the end of his life, Orwell said in a notebook:

> It is now (1949) sixteen years since my first book was published and abt. twenty-one years since I started publishing articles in the magazines. Throughout that time there has literally not been one day in which I did not feel that I was idling, that I was behind with the current job & that my total output was miserably small. Even

at the periods when I was working ten hours a day on a book, or turning out four or five articles a week, I have never been able to get rid of this neurotic feeling that I was wasting time.

Set alongside this a passage from Orwell's previously uncollected recollections of his years at prep school, *Such Such Were the Joys*, and a similar note of plaintiveness is heard:

It was in 'classics' that the real strain came. Looking back, I realise that I then worked harder than I have ever done since, and yet at the time it never seemed possible to make the effort that was demanded of one. We would sit round the long shiny table, made of some very pale-coloured hard wood, with Sambo goading, threatening, exhorting, sometimes joking, very occasionally praising, but always prodding away at one's mind to keep it up to the right pitch of concentration, as one might keep a sleepy person awake by sticking pins into him.

As a 'scholarship boy', it should be said, Orwell was singled out at school from the very start as one who was expected to work several times harder than the fee-paying boys simply in order to earn his keep, and his young childhood was, as he describes it, a horrific round of beatings and humiliations – all of them centred on success in 'the exam'. 'Over two or three years the scholarship boys were crammed with learning as cynically as a goose is crammed for Christmas.' Too patly casebook an explanation of his later, guilt-racked, industry? One certainly shies away from such an elementary diagnosis. And yet there is a sense in which one of Orwell's greatest strengths as a writer is precisely that his life does fit with explanations of this kind. That is to say, it was a life that genuinely did have 'turning points', key moments of experience which shaped the essentials of his personality for years to come. Just as one hesitates to settle for the view that Orwell worked hard just because he was beaten into working hard when he was young, so there is something objectionably uncomplex in the notion that guilt over his activities with the Imperial Police in India was the sole trigger of his down-and-out, *Road to Wigan Pier*, phase of identification with the English poor. And yet no other explanation tallies so satisfactorily with what actually occurred, and certainly Orwell himself believed it was that simple. And no explanation that did not point to something obsessive in his nature could possibly account for the *completeness* with which he immersed himself in whatever new role his experience insisted on. Such completeness, of course, led Orwell into rigid, unattractive postures: his sentimental elevation of 'the ordinary', his blanket sneers at 'intellectuals'. But it furnished everything he wrote with a deep autobiographical conviction.

Thus the very quality of obsession that made Orwell write so much also helps to explain why nothing much that is new is revealed about him by this bulk of fresh material. When Orwell fell victim to a new moral passion, there was nothing in his life to compete with it. The few private letters that are printed here are hardly private – most of them are concerned with professional or political matters; the journals he kept during the war are astonishingly free of any kind of introspection. It could be said that only a writer who was uninterested in exploring his own personality could have *employed* that personality as usefully as Orwell did, could have – as it were – sent his whole self out into the public world with such a firm sense of the moral and political reliability of its responses.

In his political writing, certainly, it was this moral firmness, coupled with a marvellously lucid style and an unfailingly rigorous intelligence, that had such a shattering effect on his opponents, and one of the many reasons for welcoming these volumes is that they make it possible for us to view Orwell's polemical activities in all their rousing detail. The turning point in Orwell's 'mature' political life was, of course, the Spanish Civil War; his involvement with the POUM militia afforded him a close-up view of political in-fighting at its messiest and most disreputable. Up till then, Orwell's politics had been vaguely revolutionary, but mainly compassionate; a combination of anger over the oppression of the poor with an admiration for working-class culture. He wanted both to change and to share the quality of working people's lives. His book reviews at this period were limitedly insistent on the necessity for writers to explore the experience of 'ordinary people'. *Ulysses* is valued for its portrait of the 'man in the street', *Tropic of Cancer* is extravagantly praised for attempting to 'get at the facts', Cyril Connolly is chastised for perpetrating the 'essential evil' of trying to escape from the dreariness of modern life, and so on.

But by the time he wrote *Inside the Whale*, Orwell had somewhat changed his tune: 'As for the writer, he is sitting on a melting iceberg' – Henry Miller is praised for having seen 'and proclaimed this fact a long while before most of his contemporaries'. Certainly this was not one of the 'facts' Orwell had previously commended Miller's work for 'getting at'. The Spanish war, the Moscow trials, had intervened, a European war seemed imminent, and Orwell's taste and curiosity were in any case too wide-ranging and eccentric for him to have been long satisfied with even a watered down version of socialist realism. The new spectre, of political censorship, was looming: the artist had the right to his despair.

At first Orwell was led, by political theorising, into an anti-war position: he feared that the war, whoever won it, would merely induce fascism in Britain. 'It is useless,' he wrote, 'to overthrow Tweedledum in order to set up Tweedledee.' He got in touch with Herbert Read to suggest that an anti-war resistance movement be set up and that they should begin stockpiling paper and printing equipment. This, in a sense, was Orwell's last fling as a left-wing activist, and one doubts whether he really believed much in it; he had probably already made his choice. By the time war actually broke out, his disgust with the efforts of the organised left in Britain to hush up what was going on in Spain, and with their refusal to countenance any criticism of the Soviet Union, had reached its pitch; and with England actually imperilled he could acknowledge his real sympathies: 'It seems to me that now we are in this bloody war we have got to win it and I would like to lend a hand.'

From this point on, although in the early months of the war he was to talk rather nebulously of 'revolutionary situations', Orwell's position was unambiguous: it involved a deep and nostalgic patriotism, a suspicion of machine-age progress, a belief in the primary need for what he called 'common decency', and a dominating hatred of all forms of totalitarianism (but particularly Russia's) and of the 'silly-clever' political theorists who won't face awkward facts. Even after the German invasion of the Soviet Union, Orwell's attitude to Nazi Germany was never as intensely hostile as it was to Russia; pro-Russian cant was no longer the prerogative of the intellectual left – it had become part of the war effort – but Orwell never once relaxed his guard. And after the war, when the facts of the concentration camps were common knowledge, his interest in the revealed horrors was a touch remote, as if now that they were over they ought not to be made too much of. The postwar years, what few were left to him, were taken up with trying to get *Animal Farm* published and with composing *1984*. As his health failed, he wrote increasingly less straight journalism.

But he had made his point. He had demonstrated 'the power of facing unpleasant facts', and he had forced others to face them too. As Conor Cruise O'Brien put it, in an interestingly equivocal essay: '. . . the cant of the left, that cant which has so far proved indispensable to the victory of any mass movement, was almost destroyed by Orwell's attacks.' In other words you can take your choice: facts and failure or a certain measure of dishonesty and the still shining prospect of success. It depends how much dishonesty you can comfortably live with, how much lying and hypocrisy the notion of 'success' can meaningfully bear. Orwell set rather troublingly high standards in such matters.

1968

Sonia Orwell and Ian Angus (Editors)
The Collected Essays, Journalism and Letters of George Orwell
Secker & Warburg

The Knocking-Shop

The recent appearance of John Halperin's Gissing biography brings to mind a project which I have long thought someone ought to tackle: a fearless update of *New Grub Street*. The job wouldn't be too taxing – indeed, in many cases, it would be all too easy to attach contemporary names to Gissing's sunken literary types: his principled dullards as well as his sleek chancers. And then there are the grim trappings of Gissing's version of the Literary Career – the foundering periodical, the doomed synopsis, the already spent advance. All in all, the book's whole world of seedy, profitless endeavour *is* worryingly up-to-date.

Even so, a Gissing of the eighties would have to make some alterations. The curse of the three-volume novel, for example, sits heavily on Gissing's greying hacks. In the eighteen-nineties the circulating libraries favoured three-volume editions of novels because readers who wanted to read on to the end would thus have to fork out three subscriptions. The publishers in turn put pressure on their authors to stretch out their plots. 'Real money' would be offered for a three-decker (enough maybe to keep your average scribbler for six months) whereas a one-volume offering would yield almost punitively dreadful rates of pay. In those days, a novel consisted of '920 pages with twenty-one and a half lines on each page and nine and a half words on each line', and that was that. If you wanted to get all experimental, you could starve. Today, of course, with Public Lending Right, it might be that novelists will start getting their own back on the libraries – a resurrection of the three-decker could triple the author's rake-off under this compassionate new scheme.

Two of the most touching moments in *New Grub Street* are when Reardon is forced to sell his books in an attempt to make ends meet – well, not meet, exactly, but at least set up some distant, mocking contact. In Gissing's day, it seems, a dealer would visit the impoverished author at his by then semi-furnished lodgings and, for a handful of guineas, bear off the best of his prize leather-bounds – the only things the poor devil really cared about: real books, not like the rubbish he and his colleagues were obliged to churn out day by day.

Here again, I think, things may well have changed for the better. For most modern Reardons, these rending scenes will instantly evoke images of Chancery Lane – or, more precisely, that small alley off the Lane where generations of book reviewers and literary men have known the confused pleasure of securing the price of their next drink(s) in exchange for a mint copy of *Giles Goatboy*, or of swopping some multi-volume reissue of John Cowper Powys for a night out on the town.

The Chancery Lane idea is (or used to be) that you can sell off review copies for half their published price. The books had to be in really good condition (hence the loving care with which one would sometimes see a reviewer handling a text which that same day he had damned as 'worthless' in the public prints) and they had to be less than four months old. In the mid-sixties, I remember, it was even possible to take *poetry* down the Lane, but I understand this is no longer so. In fact, rumour has it that things are altogether stickier now and that it is not unknown for a dealer to turn down some quite nicely priced volumes on the grounds that they are 'boring'.

In the days when I used to go down there, though, he would take almost anything. And on Fridays the Lane would be alive with reviewers struggling in from Blackheath with their holdalls, or nipping round the corner from the *Telegraph* with a fistful of Robert Hales or Arthur Barkers. One esteemed figure at *The Times* used to order a taxi for noon on Friday and when it arrived he would have a flunkey load it up with art books and American encyclopedias. He would then squeeze in beside his booty and, with twinkling eye, instruct the driver to stop off in the Lane en route for Garrick Street, or Paddington. To the novice bookman with only a Catherine Cookson and a Roland Barthes between him and the workhouse this was indeed a stirring image of literary success. Gissing would have loved it.

Now and then, of course, one pondered the doubtful morality of these Friday expeditions. After all, these books were – presumably

– sold off to public libraries for less than their published price. This meant that the author would not collect his 10 per cent (again, this was all pre-PLR). Thus, in the case of a book you had already savaged in the prints, here was an additional chastisement. Could this be just? But then, more creatively, it could be argued that the Lane simply provided an opportunity for one limb of the industry to help another, that pennies lost to the novelist brought pounds to the reviewer and that a healthy criticism could only mean a healthy . . . and so on.

Of course, many novelists are themselves fiction reviewers, and several of the Lane's best anecdotes are to do with novelist A catching novelist B attempting to sell A's latest book. Along these same lines, I know of at least one reviewer who could not bear to take his swag along in person because this would mean him once again having to view a shelf-long stock of his own most recent publication: 'It had such *good* reviews,' he'd wail, 'but now I know they didn't mean it.' A greenhorn, he had clearly not heard the one about the hapless scribe who was once seen shuffling down the Lane with a carrier-bag containing six 'author's copies' of his brand-new 'breakthrough' novel. When quizzed, he said he wanted to celebrate publication day 'in style'. Each of these yarns, it seems to me, could be gruesomely fleshed out by the author of my new *New Grub Street*. And if he cares to get in touch, I can tell him a few more.

On the topic of 'the knocking-shop' – as the Lane vendor was once widely known – I still can't quite suppress a flicker of excitement when I come across a book like *The Oxford Illustrated Literary Guide to the United States*. It has all the qualifications for a quick and unashamed dispatch to EC4: it is expensive, lavishly but boringly illustrated, virtually unreviewable except by someone as madly knowledgeable as its two editors, and almost entirely without point. Without point, that is, unless you really want to know that Thomas Wolfe rented a cottage in Boothbay Harbor in July 1929 or that Rex Stout wrote four short stories in a boarding-house in Burlington, Vermont or that in Bridgwater, Connecticut on 1 July, 1949 'Van Wyck Brooks and his wife moved to a house on Main Street in which they were to entertain many literary visitors. A Sunday supper they gave in 1957, for example, was attended by Norman Mailer, Katherine Anne Porter and William Styron.' The authors call people who want to know this kind of thing 'literary travellers' and they plead that such travellers have in the past been handicapped by the lack of a guidebook that covered the whole of the United States. Well, I'm not sure how literary travellers travel, but they should perhaps be warned that for a guidebook of this size they should also pack a portable lectern. It's about a foot square and almost five hundred pages long.

I wonder how the editors imagine their book will be used. Will the literary traveller work by place or by author? That is to say, will he happen to find himself in Blowing Rock, set up his lectern in the market square, then discover from his literary guide that yesindeedy in this vurry town John Hersey wrote his *Hiroshima*? Or should we envisage a more dogged, gumshoe type – one who picks an author and then tracks him all the way from New Sybaris to Purgatory Pond? In either case, it is hard to fathom the rewards. I mean, what does one say or think on finding oneself outside the front gate of 61 Maeaug Avenue, New London, Connecticut: is it enough simply to know for certain that John Hollander lived there from 1957 to 1959? And what of the Auden sleuth who drags himself from campus to campus ('W.H. Auden also taught here' is the *Guide*'s usual formulation) and finally ends up at Swarthmore, only to be told: 'He lived at various addresses, including 16 Oberlin Avenue, and often took his lunch at the Dew Drop Inn, now the Village Restaurant, at 407 Dartmouth Avenue'? No problem about where to eat, but even so . . .

Leafing through the *Literary Guide* is rather like gawping impotently at the For Sale pages of *Country Life*, and it would be easy to get the impression from this book that American writers live only in mansions which are situated in spacious, leafy grounds, or pillared brownstones which look as if they've been borrowed from the mayor. Page after page of enviably huge residences are on show throughout. There are no garrets, no mental institutions. There are no obvious fleabags – although, since most of the pictures seem to have been taken with an estate agent's camera, it is not always possible to slap a fair price on individual properties. The thinking here seems to be that, in addition to his thirst for history, the literary traveller will usually prefer staring at real estate that is worth staring at. A reminder, though, that even to this day, an American *New Grub Street* is not all that easy to imagine.

1983

Litfest in Oz

'Australia?' There was a punishing stress on the second syllable and the tone was one of idle disbelief: 'But *why*?' This was over seven years ago. I had just been invited to a literary festival in Adelaide; no fee, but they'd pay my Qantas. It seemed to me an Opportunity Not to be Missed. In the week or so before I set off, however, almost everybody I bumped into (including at least one Australian) seemed to think that I'd gone off my head. Nobody, I was told, went to Australia just for the sake of Going to Australia. I must be mad. Or was I 'up to something'?

I reflected at the time that 'Australia' was perhaps the only destination in the world that could have been viewed in this confidently ribald way. If I had been nipping off to Papua New Guinea for a few weeks I would probably have got congratulated on managing to see 'that part of the world'. And even if I had been going to Canada, no one would actually have pitied me. After all, I would only have been two hours from NY.

Of course, it could be argued that the Aussies bring it on themselves, with their Barry McKenzies, their Ian Chappells, their self-parodying Foster ads, and so on. And there *is* the accent: for some reason more readily mimickable than any of our own regional twangs. Theories about the Australian accent are just as snooty as theories about Australia. Some say that it is a form of cell-block Cockney, that the Kray brothers may even now be stammering their parole appeals in infant Oz. Others contend that it must be to do with the weather: that early Australians who settled some thousand miles from each other, with no contact, and from quite different racial stocks, all began developing identical cadences and speech patterns. Snootiest of all, though, is the notion that the Australian accent is what ordinary, robust Anglo-Saxon would get

223

to sound like if it were spoken in a whine – that the distinctive Oz rhythms have, over the years, captured the lilt of a steady, unearned injuredness. Try saying 'Why me?' out loud one hundred times and see what happens to your vowels.

It was, then, with many a racist slur buzzing in my ears that I set off for Adelaide. There was no cloud, though, in my Open Mind. The plane journey to Sydney (also often named – the journey, that is – as a good reason not to go) was long enough almost to convince me that I had permanently overcome my fear of flying. After you have actually lived in an on-duty jet plane for twenty-seven hours it is hard, I reasoned, to recapture that old tingle of alarm. Indeed, having organised my bed, my books, my booze, having in fact *settled in*, I could very happily have muddled along up there for a quiet week or two. At Sydney, though, they made me change into a much smaller, more precarious vehicle, and by the time I reached Adelaide I had regained the lean, demented look of a survivor.

On the plane (the second, wobbly one) I had read in a local paper that I was indeed 'flying in' that day, so it was no big surprise when I was greeted at the terminal by an eager-eyed young pressman. He grabbed my suitcase with one hand and my elbow with the other and guided me off to the Press Room. Therein, dead-centre, was a small stage flooded with television lights, and on the stage a couple of black leatherette TV armchairs. An airport interview! Reluctantly, I marched towards the lights: 'Where do I sit?' The pressman was not in the least embarrassed when he explained to me that the lights were actually for Roy Orbison and that we would be having our 'little chat' in the far, dark corner of the room to which he was now leading me. Our little chat consisted of him asking me exactly who I was, and even this thin line of enquiry petered out when the Big O, plus entourage, made his appearance. My pressman sat agog throughout the pop singer's interview and as soon as it was over he thanked me 'for everything' and shot off to watch Roy and his aides climb aboard their waiting limos.

Explaining exactly who I was took up quite a slice of my ensuing two weeks in Australia, but I could hardly complain about that, since I didn't know who any of them were. The Adelaide Festival was prefaced by a 'forum' of little magazine editors (that is to say, editors of so-called Little Magazines). I was then editing the *New Review* and was thus the foreign guest who was supposed to give the Australians an idea of how we handled these things here. Once the event got going, though, it swiftly became clear that how we handled these things here was of no interest whatever to the dozen or so tense figures round the table. Each of them had something on his mind, something very local and very specific, and each was determined to be heard. The Gough Whitlam spirit was still alive, and much of the talk was therefore about cash: about how much more of it each magazine felt that it deserved. This was more or less to be expected. What made the thing somewhat eerie was the general air of rancour, of scores being settled, long-held grievances off-loaded. With one or two exceptions, they did not seem to like each other much, and none of the dislike was secret. In theory, very bracing – but it wasn't. I kept trying to work out who was on who's side, and to identify ideological blocs, artistic differences: with so much hostility in the air, there had to be a pattern. In the end, though, none of it fell into place.

When I described all this later to an Australian non-editor, he was much amused. Australia, he patiently explained, is a big country. The editor of *Sperm* from Melbourne had never before met the editor of *Blaze* from Perth, and it was well known that *Sperm*'s grant was cut because the editor of *Blaze* was having a really sick affair with a poetess whose last book *Sperm* had dumped on; the editor of *Blaze*, as everyone knows, was a big friend of X on the Queensland Arts Council . . . and so on. It may be a big country, I suggested, but it's a small world. No, no, he said, the distances do matter. Hardly any of the people at that forum had ever met before, and they had probably been slagging each other off in print for years. It was usual enough for the 'established' literary figures to meet each other and adjust their literary politics accordingly, but the smaller fry's sense of exclusion, and hence their integrity, was bolstered by geography. If I had been there longer, he consoled me, I'd have known the score.

Well, thanks. It had to be confessed, though, that the score I did know was the wrong one. The only Australian literary magazines I was familiar with were the *Meanjin Quarterly* and *Overland*. When I announced this to the forum I was heckled with what sounded like genuine contempt: even though the editor of one of these publications was seated at the same table. During the course of the next week, I was to make several similar errors. Names like Patrick White and A.D. Hope were greeted with candid derision, and nobody had heard of Clive James. When, at one of the actual

Festival's talk-ins, I said that it was odd to find Peter Porter missing from various standard anthologies of Australian verse, I was given the clear impression that P.P. had simply got what he deserved. Among poets there was much talk of an 'Australian identity'; one way of asserting this identity was to be indifferent to anything that was going on in London. A rather specialised branch of the 'identity' lobby spoke of the new affinity it felt with Californian poets like Robert Duncan. Again, the word 'geography' was used: it made geographical sense for Australians to cosy up with San Francisco.

To balance the provincial angst, there was also a number of sneering cosmopolitans, but they tended not to sit on platforms. They were to be found hanging around in the bar; and once they found out you were from 'Europe' they would tell you about the year they spent in Florence, and how they couldn't wait to get back there, or to Paris or to London, for some real culture. Look at them all, they would say, gesturing towards the marquee where some fiercely local debate was in progress, and they would look seriously cheated when one said (not quite truthfully) that it was much the same in London.

I was not the only non-Australian at the Festival. Indeed, some of the fortnight's more amusing moments were provided by my foreign colleagues. Two days after I arrived in Adelaide, Ted Hughes and Adrian Mitchell were scheduled to arrive from London, and there was a slight panic among the organisers when neither of them showed up at his hotel at the appointed hour. News finally arrived that, yes, they had in fact arrived at the airport but that each had been hijacked by a group of fans. Hughes had been transported to a cattle ranch (or was it a pig farm?) to check out the local livestock, and Mitchell had been met by a small band of anarchists who had whisked him off for an inspection of a nearby penitentiary. It's tough work, being true to one's own subject-matter, and the pair of them looked distinctly drained by the time they were released into the hands of their official welcomers. Mitchell, however, recovered pretty smartly. He was soon to be heard reciting an indignant poem about prison conditions in South Australia. Another comedy lay in the rampagings of the local Women's Libbers. Hughes was an early target – it appeared that he had not been nice enough to Sylvia Plath. When I quizzed one of the harpies on this score, it turned out that she was getting all her facts direct from the poem 'Daddy'. 'That's good enough for me,' she squeaked. 'And anyway, you just have to look at him. Macho bastard.' Hughes himself stayed cool.

So too did Robie Macauley, the American delegate – so cool, in fact, that it took the sisters all of a week to discover that he was not just a mild-mannered US author. He was also, they learned, the fiction editor of *Playboy*! The anti-Hughes campaign was dropped instantly, and poor Macauley (who was only there to grab some sun) became hate-object number one. Every time he appeared on a platform they would barrack him, and at question time at least six amazons would leap up to grill him about sexist centrefolds. Macauley would blink at them, then try to mumble something about the relatively high quality of *Playboy*'s fiction, or about how for him it was all a way of getting good money into the pockets of good writers. It was no use. In his opponents' eyes, he had *become* Hugh Hefner. I advised that there must surely be a way in which he could turn this error to his advantage. Neither of us could quite think of how.

All this was in 1976, and I suppose it's different now. I wonder, though. Leafing through the catalogue for 'Australian Publishing – A Decade of Achievement', I kept coming across turns of phrase that jolted me back to that marquee in Adelaide. Even the exhibition's subtitle had something of this same effect. And I was stirred to near-affection by the blurb for an anthology of Australian SF: 'This collection of Australian Science Fiction mirrors the nation's apprehensive fascination with its own unexplored emptiness, and its fear of forfeiting its never-too-clear racial identity.'

1983

How to Hoax

Years ago, when I was serving as an anonymous hack on the *Times Literary Supplement*, one of my duties was to pen sprightly paragraphs for a weekly books column. The idea was to mop up publications which were not considered worth full-scale reviews but which nonetheless had to be 'covered' by a journal of record such as ours. Things like: *A Dictionary of Spy Writers* or *The Balladeers' Handbook* or *Henry Williamson: My Friend*. Usually, there was a brisk supply of such material and it was easy enough to knock out the required eight or nine paragraphs per week.

Sometimes, though, there would be nothing: no *Murderer's Who's Who*, no Yorkshire verse, no New Zealand little magazines. To guard against such barren stretches, we invariably had one or two 'timeless' items on the go: foreign stuff, mostly, since no one knew when that was out of date, but now and then something solidly domestic – jokey items on the philosophy of crossword puzzles, or shrewd, relaxed meditations on what ought to be done about the Regions/Writers-in-Residence/The Open University. You could always find a current peg for material like this – 40 per cent of 'on the one hand', 40 per cent of 'on the other', and a final, plangent 20 per cent of 'It is to be hoped that . . .' Child's play, really, provided that you remembered to change the names and dates.

To liven things up (it must have been a Friday, after lunch) we decided to compose a spoof poem and submit it to one of those 'Poems Wanted' publishers who advertise in all the weeklies. To a literary editor, the phrase 'Poems Wanted' has an outlandish, almost eerie twang. I can't remember how our poem went but it was made up of extremely well-known lines out of, I think, the *Faber Book of Modern Verse*. It might even have read:

April is the cruellest month
Because
It makes me think
Continually of those who were truly great
So it's no go
My honey love, it's no go my poppet.

It might even have been called 'collage'. The point is, we were almost begging to be rumbled.

Anyway, we sent the thing off under a daft pseudonym and, within days, back came a cordial acceptance. The publisher (call him Arthur Daley) would be glad to include our 'splendid' composition in *Best Poems of 1969*, or whatever year it was. The catch (described by Daley as the bonus) was that we would be expected to purchase eight copies of the book when it appeared. Although it wasn't spelled out, the deal was clear: no purchase, no publication. We calculated that with, say, two hundred poets buying eight copies each, this rather shoddily printed anthology would chalk up a decent profit before a single copy reached the shops; if shops indeed figured in Mr Daley's plans.

So we wrote it all up, mingling tired mockery with almost prim reproof, and bunged it into the column during a slack week. There was much applause all round, as if we had dealt the philistines a telling blow. For my part, I was at first simply glad to have filled the space with something that had been quite fun to do. Later, though, I did begin to wonder. After all, who had we damaged, if damage had been done? Not the publisher, certainly: poetry might be a tidy little earner if you play it right but Arthur could as easily switch to monogrammed nappy-liners or one-legged tracksuits. By the time our piece appeared, he had probably already diversified, moved on. No, the most likely victims of our little jape were the two hundred 'poets' who had no doubt been quite happy with the way things were – only too eager, probably, to fork out for eight copies of a book they could pass on proudly to their grannies, ex-husbands, and the like. These sensitives were now exposed as shoddy self-deluders. Auden understood about the real, the hidden and depressed, readership for poetry: these poets of 1969 were even more hidden, more depressed and very likely ate in even nastier cafeterias than the types Auden had in mind. They had probably never even heard of

Auden. Who were we to bully such harmless dabblers into rough self-knowledge?

After a day or so spent musing along these pious lines, it dawned on me that I must surely be suffering from hoaxer's backlash, that sour and anxious sensation I remember seeing registered on the faces of a gang of bloods at my Oxford college just after they had finished booby-trapping a swot's room, and on the less well-bred faces of my barrack-mates in the Air Force when they sent the weediest of our colleagues out on a fake-date with the CO's daughter – what fun it had been watching the poor slob dab after-shave into his armpits, and how blissful the moment when, with a chuckle that could only be described as 'debonair', he decided finally to wear the flowery tie and not the striped . . .

Do all hoaxers end up feeling a bit wretched, after the event? Did the inventors of Ern Malley experience a few spasms of discomfiture after their spoof poet had taken the Australian literary scene by storm? I suppose not – after all, this was a high-minded hoax, an act of Criticism, really: its authors could boast that there was nothing in it that was petty or vindictive. And what about Dr Johnson's pal, the awesomely resourceful George Psalmanazar whose fraudulent study of Formosa got him a job at Oxford, teaching missionaries to master his faked-up Formosan tongue? George was made to suffer for his cheek, and in time he did repent – but he too could surely have pleaded that his jests had served a highish purpose.

Higher, certainly, than the purpose served by our own most recent literary hoax. I have before me a press hand-out from the firm of Michael Joseph:

WE BELIEVE THAT NEVER BEFORE HAS A CELEBRATED WRITER OF FICTION SO SUCCESSFULLY DISGUISED HER IDENTITY AND CREATED SUCH AN EXPERIMENT IN PUBLISHING. AND NEVER BEFORE HAS A WRITER AT THE HEIGHT OF HER POWERS WRITTEN TWO SUCH POWERFUL AND MOVING BOOKS IN ANOTHER PERSONA.

The story is now well known. In 1982, a writer who called herself 'Jane Somers' submitted her 'first novel' to three London publishers. Two of them – Cape and Granada – turned it down. The third, Michael Joseph, published it in 1983 – under the title *The Diary of a Good Neighbour*; they said that Jane Somers had already written some romantic fiction and was well known as a journalist. The book got 'mild reviews', according to my hand-out, and 'sold moderately'. It was published in America, and translated into three languages. Earlier this year, Jane Somers's second book appeared, entitled *If the Old Could*, and shortly afterwards it was revealed that Jane Somers was just another name for Doris Lessing. Now both books are reissued in a single volume under Lessing's name – with a rather dotty introduction explaining why she had gone to all this trouble.★

The explanation is in two halves: one half is severe and public-spirited, the other is girlish and bewildered. On the public front, Lessing contends that she has revealed important truths about the state of publishing and reviewing: it's all so mechanical and yet it's all so name-fixated – by means of her hoax, she has established that a known author gets more respect than an unknown. Well, thanks for telling us. She also wanted to help these said unknowns by demonstrating that even somebody as gifted as herself could, when rendered nameless, be treated with institutional disdain. And, as if all this were not sufficiently confusing, she (parenthetically) rather liked the idea of exposing the shoddiness of her regular reviewers. 'Some reviewers complained they hated my Canopus series, why didn't I write realistically, the way I used to before; preferably *The Golden Notebook* over again? These were sent *The Diary of a Good Neighbour* but not one recognised me.' *That*'s pretty shoddy, you might think; after all, these people are supposed to be her fans. A sentence or so later, though, Lessing herself lets these (and, I should say, all other) dunces off the hook: 'it did turn out that as Jane Somers I wrote in ways that Doris Lessing cannot . . . Jane Somers knew nothing about a kind of dryness, like a conscience, that monitors Doris Lessing whatever she writes and in whatever style.' And it is here that the girlishness intrudes. What she seems to be saying now is that when Doris Lessing becomes Jane Somers she stops being Doris Lessing; it is only afterwards that she becomes Lessing enough to blame people for thinking Somers is not her:

Some may think this is a detached way to write about Doris Lessing, as if I were not she; it is the name I am detached about. After all, it is the third name I've had: the first, Tayler, being my

---

★ *The Diaries of Jane Somers* (Michael Joseph, 1984).

father's; the second, Wisdom (now try that one on for size!), my first husband's; and the third my second husband's. Of course there was McVeigh, my mother's name, but am I Scots or Irish? As for Doris, it was the doctor's suggestion, he who delivered me, my mother being convinced to the last possible moment that I was a boy. Born six hours earlier, I would have been Horatia; for Nelson's Day, what could that have done for me? I sometimes wonder what my real name is; surely I must have one.

This is territory remote from the public-spirited, and rather more interesting, but Lessing doesn't linger there for long. The drift of her preface is that she has somehow done everyone a favour. But what, in the end, has been achieved? Publishers and reviewers can hardly be reviled for not having 'heard' the authentic Lessing cadences. As she admits, she wasn't using them. Nor can they be blamed for not doing well by the aspiring Somers. Having now read both novels, I am surprised that the fledgling didn't have a rougher ride. In fact, if Lessing has proved anything, it is that she has a gift for manipulating the very machine she has laboured to 'expose'. In hype terms, thanks to the hoax both titles are now doing very nicely.

Far better, certainly, than they deserve. The first novel has some arrestingly beastly descriptions of old age, but creaks horribly when it tries to describe the innards of a swinging women's mag. And the heroine's stylish metropolitan know-how is registered with gauche unease. The second book takes a few wild swings at feckless youth, but its main artery is Mills and Boon:

> And then, my life with Richard. It really is another life, and I fly into it, my heels winged. Sometimes I arrive at our rendezvous with my hands full of flowers, somewhere to put my joy. Richard laughs when he sees them, straight into my eyes, so that my eyes dazzle with it, like too strong sunlight. He takes flower after flower, putting them in my hair, my belt, my buttonhole. I stand bedecked and people look, at first ready to be critical, but then getting the benefit of the spin-off of our enjoyment.

It's true that the character doing the talking here writes romantic novels (she is, indeed, called Janna Somers) and it is just possible that we are meant to think that she's gone off her head. But not really –

here is another character (the sophisticated magazine's sophisticated editor) on his newborn child:

> Janna, this is my fourth, and God forgive me the best! I know you shouldn't like one more than another, and in a sense I don't, they are *miracles*. I simply can't believe it, how utterly amazing and marvellous each baby is, each in its own way . . . When little Caroline was born – although I had seen it all three times before and every time it was just the most *perfect* thing – when this little being appeared, and they put a towel around her and put her *straight* in my arms, because I am afraid poor Phyllis was not with us at just that moment, she opened her eyes and looked at me. She wasn't crying or shocked or anything like that – I know now because after all Caroline is my fourth.

He burbles on like this for four pages – he has forgotten, for four pages, that our heroine is childless; the whole soliloquy is a set-up for Janna to surprise herself with a sudden unstylish burst of tears. 'Then he was up in a bound, and he had his arms about me. "Oh Janna, don't don't, I am so sorry. Of course, I had forgotten, you haven't had children, oh poor Janna, I am sorry, how awful of me."'

It is at moments like this – and there are lots of them – that one begins to wonder if Lessing hasn't perhaps pulled off a hoax within a hoax – a new way of packaging old pulp.

1984

Thinking Big

In the current issue of a magazine called *The Face* there is an article on Norman Mailer's recent visit to this country. He was here, it seems, to promote *Tough guys don't dance*, his latest novel: he did some 'major' TV interviews, a bit of radio, and – towards the end of his stint – he called a press conference in order to complain about the low quality of the reviews he had been getting. His tone was querulous. He felt that we (I myself was one of the 'wimp' critics he objected to) had been made nervous by his powerful masculinity and, to cover up our fear, we had tried to get macho with his book. Mailer was angry, says *The Face*, and he was spoiling for a fight.

What is it with these New York lit-celebs? A year or two ago, Gore Vidal published a book-length essay of complaint in the *Spectator* after his new volume of essays had been underhailed by the London reviewers. Again, I was named among the guilty men and Vidal's tone, like Mailer's, was shrill, vengeful and tremulous with self-regard. It was not that the reviewers had been 'wrong' about his book: it was simply that, in one way or another, because of something feeble or unhealthy in their personalities, they were not 'adequate' to cope with the full majesty of Gore's achievement. It was a size thing, as it always is with these Americans. British critics just aren't big enough to grasp what's going on up there.

In one sense, people like Mailer and Vidal are indeed built to a larger plan than most. I've looked up the reviews I wrote and in neither case, it seems to me, does the discussed author have grounds for more than – at worst – a middle-sized pang of resentment. Indeed, the Vidal review now strikes me as quite kindly. Well . . . big men, big egos, you might say. But that won't really wash with these two, as it might have done with innocent, out-of-town megalos like Steinbeck or O'Hara. Both M and V take pride in the pitiless, almost imperial candour with which they have despatched upstarts and rivals to the outer darkness. Indeed, they have often entertained us with their lordly put-downs of each other. 'You demagogue!' roars one. 'You narcissist!' retorts the other. No, these are city boys, big fish. And yet here they are whimpering because a few British book-reviewers can't quite bring themselves to kiss their feet. It's hard to fathom.

And yet it becomes not so hard after a week spent toiling through a couple of weird new publications from the States: *Mailer: His Life and Times*, by Peter Manso (Viking), and *Conversations with Capote* by (can this be the correct spelling?) Lawrence Grobel. Each book goes far, and unpleasantly, beyond mere feet-kissing, and each offers a neat image of the sort of literary-critical milieu in which the Mailers and Vidals feel most relaxed: a milieu in which their kingship is acknowledged, in which other people are either sycophants or foes or, now and then, pretenders to the throne. These last are dealt with savagely, in chic one-liners which the sycophants can busily sculpt into headstones.

Manso and Grobel belong to a strange new breed of sycophant: 'oral historian', or 'professional interviewer' – that's to say, their tape-recorders are so microscopically discreet that they can be comfortably fitted into a pint bottle of *Old Grandad*. The Manso book, it must be said, is riveting. Like eavesdropping, it oughtn't to be, but it is: seven hundred pages of gossip, all of it first-person, on-the-spot and awesomely ready to assuage even the most shamefully low-level brand of curiosity. And yet, because all of it is tinged with homage, we end up knowing not much more than before. Now and again, Manso provides a third-person narrative link between the slabs of tape-recorded speech, but mostly the book is a *This is your life* presentation of Old Norman, as seen by his buddies through the ages. Norman himself takes a small part, humbly shuffling his feet at centre-stage, and the main action is provided by ex-wives, hangers-on both ex and current, by agents, publishers and magazine editors – in short, both those who have given and those who have received. There is a half-hearted attempt to elevate the proceedings by including testimony from the likes of Irving Howe and Alfred Kazin, but even they tend to get dragged down into the mire. (Who else but a really professional 'professional interviewer' could have persuaded Diana Trilling to reveal that she has 'often wondered what Norman was like in bed'?) The book's favourite subject, in the end, is money, and to follow the plot we need to involve ourselves quite early on in the drama of Mailer's 'cosmic' finances, but there are some spicy bits on his mad escapades of the sixties as well as a few *House and Garden* glimpses of How He Lives Now. And the Jack Abbott fiasco is covered in some detail.

The same cannot be said of *Conversations with Capote* (Hutchinson). Here the indiscretions verge on mania, and it seems unlikely that even Capote would have allowed them to see print if he had lived. One suspects that he was drunk or drugged whenever Grobel came to call, and he needed almost no encouragement at all to play his queen-wasp act right to the limit:

Oh, Saul Bellow is a nothing writer. He doesn't exist. Tell me *one* book of Saul Bellow that's in *any* way memorable, even a chapter that's memorable.

I've always liked 'Henderson the Rain King' for one.

Oh no. Dull, dull . . . I think he's a dull man and a dull writer. Hello, Saul, how are you?

Do you feel that way about Philip Roth?

Oh, only more so. Philip Roth's quite funny in a living-room but . . . forget it.

Bernard Malamud?

Unreadable.

What about someone as prolific as Joyce Carol Oates?

She's a joke monster who ought to be beheaded in a public auditorium or in Shea or in a field with hundreds of thousands (*laughs*). She does all the graffiti in the men's room and the women's room and in every public toilet from here to California and back, stopping in Seattle on her way! (*laughs*) To me, she's the most loathsome creature in America.

Have you ever met her?

I've seen her, and to *see* her is to loathe her. To read her is to absolutely vomit . . . She's too . . . oooogh! (*shudders*)

Prodded by Grobel, Capote shudders on through a long list of eminents, both past and present: Frost, Dostoevsky, Faulkner, Gertrude Stein ('I am a pot of shit, I am a pot of shit, I am a pot of shit'), and after about fifty pages one simply wants to look the other way. During the last two years of his life, Capote was uninterviewable, and Grobel must have known it when he fixed up this 'definitive, in-depth' chat with 'the great writer'. On the other hand, it could be argued that Capote got what was coming to him: that a writer who builds his career on manipulating gossip ought not to be surprised if his deathbed is wired for sound.

A relief, then, to turn from all this deranged big-talk to some sturdy English self-effacement. John Haffenden is steadily becoming the closest we have to a domestic version of the Mansos and Grobels. He has already published a book of earnest conversations with a dozen or so poets and this month he gives it a companion: *Novelists in Interview* (Methuen). Plodding and decent, and often more 'up' on an author's work than the poor author seems to be, Haffenden must be called exemplary in his approach. The focus is almost always on the text and the interviewer's demeanour, although steadily cordial, is not self-abasing. Indeed, Haffenden gets quite strict if an author resists his high estimate of his or her output. This can be comic and endearing. When Haffenden praises Anita Brookner for her 'integrity', she offers to make him a present of it. Similarly, when he tries to cheer her up by reminding her that she is, after all, 'successful': 'I dispute that,' Brookner snarls (or maybe sobs, it's hard to tell with transcripts), 'I feel that I could get into the *Guinness Book of Records* as the world's loneliest and most miserable woman.' Since her first novel, she contends, 'It's been downhill all the way . . . I hope this latest novel, *Hotel du Lac*, will slightly redeem me in the public eye.'

There are not too many sparky moments of this kind, although some light entertainment can be had from studying Haffenden's small background introductions to his fourteen writers' lives and works. Chiefly, these are bibliographical and critical, but each one contains a human flourish to remind us that even interrogators have to live. Haffenden, it transpires, must be working part-time for an estate agent. Angela Carter, we thus learn, lives in 'a rumpled terrace house to the north of Clapham in London', whereas Iris Murdoch, when she's writing, chooses to make do with a 'compact top-floor pied-à-terre'. V.S. Pritchett is encountered in 'a handsome terrace to the north of Regent's Park', and Emma Tennant in 'a comfortably and attractively bruised Victorian house off Ladbroke Grove'. Russell Hoban's 'terraced house' is also 'comfortable' but it seems to be a shade down-market, 'fronting Eel Brook Common'. Salman Rushdie's residence also rates a 'comfortable', but he's in Tufnell Park. David Storey's pad, on the other hand, is fashionably situated but Honest John Haffenden would be lying if he didn't tell you it was merely 'roomy'. Top marks go to Pritchett and to Malcolm Bradbury, who wins a hard-to-come-by 'elegant' for his Victorian house, with bonus marks for having made Haffenden approach it by way of an impressive 'gravel drive'. As to the places Haffenden would least like to move into, these are occupied by Fay Weldon ('a small modernised terrace house in Kentish Town') and Martin Amis ('a flat in a solid and gabled Victorian edifice . . . it looks as if it has just been burgled'). The wisest of all interviewees, though, turns out to be David Lodge. Perhaps he had heard of Haffenden's obsession, or maybe if you are called Lodge you tend to know about these things. Anyway, there is a note of pained defeat in poor Haffenden's run-in to their interview: 'I talked to him in March 1984 in his large standard office – burdened bookcases, attendant chairs, the bare expanse of a seminar table, all evenly lit by big modern windows providing a view of grass and paths and student processes – at the University of Birmingham.'

On this evidence, John Haffenden might turn out to be the only man in England who doesn't chuckle his way through the second volume of Clive James's memoirs – *Falling Towards England: Unreliable Memoirs, Part Two* (Cape). When James arrived in England in the early-sixties, he had no money, nowhere to live and not very much to wear, apart from a white nylon drip-dry shirt, some Hawaiian leisure-wear and a pair of Hong Kong rubber sandals. Mostly, though, he had Nowhere to Live, and if he hadn't already – at Southampton – learned to hate England for its weather, he would in any case have been swiftly crushed into homesickness by its flinty landladies, its rat-trap furnished rooms. Not that he always had a furnished room: in those days, Clive was a familiar sight in certain quarters of Earls Court and Tufnell Park – a bundle of bread, booze and borrowed blankets that you tripped over when you went to make coffee in the morning. At one point, he is to be found crouched in a coal-barge; at another, he sets up house in a brown paper bag. And when he does find a more or less regular 'hired box' in which to stretch his frozen limbs, it turns out that the room won't stretch that far.

To go with the weather, and the housing, we also managed to clobber the vivacious immigrant with our class-system, our unyielding girls, our not-so-fast fast food, and so on. No one would give James a job, not even the jobs he'd vowed never to accept. The magazines that accepted his poems somehow managed to find reasons for not printing them. His teeth were beginning to crack up. Clive was never less ebullient; the Flash of Lightning reduced to a thin drizzle. And when things start getting better, he somehow contrives to make them worse: some of the funniest stories are to do with the jobs he did get and was fired from, or simply never went back to after having engineered some king-sized cock-up. Throbbing beneath all of this – as readers of *Unreliable Memoirs: Part One* can happily envisage – we hear the steady beat of Aussie lust. Clive is a poet now, so we must bear with him when he describes bumping into Millicent at the coat-rack: her 'breasts struck me physically. It felt like being run through twice with an angel's tongue.' Similarly, when he cops his first good stare at Pandora's lovely legs: 'whereas Millicent's legs had merely been poetic, Pandora's were rhapsodic. They came tapering down out of the hem of that glorified Black Watch kilt like a pair of angels diving with their wings folded, did a few fancy reverse curves of small radius so as to recreate the concept of the human ankle in terms of heavenly celebration, and then . . .'

There is quite a lot of this angelspeak throughout the book but since – in real life – young Clive is getting so little of what he craves, most readers will be glad to let him have his fling. In fact, by the end of the book, most readers will forgive him most things – even the over-solemn way he apologises for once having been left-wing. Not so physically rich, nor so abundantly confident of its effects, as *Unreliable Memoirs: Part One* – after all, nowhere but Australia could quite measure up to James's hunger for hyperbole – this sequel is nonetheless a comic triumph, full of terrific jokes and brilliantly sustained set-pieces. Clive may not have managed to sweet-talk Millicent and Pandora into sharing his paper bag, but that was long ago. He ought to try them again, because his pitch is getting close to sounding perfect.

1985

Undelivered: Cyril Connolly's Horizon

In 1939, London's three most interesting little magazines ceased publication – *The Criterion, New Verse* and *Twentieth Century Verse*. No one was greatly surprised – after all, lots of other things were closing down. It was difficult to see how any sort of literary 'centre' might function in wartime conditions or in the mood of nervous depression that afflicted most intellectuals of the day. Auden and Isherwood had left for America and the Thirties movement which had invigorated editors like Geoffrey Grigson and Julian Symons was thoroughly defunct.

If there was to be a Forties movement, what would it be like – apocalyptic, introspective, religious? It was hardly likely to be political or patriotic, and yet the urge towards a public sort of literature was ingrained in most young writers of the time: what would they do now that the old Life versus Art debate seemed pointless, if not risible? If anyone *was* mad enough to want to start a magazine in these circumstances (with impending paper shortages, scattered contributors, bombs over Bloomsbury to be thought about as well) what would he find to print that might bear usefully upon the coming chaos?

Horizon's first issue went on sale around Christmas 1939. Its editor, Cyril Connolly, was already a noted expert on defeat, having made a name for himself with a how–not–to book for aspiring writers, called *Enemies of Promise*. Connolly had also published a novel and was a well-known wit-about-town, an elegant writer with a vanity problem, a bit over-fond of restaurants and women and – at thirty-seven – seemingly forever on the brink of not delivering the masterpiece everyone had been waiting for since . . . well, since Eton, really, where his teacher said to him: 'You've got a Balliol scholarship and you've got into Pop – you know, I shouldn't be surprised if you never did anything else the rest of your life.' Connolly liked telling stories like this about himself, if only in order to draw admiring attention to what he actually had done – which was a good deal more than nothing: *Enemies of Promise* chills the blood pretty effectively, even today.

'Early laurels weigh like lead' was just one of many Connolly-isms trotted out to excuse some failure of energy or commitment. 'I work best in scraps,' he'd say, 'and besides, a little of me goes a long way.' The self-denigration invariably had a somewhat boastful ring, but then Connolly's overall posture was not without a certain aptness for the early-forties: tired, disenchanted, responsive only to the very best but vaguely doomed. Five years earlier such languor would no doubt have seemed heartless and irresponsible. In 1939, it didn't exactly capture the spirit of the age, but it did capture a mood that many people, off and on, had had a taste of and could not deplore.

Horizon's first editorial could hardly have been glummer: lack of purpose was to be the order of the day: 'However much we should like to have a paper that was revolutionary in opinions or original in technique, it is impossible to do so when there is a suspension of judgement and creative activity.' Why then should 'we' wish to have a magazine at all? This was the obvious riposte and in issues to come Connolly was ever ready to ask this same question of himself. In his monthly column 'Comment', he was forever grumbling about the difficulties and the tedium of it all, meanwhile confiding to his journal that 'An editor frays away his true personality in the banalities of good mixing, he washes his mind in other people's bathwater, he sacrifices his inner voice to his engagement-book.' From time to time, in the magazine, he would berate big-name writers for not helping out with contributions, and chastise subscribers for not resubscribing: 'If we can go on producing a magazine the least you can do is read it.'

When Connolly sent out a questionnaire asking readers to say what they thought of *Horizon*, several of them accused him of 'indecision, inconsistency, waveringness'. This was music to the jaded ear, and Connolly was almost buoyant in reply: 'Our doubt is our passion,' he said, 'and our passion is our task.' From time to time, he took a perverse pleasure in mocking his active-service readers for their dullness and solemnity. The war, he proclaimed in one issue, was inimical to the making of good literature – when

241

a writer becomes a 'Warrior', his tendency is to stop writing. And to a soldier-contributor who complained of *Horizon*'s remoteness from wartime concerns, Connolly snapped back rather testily: 'Unless the dashing captain has now left these shores, it is he who is under the obligation to us for carrying on through the craters, and amid the looped and windowed raggedness of our offices, to provide him and his stern followers with something to read in their quarters in the West Country.' 'Dashing', 'stern', 'intrepid': these were Connolly's favourite jeer-words for the lads in uniform.

After a bit, *Horizon* did fall in with the war effort (it had to be careful because of paper-restrictions) but its truest voice was that of the beleaguered and misunderstood custodian: protecting the old civilian values until such time as they could be enjoyed properly again. This must have been irritating stuff to read for soldiers at the front line, but it also had a strong seductive power: the fighting men needed to be reminded now and then of 'what they were fighting for' and to some of them *Horizon* brought reassurance that the old life of books and art was still intact, that Cyril – for all his self-indulgences – was holding things together.

Certainly Cyril liked to take this line. His editorial ill-temper had a guilt-component and he was often all too eager to tell the world that living through the Blitz was no fun either. It was not in his nature, though, to pretend (for long) to any great nobility of spirit. Hence the wavering: *Horizon* is hard on itself but quickly takes offence when its usefulness is called in question. It was all right for Connolly to say 'It is unfair to judge art in these philistine conditions', or 'The war is not conducive to good writing – that can wait till afterwards', but woe to any outside critic who didn't understand that much of this was just a pose, that Connolly's dignity required that he be seen from time to time strolling along tight-ropes: after all, was he not in a 'reserved occupation' (the editorship of *Horizon*), always likely to be mocked for cowardice if he was thought to be over-zealously protecting his position? Towards the end of the war, Connolly addressed a remarkable 'open letter' to the soldiery:

> Of course all the time you had to fight. Don't think I am unaware of all this fighting, it is just that which churns the guilt round and round till it curdles into a kind of rancorous despair. You were

always fighting for me, in the favoured places of the world, and writing me your friendly unpatronising letters which I have to answer. Oh, why can't I fight for myself?

After the war, *Horizon* continued to flaunt its inconsistencies, but these now seemed merely to depend on where Cyril Connolly happened to be, and on whether or not he was having a good time: there was a bout of Francophilia, a peculiar Swiss number, a special feature on how hard it was to earn a living as a writer, a rather sycophantic issue on America (its 'wonderful jeunesse' – and, incidentally, its wonderful food parcels, for which Cyril cheekily advertised in one issue of the magazine). By the late-forties, *Horizon* was speeding eagerly towards its 'long desired shade'. It was indeed a wartime magazine, although it survived until December 1949, when it famously (but not for the first time) remarked that 'it is closing time in the gardens of the West'.

The usefulness of Michael Shelden's archly titled book is more biographical than literary-critical. Professor Shelden is full of praise for Connolly's 'elegant prose and witty, perceptive insights' but his own text often seems rather plodding and wide-eyed. He always seems more intrigued by the gossipy background to *Horizon* than by the magazine itself. Connolly's 'romantic life' is chronicled in some detail and gets more splendidly complicated with each new memoir that appears. But then, imagine those inconsistencies, those waverings carried over into the field of personal relations. There are informative sketches of various of the magazine's helpmates and hangers-on: we hear one or two not altogether kindly anecdotes about Sonia Brownell (later Orwell), who rather fancied herself as editor-in-waiting and was always encouraging Connolly to extend his holidays abroad. She once sent back Theodore Roethke's 'The Lost Son' with the remark: 'It seemed to us that your poetry was in a way very American in that it just lacked that inspiration, inevitability or quintessence of writing and feeling that distinguishes good poetry from verse.'

The real hero of this book, however, is not Connolly; nor is it *Horizon*. Shelden's keenest interest is reserved for the personality and the predicaments of Peter Watson, who put up the money for the magazine and stuck with it in spite of Connolly's moodiness and without ever, it appears, having a sure grasp of what the whole thing was supposed to be about, or for. But then, who did? Watson comes across as both brave and pitiable, a wealthy homosexual with a masochistic fondness for bullies and exploiters. A decent man, modest, generous, anxious (perhaps over-anxious) to be 'of service to the arts', he is treated appallingly by almost everyone he has to do with. We certainly groan for Watson as he plunges into yet another dangerous alliance, but is he interesting enough for us to be treated to such large slabs of his intimate love-correspondence? Well, just about, perhaps – although let us not delude ourselves that we are learning much here about literary magazines.

1989

MICHAEL SHELDEN
Friends of Promise: Cyril Connolly and the World of 'Horizon'
Hamish Hamilton

Tambidextrous:
The Presence of Poetry London

The twenty-three-year-old J. Meary Tambimuttu arrived in London from Ceylon in January 1938, armed with an introduction to T.S. Eliot and possessing also 'a sunburst of a smile', 'dark rock pool eyes' and a 'belief in poetry as one of the great emotional expressions of mankind if not the greatest'. The monarchist Eliot was perhaps impressed by Tambi's claim that he was a prince in his own country. Also Tambi claimed to be a Christian: his initial 'J' was said to stand for 'Jesus'.

Whatever the chemistry, old Possum took a shine to this exotic young literary operative, with his grand talk of spiritual regeneration, East–West cross-inspiration and the like, and encouraged him to start up his own poetry magazine. Or so Tambi reported to the new friends he was rapidly collecting in the pubs of Charlotte Street and Rathbone Place: 'T.S. Eliot says I'm going to be a great poet. I could have cried when he said that. He's so kind.' In 1939, Tambimuttu brought out the first issue of *Poetry London*. Within a year, the Sinhalese prince had established himself as monarch of Fitzrovia: a disorderly and dissipated province, to be sure, but sorely leaderless and much in need of its own periodical.

Even the most sceptical of chroniclers (none of whom are to be found in this anthology of largely Fitzrovian salaams) seem to have found Tambimuttu a rather magical presence in those days. He was a high priest of the Self in a period when selflessness was supposed to be the order of the day. 'I love ecstasy,' he would declare, 'I am not a man. I am a spirit. I am everyone. I am everywhere.' When asked his views on politics, he would ostentatiously consult his navel; when introduced to a military man, he would 'gurgle' at the multi-coloured medal-ribbons – 'an

245

aesthetic gesture, merely. Otherwise the war – happily – might never have been.'

'Spirituality' is the word most often used about him by his London admirers, as in: 'There was a dimension we could guess at but could not share.' Not far behind 'spiritual' come 'mystical' and 'childlike' – these qualities evinced more by the man's 'aura' than by anything he said or did. And on top of all this, Tambi was a high-performance drinking man: the Western mind was awed by the spectacle of 'a spiritual man who spent a lot of his life in pubs, drunk or semi-drunk, and was unashamedly promiscuous'. When consulted on this point, Tambimuttu (who at school had been a Roman Catholic Boy Scout and had read deeply in the works of Horatio Alger) would speak loftily about life's 'passing show'. The mortal Tambi housed, in addition to the beer, 'a deep inner current flowing like some great Indian river towards distant, yet-to-be-explored territory'.

Tambi was full of spirit-talk (of both varieties) and he saw it as his mission to rid Western culture of the odious and all-pervasive influence of Intellect. In issue one of *Poetry London*, he contributed the first of several lengthy and very hard to follow Letters to his Readers. He declared himself to be against all forms of critical reviewing; criticism, he said, is 'the manifestation of the emasculated public school mind'. Poetry belongs to all of us. 'No man is small enough to be neglected as a poet, every healthy man is a full vessel.' He half-admitted that some vessels might be bigger, or fuller than others, and that Dylan Thomas was perhaps the biggest and fullest of them all, but this sort of instinctive judgement should not be thought of as at all literary-critical: 'The critic is not our concern. Let him get squashed under his microscope. As Shakespeare did, we will give the public what they want and to hell with the critics.'

At moments like this, it was clear that the holy man had a vicious turn of speed when he was in the mood, and in subsequent issues of the magazine he had a none too spiritual way of foaming at the mouth whenever he came across the names Julian Symons (editor of *Twentieth Century Verse*) or Geoffrey Grigson. Grigson was chief villain because it was he above all, in his magazine *New Verse*, who had turned poetry into something 'mental' and 'cultural' (two of Tambi's key hate-words). He had also helped to deafen the ears of English poets to 'those rhythms and sounds that have a mystical, mantric appeal'. It was Tambimuttu's aim to restore the mysticism and the mantra, and in the first few issues of *Poetry London* it seemed that he proposed to assume the burden single-handed. His epic poem, 'Out of this War', began to appear – a kind of *Waste Land* rewritten by D.H. Lawrence with incidental music by D. Thomas. Civilization, it told us, was in disrepair because we have paid too little heed to the 'roaring of our blood', 'the generous flame of our most powerful intuitions'. After Dunkirk, Tambi's response went (in part) as follows:

> Descend O warmth into this frigid sex
> and wax the blood to a rigid flame
>
> Propose a meaning for the thousand dead.
>
> Give us back the robe of splendid sap
> Lap us in the gold, the power and ooze
>
> Of rounded hours in the melon's belly
> Singing gills of the sunfilled juice.

This, then, was the kind of poetry Tambimuttu wanted for his magazine and, after a year or so, he began to get it, by the yard. Large stretches of *Poetry London* make for lurid reading, with Intellect in thorough disarray. On the other hand, simply by being there, in London, with a magazine, Tambimuttu also got some fine poems by Alun Lewis and Keith Douglas – for each of these poets, Lewis in India and Douglas in North Africa, it mattered a lot that they were getting recognition in the capital. To each of them, Tambi might have been a bit of a joke, but they were grateful for his presence.

After a while, *Poetry London* began to print poems from the Auden line – even from J. Symons. Having taken a stand on behalf of Poetry for the People, Tambi's policy seems to have been to accept almost everything that arrived: many of the poems he took never saw print because he would lose sheafs of manuscripts, it is said, when he went on his almost nightly pub-crawls. Some proffered texts took up permanent residence in the (never-used) chamberpot beneath his bed. Several of the stories related in *Bridge Between Two Worlds* are to do with the magazine's chaotic bureaucracy, but they are told fondly, even protectively. It seems clear that

Tambi was able to charm his way out of even the tightest of editorial corners.

He was adroit, too, in the matter of collecting patrons for his magazine. When *Poetry London*'s first benefactor, one Anthony Dickins, fled penniless into the army, Tambi had the (also soon to be defunct) publishers, Nicholson and Watson, waiting in the wings. Under their protection, he produced a line of Editions Poetry London in which he was able to indulge his rather sophisticated taste for typography and book-illustration. In this area, also, he had the knack of charming the lyre-birds from the trees: many of Tambi's literary publications are now most prized for their contributions from Graham Sutherland and Henry Moore.

When *Poetry London* expired, in 1944, Tambi made sure that it went out with a bang. Somehow he got the money together for a gigantic final number and stuck into it all the poems he had accumulated but not printed since the thing began. He then, the story goes, held a big party for the contributors, paid for it with their fees and after that got each of them to ask for an individual receipt so that he could claim the whole lot back on expenses. Some admirers that night must have at last experienced the full significance of Tambi's edict: 'I am everyone. I am everywhere.'

At the end of the war, as critical standards began to reassert themselves in London, Tambi set off to try his luck in America. But *Poetry London–New York* never really found a niche in either city. The Americans (as someone in this anthology points out) were more familiar with 'gurus, shamans and avant-garde entrepreneurs', and in any case Tambi's act needed a background of sirens and pub blackout. In the sixties, he latched on to the Beatles during their Hare Krishna phase and managed to squeeze out two issues of *Poetry London/Apple Magazine*. And at the time of his death in 1983 he was still hustling: his final project was to promote the idea of an Indian Arts Council in London. In that period of controversial government subsidies for magazines, it would have been just like Tambi to have acquired his personal Arts Council. It was not to be:

Tragically, after the first two inaugural meetings, which were supported by Sri Varadarajan and S. N. Chakraborti of the Indian High Commission . . . and many leading figures representing

248

the art and culture of the Indian subcontinent in London, as well as personal friends, Tambimuttu had a fall in his office. A few days later he died in hospital of a heart attack.

His very last book-publication wheeze, incidentally, was 'the preparation of a special book to mark the wedding of Lady Diana Spencer to Prince Charles. Unfortunately, it was never published, since the promised funds did not materialise.'

The present book also seems to have had trouble assembling the necessary funds. The editor, Jane Williams, speaks on her Acknowledgments page of 'many difficulties and crises during the past few years as slowly the book has come together', years in which she has at times 'felt daunted and like giving up'. There is something ragged and quite likeable about the final product: like an ill-planned party, it seems both padded out and over-crowded. There are pious fragments from 'name' writers, soppy and pretentious items from old girlfriends and pub-cronies, and some gratuitous bouts of Indian philosophy. There are also extracts from Tambi's own uncompleted autobiography, and facsimile pages from the magazine. Tambi comes out of it all still looking like something of a charlatan, but we ought not to grudge him this *festschrift*: if nothing else, the book gives us an idea of how he got away with it.

1989

JANE WILLIAMS (Editor)
Tambimuttu: Bridge between two worlds
Owen

What's Wrong With Desmond?

The titles of Desmond MacCarthy's books must have seemed to him unassailably offhand – *Remnants*, *Portraits*, *Experience*: titles nicely in tune with his well-known view of himself as a chap who could surely have done better. One of his favourite lines of poetry was Hartley Coleridge's 'For I have lost the race I never ran' and early on in his career he got used to being spoken of as having squandered a great gift. Part of MacCarthy's charm was that he had no serious quarrel with this view. In 1932, he decided – was persuaded – to issue a selection of the book reviews he had been turning out for over twenty years, for the *New Statesman* and the *Sunday Times*. It was typical of the man that he should call it, simply, *Criticism*.

This time, however, MacCarthy had picked a bad year for offhandedness: 1932 was the year in which F.R. Leavis's *Scrutiny* was launched. 'Criticism' was no longer a word to be murmured with self-deprecation. It had become an enterprise, an undertaking, a means of finding 'solutions' for 'problems' in the present culture. In *Scrutiny*'s second issue, Leavis published an article that asked: 'What's Wrong With Criticism?' Desmond MacCarthy's modest compilation handily supplied some of the answers. Leavis wrote: 'If a literary tradition does not keep itself alive here, in the present, not merely in new creation, but as a pervasive influence upon feeling, thought and standards of living (it is time we challenged the economist's use of this phrase), then it must be pronounced to be dying or dead.' By this reckoning, Desmond's twenty-odd years' worth of literary journalism seemed, shall we say, off-colour.

MacCarthy had perhaps been a trifle provocative, in his introduction to *Criticism*, when he boasted that his reviews were 'clearly not the work of one who believes that the critic ought to turn personal impressions into general laws' and, true enough, a year earlier – in *Portraits* – he had rapturously hymned Oxford's Walter Raleigh as 'the most spirited of professorial critics'. Even so, it was evident that for Leavis the real crime of this powerful weekly 'critic' was his deep disinclination to take criticism seriously. According to MacCarthy, 'the first step to culture is to learn to enjoy, not to know what is best'. Indeed, he doubted that anyone *could* know 'what is best'. For his book column in the *New Statesman*, he had signed himself 'Affable Hawk', but not because he wished to suggest any hint of beakiness. His predecessor on the column had been John Squire, whose pseudonym was 'Solomon Eagle'.

It is easy enough to see why, for such as Leavis, MacCarthy might be perceived as the apotheosis of indolent metropolitan bookmanship. *Scrutiny*, after all, was in some measure aimed as a 'serious' riposte to MacCarthy's own profoundly dilettante *Life and Letters*, a periodical of which, in 1931, Max Beerbohm had felt moved to exclaim: 'How it makes one ache to be living in those days of serious refinement and happiness! How it cheapens this thin, sad, hectic little era.' And 1932, the year of *Criticism*, was also the year of Leavis's *New Bearings*. Maurice Barings, it had to be admitted, were much more Desmond MacCarthy's kind of thing.

And yet, somehow, poor MacCarthy: first Leavis and then, shortly afterwards, Geoffrey Grigson, who reserved a large cage for him in *New Verse*'s private zoo. (Roy Campbell's notorious assault on Grigson was in fact prompted by something Grigson said about MacCarthy.) It must have seemed to Desmond faintly baffling that these fierce fellows should be getting so worked up about him. He had always been an easy-going type, well liked at school and able to move easily between Bloomsbury and Chelsea. Although Virginia maybe condescended somewhat, he knew that she was very fond of him. But then, everybody was.

And it was not as if he really *wanted* to write book reviews. In 1905, after Eton and Cambridge (where he served as an Apostle under G.E. Moore and thus first weakened his creative powers: too much 'What *do* you mean by that?'), MacCarthy drifted into literary journalism via small magazines set up by rich and dotty friends. The idea was that such jobs would keep him going while he touled on the large and brilliant work of fiction that was at first confidently expected of him by his Bloomsbury acquaintances and chums, both old and young.

'When I first saw Desmond,' Leonard Woolf later recalled, '. . . he looked like a superb young eagle who with one sweep of his great wings could soar to any height he chose . . . Why did he never fulfil his promise? Why did the splendid eagle degenerate into an affable hawk?'

This was a question that dominated MacCarthy's life, both professional and private, for some twenty years – until he reached the age of about forty and was able to lament without much fear of contradiction: 'I was born to be a good writer and a rare friend. Idleness and fecklessness have spoiled me for myself and others.' By this time it had dawned on him that even his best friends, indeed especially his best friends, seemed to prefer his conversation to his written work. Why not make his written work sound more like conversation? As his talk, both on the printed page and at table, became more beguilingly flute-like, so his eternal Chapter One became more leaden-seeming: 'Henry has fallen in love on the platform of Paddington Station and is just passing Sutton's Seeds on his way to Eton.'

MacCarthy married at twenty-nine and his bride Molly was not slow to join the chorus of reproach. She was herself a writer of real verve and in her letters she spared him very little: 'It is no use vaguely sitting down "to do a little work,"' she'd say. 'The time has come when you must simply *fling* things into the press or you will never do anything at all. I do really think you are behaving feebly and in an unmanly way.' Desmond seems not to have minded being told these things, nor was he at all put out when, later on, Molly put him in *her* novel, *A Pier and a Band*, as the character Fitzgerald, who 'seemed to take no pains whatsoever to keep himself up to the mark . . . He might have been impressive if he had shown the slightest desire to be so.'

For several years 'What's Wrong With Desmond?' was the cry and many similes were strained for: he was like a 'sieve, a drain, a wastepaper basket', or 'like a wave that never breaks, but lollops this way and that way', or (and who can blame him here?) 'like a dog who runs out when the door is open'. Was it innate laziness, was it that he loved life too much and literature too little, was it that he was too gregarious, too hard-up, too ready to suffer bores gladly, too talkative, too Irish? MacCarthy, although he called himself Anglo-Irish, was by parentage half-English and half-Prussian. There was an Irish background, though, and people liked to make mention of an 'Irish grandfather, who sold off priceless land in Kensington, which would have earned the family a fortune in rent, and spent the proceeds on an unsuccessful lawsuit to recover worthless ancestral acres in County Clare'. Desmond, it was believed, had similar difficulties when it came to assessing his own worth.

Perhaps he married the wrong woman. If he did, nobody said so, although it was well known that there was no sexual bond between Desmond and Molly and that she, quite early on, had allowed herself to be talked into a 'trivial' affair with Clive Bell. Desmond, whose own early dalliances were theoretically intense but not physically consummated (all the girls liked him far too much for *that* to be allowed to spoil it), was probably far more upset by this than he admitted. The upshot, at any rate, was that he spent more time out on the town, or at smart country-house weekends, while the nervously delicate Molly sat resentfully at home. She had a hearing ailment, too, which progressively got worse: 'the deaf wife of someone who thrived on conversation and theatre-going'.

Clever Hearts is an intelligent and sympathetic account of the marriage, co-written by the MacCarthys' grandson and his wife, and seems in no doubt that, for all their quarrels and estrangements, Desmond and Molly were a perfect match. It is certainly true that the pair stuck together and were very close towards the end (after Desmond had put a stop to the one non-trivial affair that did threaten to break up the marriage) but rather too many of their energetic years seem to have been spent in useless conflict. If the question really is: Why didn't Desmond deliver? then we perhaps ought not to shrink from wondering what might have been if he had married someone else. After all, he did once advise Cyril Connolly to marry a woman who attracted him in preference to one he rather liked. And easily the most affecting document quoted by the Cecils is a letter from Molly on the matter of her sexual loneliness:

You see at the bottom of it all is something that I daily want to tell you in a *serious* way but feel sensitive about saying . . . that I myself have felt almost *daily* for about a year a great wish to go to bed with you but am too proud seriously to ask it.

You seem so cold that it has passed by quite unrealised by you that in the last three years I have only twice been to bed with you. This at the most passionate age of my life (I can tell from my feelings) when I feel force of life dying within me of starvation, deafness coming, morbidness getting a clutch on me. But I do not reproach. I suppose it *can't* be helped that you cannot wish it for yourself, but I think you ought to face this with me with dignity and seriousness. (I have been hurt that you have not realised that under light words, I have been feeling *acutely* really.)

I feel that I have lately been relegated to the light chaffy side of you. You do not give me *any* serious life at all . . . But dearest I love only you in this world, even more than Bumpy (their son, Dermod) – if I lost you I would simply *lose* life; therefore you *must* help me to make your life happy by helping me to be generous . . . But how to do it? Oh God. It is no use the way you pass it off in chaff . . .

And what did Desmond make of this? There is no record of his response but written on the letter's envelope there is a further plea from Molly: '*Don't* leave this about. Found in the bathroom.'

The Cecils are too fond of their subjects to take sides, but their tendency is to accept that Desmond was indeed the charming, exasperating failure he was said to be – a judgment that rather depends on believing in his original high gifts. To the uninvolved, the truth seems to be that of his type – the type being, I suppose, post-Edwardian belles-lettrist – Desmond MacCarthy was a stylish and mostly honourable performer. He could be a witty, sometimes moving memoirist – on Henry James, for instance, or on the mood in London at the declaration of World War One – and several of his essays thoroughly deserve (as he might well have put it) not to be forgotten. Also, when he took the trouble, he was a persuasively 'close reader' (see his articles on Yeats and Chekhov). His pieces often tailed off near the end or they might wearily jettison some critical point rather than risk seeming to enforce it. Partly this was to do with his famous indolence and unreliability: many a piece was written with the night-printer at his elbow. Partly it came from a journalist's fear of boring his reader, from suddenly realising, two-thirds of the way through, that he had bitten off more than his thousand words could chew.

Of course, academic critics like Leavis would have been fortified in their contempt by special pleadings of this sort: if you really are a journalist, don't call yourself a critic. And, they might have added, if you *are* a journalist, then kindly tread with caution when you are dealing with current events. MacCarthy in the late-twenties–early-thirties believed himself to be living through a 'rather silly' literary period. Gertrude Stein was one of the few authors able to ruffle his affable old feathers – 'How, one asks in amazement, can anyone suppose this sort of writing to have any value?' – and there was always just a trace of this amazement in his attitude to Eliot and Joyce: enough of a trace, anyway, for him to get sneered at for his fuddy-duddy views.

In fact, MacCarthy was fully alert to the importance of *Ulysses* and *The Waste Land*; he clearly knew what they were meant to be about and how they differed in quality from the works of Gertrude Stein (*Ulysses*, he wrote, 'contains more artistic dynamite than any book published in years. That dynamite is placed under the modern novel'). His problem was that he found nothing in these writers to *enjoy*, and he genuinely distrusted those who said they did. Unfortunately, it was a short step from debunking the Literary Snob (as he often did, and quite amusingly) to finding himself custodian-elect of middle-brow literary opinion.

MacCarthy continued reviewing for the *Sunday Times* until he died, age seventy-five, in 1952, knighted at the last for his services to Criticism. By the late-fifties, when I first came across his name, he had been completely written off, or so it seemed. His books were out of print and Leavis's influence was at its peak. It was not until 1984, when MacCarthy's son-in-law Lord David Cecil edited a new selection of MacCarthy's writings, that it occurred to me to find out about him for myself – i.e., to read something he had written. There was no great revelation: it was just that he turned out to be a good deal sharper and funnier, and more stylish in his prose, than I had been led to believe – and far more likeable. And this was a good, if shaming, lesson in the ways of literary prejudice.

1990

HUGH AND MIRABEL CECIL
Clever Hearts: Desmond and Molly MacCarthy, A Biography
Gollancz

PART V

SPORTS AND PASTIMES

The Comic Strip

Raymond's Revuebar is usually thought of as Soho's superior strip club. It stages not mere skin shows but Festivals of Erotica, it sells Dunhill or Lambert and Butler cigarettes, and it gets itself listed in the daily papers under Theatres. Svens and Ottos have no need to look shifty when they sidle into Raymond's. This is no quick stop-off for provincial wankers. Raymond offers leisured pornography for the international connoisseur.

This summer, though, the joint has worn a faintly puzzled look. At the front door, visitors have been greeted with two contrasting slabs of art-work – one celebrating the genteel enticements of *les girls*, the other showing a large Blitz-vintage bomb descending on a city centre. The bomb carries a chalked slogan: 'Have a nice day.' On the night I went there, the tuxedoed bouncer was having a hard time explaining to the punters that Raymond's Revuebar was now in fact *two* theatres. 'Turn right for the Festival of Erotica,' he'd instruct the plumply cufflinked; 'Upstairs for *The Comic Strip*,' he'd tell anyone in jeans. Raymond, you see, had leased his Boulevard Theatre to an 'alternative comedy' ensemble, and for two nights a week his de-luxe foyer had become a jostle of conflicting styles. The bouncer boasted that he could tell at a glance who'd come for what: the problem was making sure everyone ended up in the right place.

The idea of satire in a strip club began a few years ago with the Comedy Store in Meard Street: here, on weekend evenings, amateur comics were invited to try out their acts on audiences made tolerant by the sleazy ambience and the prospect of a late-night drink. Most of the seven *Comic Strip* performers had built up small reputations at the Store (or at the Elgin pub in Ladbroke Grove) before moving into Raymond's. For them, this was a step-up

259

to the big-time: four pounds a ticket and a stone's throw from Shaftesbury Avenue. Raymond's, though, was still 'alternative' enough for them to mount a show which Shaftesbury Avenue wouldn't even dream of putting on: a show more 'offensive', I would think, to those who use words like 'offensive', than anything *les girls* were offering next door.

The Comic Strip's compère and guiding star is a Meard Street veteran called Alexei Sayle, a portly, spring-heeled Liverpudlian with a convict haircut, a Desperate Dan chin and an Oliver Hardy silkette suit well buttoned at his bulging gut. A rock version of the theme from *Crossroads* starts the show, and Sayle hurtles on to the stage, spraying the audience with saliva, sweat and a deluge of fucks, cunts and bastards (flat 'a' – *bas*-tards!). A big man who can move like lightning; a pathologically aggrieved pub lout who's read some books; a 'cheeky monkey' from the Kop. Sayle's posture is manically contemptuous, his rhythm a hysterical crescendo of obscenity with spat-out satirical asides. Both the stance and the timing are near-perfect, and within seconds he has the audience agape. Most of them, it seemed, had never been called *cunts* before.

'Silly fuckers from Hampstead and Islington' who have been conned into paying 'four fucking quid' in the hope of seeing something 'alternative' (Sayle whines this in a poncey voice), or 'political' (this in a yobbo-radical-type grunt): so much for the fans. You've come to the wrong place, Sayle taunts. Just because he happened to look like a 'fucking East German playwright' they needn't expect any Berlin-in-the-Twenties *significance*. His own philosophy of life was simple: all you need is 'to have a fucking good grip on your *temper – cunts!!*'

If anything was to be learned from a night out at *The Comic Strip* it was that bad language still has an awesome potency. It was obvious to everyone that Sayle was getting laughs for some really rather thin material, but the laughter never stopped: the hectic speed and the vein-popping intensity of his delivery was part of the secret – but it was the 'fucking' element that really guaranteed his triumph:

I can't understand why they're always picking on the Afghans – fucking nice dogs. Who ever heard of fucking Toxteth – Tox-*teth* [saliva spray] before the fucking riots, eh? That Willie

260

Whitelaw, half-man, half fucking bumblebee, the wanker. The proceeds of tonight's show are going to my favourite London charity: 'Help a London Child – kill a Social Worker'. Toxteth – two hundred fucking *years* some of those cunts have lived up there. What about the fucking Soho *Vikings*, eh . . .

And so on. It may not look much on the page, and has perhaps been imperfectly transcribed (Sayle's-pace is about fifteen words a second) – but think how enfeebled it would be without the 'dirt'. As Rik Mayall (on *The Comic Strip* bill as one half of a duo called Twentieth Century Coyote) patiently explained to me: 'The rhythm – that's one of the reasons why we swear a lot on stage. The rhythm of the thing is very careful – the laugh has to come just right. It's almost poetic – if a sentence is not quite long enough before the laugh, we put in a "fucking".'

He might have added that the swearwords also inject meat and venom, an illusion of anything-goes rebelliousness: if you can say *that*, then surely nothing's sacred. It is only after the show is over that you register what *hasn't* been treated with contempt. Women's lib, gay pride, black power – indeed any cause likely to be favoured by the average 'silly fucker' from Islington or Hampstead. Such audiences don't mind being mocked for their yoghurt and stripped pine – but it might have been a different story if *The Comic Strip* had ventured an assault upon their reflex liberalism. Rik Mayall acknowledges all this:

> The next stage, yes, is to get to where you can take the piss out of anything. At the moment, though, with Brixton and all that you can't go around saying: Who are these niggers with big fat lips? It would be great if you could. Short people, tall people, people with big ears, why not people with black skin? It's when you get too specific – so it's *just* blacks – that it gets wrong. At the moment I suppose we feel that you don't take the piss out of the man at the bottom.

Mayall, who has written an MA thesis on Pub Theatre, teamed up with Ade Edmundson at Manchester University, and the pair of them spent a few years touring the college circuit before hitting London. Twentieth Century Coyote is perhaps the least 'meaningful' item on the bill: Mayall and Edmundson specialise in on-the-edge neanderthals like the Dangerous Brothers or (played by Mayall) the catatonic Kevin Turby. Kevin's *tour de force* is a long, intricately plodding monologue about His Average Day. He gets up very late and goes down to Tesco's where he buys some cornflakes which he then takes home and puts into a plate before sitting down at a table with the flakes in front of him . . . etc. 'I was just sitting there eating my cornflakes. I don't know how many I had had. Fifteen, sixteen, maybe. I wasn't counting.' All this is delivered in a bombed-out monotone: you couldn't really call Turby one of the unemployed because the simple business of getting through the day demands his total concentration, his entire stock of 'resources'. There is, to be sure, a great army of the unemployed, but, as Turby makes clear, there is also an army of the unemployable.

Much of Twentieth Century Coyote's act consists of making jokes about old jokes. The Knock-Knock routine, for example, is maybe the most easily graspable of all 'response-jokes'. For the Dangerous Brothers, however, it's a tough one: the brothers' combination of low intelligence and a short fuse turns any sort of inquisition into a threatening 'set-up'.

> 'Knock knock, open the door.'
> 'Open the door – who?'
> 'Open the door please I want to come in.'
> 'Open the door please I want to come in – *who*?'
> 'Look, just OPEN THE FUCKING DOOR, WILL YOU?'

And by this stage the pair will come to blows – Mayall extraordinary to watch with his electrocuted stare and clockwork arms, Edmundson almost coquettish as his cringing victim. And the fighting, of course, isn't custard-pie. It's kneeing, nutting, nipple-twisting stuff: a punk version of the traditional music-hall chastisement.

Coyote operates a similar trick with the famous gooseberry joke, which is: 'What's round and hairy and goes up and down?' 'A gooseberry in a lift.' Adrian Dangerous doesn't get it. 'How did a gooseberry get in a lift?' he wants to know. 'How do I know, it's a fucking joke, it's *implicit*.' 'Yuh, well, how does a fucking *gooseberry* push the button in the lift? Gooseberries don't have *arms*.' '*Bast*ard, how many fucking gooseberries do *you* know?' Nervous pause from Adrian, then (boldly): 'Three.' 'All right then, let's have the fucking *names* of these gooseberries you're so matey with.' 'What?' '*Names*, you cunt.' 'Names? Well, there's Derek, int-there? Derek Gooseberry.' 'Derek Gooseberry. All right, where is he? Go and get the bastard.' 'He's got a headache.' 'A headache! That's very fucking convenient.' Mayall is now advancing and there is a giggling masochism in Edmundson's retreat – this time he'll make the beating *really* bad. 'Anyway the point is: Derek has got fuck-all arms.' Mayall is now on the brink, eyes like ray-guns, both fists twitching: 'So fucking what if he's got fuck-all arms, he could have jumped up and NUTTED the fucking button, couldn't he?' and even as the first savage blow connects, Edmundson screams out his last request: 'BUT HE'S GOT FUCK-ALL LEGS!' And yes, the beating really is quite bad this time.

The Comic Strip's other double act, the Outer Limits, is more hooked into the media than is Coyote, and more conventionally slick. Peter Richardson and Nigel Planer have been together now for eight years – 'We do everything together. We piss into each other's mouths' – but for most of that time they played music, with the jokes as decoration. Now a lot of the jokes (many of them too esoteric for my tuned-out ear) are to do with current or quite recent pop: a big-band crooner's delivery of hits by groups like the Stranglers and the Sex Pistols was greatly enjoyed by experts in the audience, and there was a funny routine about a music agent who has huge hi-fi speakers instead of pillars at the front door of his mansion. On the whole, I found it easier to get into their film and TV spoofs: a hard-core disaster movie in which a hijacker decides not to go through with it because the in-flight pic is *Kramer versus Kramer*, and a mincing version of Starsky and Hutch –'those soft-talking, go-getting, bum-kissing boys of the Nancy Squad'. Although Sayle at the beginning of the show had pronounced the Art of Mime to be a 'Wank', the Outer Limits are brilliant at turning four square feet of stage into worlds of their own invention: as if to prove this, they make their most dazzling routine a mock Space Invaders set-to. In persona and physique the two are well matched – Planer cherubic and elastic-limbed, Richardson sly and demonic – and Planer, it should be said, would make a more than passable rock singer.

Peter Richardson is, in fact, the producer of *The Comic Strip* and he paces the evening with real skill. In between the frenetic stuff he places two low-keyed solo acts: one by Muppet writer

Chris Langham, who has a cool line in 'disabled' jokes and does a gripping owl impersonation, and Arnold Brown, an appealingly depressed Scots Jew: 'Two racial stereotypes for the price of one'. Brown is one of those 'What am I doing here?' comedians, doleful and wry, not really expecting the audience to pick up more than a third of his material. For Arnold, all is bleak – and barely worth the effort; his catch-phrase is 'Why not . . .?' (as in: 'I'm Arnold Brown, I come from Glasgow' [lengthy pause] 'Why not?'). He ranges from a deprived childhood ('There I was sitting in my tenement, trying to work out the meaning of the word "serendipity"') to a still-deprived maturity. The recession is a kind of gift: it means that Arnold is living in a world he understands, a world of 'second-hand food shops' and 'waiting-lists for people wanting to vandalise telephone kiosks'. A good deal older than his colleagues, Brown gloomily acknowledges that the times are bad enough for his time to have finally come. I hope it has.

And yet it is hard to see how *The Comic Strip* can 'make it' without cleaning up and thinning out their best material. They are already moving into the area of 'alternative success': an uncensored LP has just been released, a film is being made by the producers of *The Great Rock and Roll Swindle*, and the group is currently on tour around the revue-bars of provincial England. The lucrative working men's clubs are, they say, out of their range ('they don't like non-racist jokes – it's still all niggers and mothers-in-law'), and it need hardly be said that television would try to turn Alexei Sayle into Les Dawson. Still, for the moment, they must surely be the funniest live act in Britain: they have spleen to spare and they are obviously having a good time. It would take a *really* silly fucker to predict what they'll do next.

1981

Just the Job: Cynthia Payne's Comforts

'To me it's just a job. They get on, they get off and get dressed and that's it.' Thus Sharon of Birmingham, one of several matter-of-fact working girls interviewed by Eileen McLeod for her study of *Prostitution Now*. Most of McLeod's interviewees would go along with Sharon's view of her vocation. Here's Carol: 'When they give me the money I say, "Look then get on with it I haven't got all day," and they say, "I hope you're not going to rush me," and I say, "Look cock, you've got a certain amount of time here I don't expect you to be in and out in two minutes, but I don't expect you to spend two hours here"; they say, "Fair enough."' 'Fair enough' may indeed be what they say to Carol, but it's probably not what they are saying to themselves. Yet there they are again, the punters, once more forking out good money for bad sex. Carol and Sharon have little need to brood on the niceties of customer-relations.

Nor do they ever seem drawn to speculate on why chaps keep coming back for more – more of what the girls themselves perceive to be an almost derisively brusque freeze-off. So far as Carol and Sharon are concerned, it's all a matter of 'relief' or 'despunking', something that men have to have done to them from time to time. As a car needs to be filled up, a man needs to be emptied. And the fact that necessity is involved does not in the least soften the working girl's view of what she's up to. On the contrary, it makes her all the more secure in her contempt, all the more confident that business cannot fail to prosper – supply and demand nicely balanced by Nature in favour of the supplier.

As for the men, most of them probably know very well that prostitutes despise most of their clients, that some simply despise men, and that the whole transaction is likely to be, shall we say, offhand. Some keep at it, presumably, because they keep hoping that they will get lucky – that tonight, unlike all the other nights, they will chance upon a true 'lady of pleasure': a healthy whore who likes it, and who quite likes them. The fantasy of purchasable and yet genuine (just for you) sexual compliance has brutally deep roots. As to the others who 'go back for more' – well, in many cases, Carol and Sharon are probably correct about 'despunking'. Quite a few, though, revisit the house of shame in the hope that Sharon will be just a touch *more* hostile this time, that Carol's irritability will have sharpened up a bit since Thursday. These men go back for a sweet taste of 'just what I deserve' and would flop dreadfully if Sharon suddenly went soft on them, or if Carol let them play on into extra time.

Or so I hazard after reading the confessions of Cynthia Payne, the 'madam' jailed in 1978 for running 'a disorderly house' in Streatham. The police raided her place during a Christmas party and picked up seventeen women and fifty-three 'middle-aged to elderly' men, including clergymen, MPs, barristers and diplomats. Only Cynthia herself was punishable by law: Messrs Bedwell and Lovejoy simply had to give their names to the police. The press raised a few murmurs, and a few laughs, on Cynthia's behalf. Her own attitude was summed up by the wall motto in her kitchen: 'My house is CLEAN enough to be healthy . . . and DIRTY enough to be happy.'

The oddity of Cynthia Payne is that she would take a dim view of the Sharon/Carol line on prostitution. She seems to have liked most of her clients, she talks of providing a useful 'social service', she has done excellent work with the handicapped, and altogether takes pride in having encouraged her girls to be 'loving on the bed': 'Most women on the game don't even kiss the punters, let alone do what my girls do. I don't order them to kiss, but they know I'm grateful if they do.' Cynthia also goes to extraordinary lengths to accommodate unusual 'kinks'. If a bank manager, say, wishes to be pelted with mud, Cynthia will somehow get the mud together, or at least make do with a bit of vaseline and the contents of her Hoover bag. If a vicar wants to do it with an angel ('I crave an ample angel' was how the Reverend worded his request), she will rush about in search of the necessary props: a big blonde, a flowing cotton shift and a pair of golden wings from the theatrical costume shop. And in each case she will get a real sense of fulfilment from the outcome. The muddy bank manager she describes as:

> in his seventh heaven. Some of the stuff stuck to him, which was exactly what he wanted. He looked bloody horrible by the time we'd finished with him, like a monster from the deep. He thanked me after we cut him down . . . I called him a disgusting sod and ordered him to wash. That clinched it. He was squirming with pleasure.

As for the vicar, on meeting up with his 'divine messenger' he 'started to salivate in an alarming manner'. The angel was then 'most ferociously deprived of her wings'.

How then does Cynthia maintain this high standard of hospitality, this cheerily (and, come to think of it, literally) painstaking determination to 'fix up' her eccentric clientele? Her 'biographer' Paul Bailey clearly believes she has that fabled 'heart of gold', that she is a kind of Lady with the Red Lamp, imaginatively caring for the wanking-wounded, the casualties of the sex war. But there are many differences between her set-up in Streatham and the predicament of street-walkers like Carol and Sharon. For one thing, she doesn't – or didn't during her years as a madam – need to simulate any sort of submission to the horny male. In the main, her punters seem to have been bondage-buffs, slaves in search of a leathery dominatrix or freaks whose peccadilloes involved very little close contact with the bodies they had bought. Most of them were 'upper-class loonies', wishing to repeat some bad experience they had with Nanny. One will turn up with his own 'punishment chair', another will plead to be allowed to do heavy housework in the nude (with the odd lash if he bungles it), a third will carry a page of dialogue which he will want his girl to read but with him: the climax comes when she beats him for not washing out his ears. When Cynthia describes these goings-on she sounds like some kindly old repertory bore: director, stage manager and wardrobe mistress – 'Remember the Angel! Gawd, that was a laugh . . .'

Cynthia's other clear advantage over ordinary working girls was that she specialised in the elderly: 'I don't cater for young men any more, unless they're transvestites or slaves. Blokes under forty are all Jack-my-lads who think their pricks are

267

bloody priceless.' The types who went to her in Streatham all had one reason or another to feel out of the mainstream of sexual conduct. Even those who didn't want a beating would probably not have had the cheek to turn one down. Certainly, there was no chance of any of them coming on like 'Jack-my-lad'. With male subservience made explicit, Cynthia could afford to be compassionate and bountiful. One of her favourite clients was a sixty-two-year-old virgin. In Paul Bailey's warming words: 'Old Humphrey was one of several beneficiaries of Cynthia's special discount scheme for pensioners. He is seventy-six now. He is adamant that meeting the Streatham madam ensured him more than a decade of unexpected happiness.'

According to Bailey's biography, the madam was not always so obliging. Indeed, her own sex-life before she got into 'partying' was spectacularly joyless. A succession of layabouts and con-men had their evil way with her when she was in her twenties: there were messy abortions, a fond but faded sugar daddy, and one near-true-love: the disreputable Sam, a 'carnival bloke' when newly 'despunked' but of repellently prodigious appetite. 'I remember crying once when he was doing it because I didn't want it and I said so, it was that time of the month. He took no bloody notice. When the prick is hard, the brain is in the balls.'

As a prostitute, Cynthia was a grudging performer, a Sharon or a Carol – 'I used to lay there like a log.' It was only when she drifted into the role of impresario that she developed the social awareness which enriched so many lives in Streatham. At first, she claims, she laid on her lunchtime sex-parties because 'I love entertaining. It's my greatest pleasure in life.' She would advertise in contact magazines and set up lesbian displays for her 'older' clients. She also provided food and drink – and gave the left-overs to the neighbours. 'It was years,' she says, 'before I came up with the idea of an admission charge . . . In those days I was always out of pocket after a party. Everything was free: the booze, the grub and the fucking. I'd laid it on just for the fun of it.' When she did start charging, she did all she could to maintain the party spirit – her grizzled punters would be asked to buy vouchers at the door: a way of avoiding any squalid sterling transactions in the bedroom, and the source of later jokes about Sex in Exchange for Luncheon Vouchers. Her greatest triumph came when her father visited the house. A violently puritanical presence in her childhood, Dad had been revolted by Cynthia's slow drift into prostitution; there were occasions when he could have helped her, but hadn't. The first half of Bailey's book is full of her pathetic letters home, and of her complaints against her father's fierce self-righteousness. And then:

> Dad turned up one night on my doorstep, really far gone in his cups. He could hardly stand up, he was so bloody squiffy. I let him in, and I said, 'For Christ's sake, Dad, what are you doing in London this late?' It was after midnight. 'I want a girl,' he said.

Cynthia tells him he is drunk, that he will feel different in the morning:

> I was convinced that he would be thoroughly ashamed of himself when he woke up, he was that kind of man. Either that, or he'd forget that he ever asked me. Anyway, he came into my bedroom the following day and he said to me, 'Cinders, I meant every word of what I said to you last night.' I was bloody flabbergasted. He was stone cold sober by now – it wasn't a drunkard talking any more. 'I want you to find me a woman. You specialise in looking after the needs of older men – well, Cinders. I'm an older man, and I need a woman.'

She asks for time to think it over and Dad begs her not to take too long: 'I've never known him to be so bloody nice to me. Typical man, I thought – all smarm when he wants his oats.' She broods on the whole business for a bit – 'it wasn't as if he helped me when I was desperate' – and then, grand old trouper that she is, 'I had one of my brainwaves':

> I remembered Mavis, who'd been my sister Melanie's best friend at school. She'd worked for Dad for a while and he'd fancied her something rotten . . . He wanted to make a pass at her, but he thought that because she was so ladylike she might take offence. And he didn't have a bloody clue, and no more did Melanie, that when he came and asked me to organise a bit of the other for him that Mavis was one of my girls. I've sent dozens of blokes to Mavis and they've all come back raving about her.

She's a genuine French polisher, the real McCoy. She gives the most bloody wonderful blow-job it's possible to have. She's an artist at it.

So Mavis it is, and Dad – when next seen – is indeed gleamingly French-polished, and an utterly changed man. He becomes a regular client at Cynthia's parties, and at last treats his daughter with respect – not quite grovelling, perhaps, but near enough: 'He was a nice old boy at the end because he was having it off whenever he felt like it. It just goes to prove what I've always maintained – that men are much more pleasant and considerate so long as they are regularly despunked. If they're not getting their oats, they're bloody pests.'
Cynthia is now out of jail, still lives in Streatham and still gets her housework done by Slave Philip and her garden fixed by Slave Rodney. Her former clients, Bailey says, are 'waiting in the wings'. Her dream is to open a home for the elderly – men and women:

I'd be matron. There would be special wards for the disabled. If people wanted sex, they could charge it to the National Health – the ones who can't afford it, I mean. I'd have slaves to do the cleaning and Mistresses to see that they don't cut corners. I'm surprised that no one's thought of it before.

Martin O'Brien is exactly the sort of Jack-my-lad who would have been barred from Cynthia Payne's premises. In *All the Girls* he sets off round the world (or parts of the world) with unlimited funds and a grimly limited mission: he will sample whatever prostitution has to offer – from Caracas to Bangkok, from Sydney to Moscow, from Manuela to Magda. It all gets tiresomely repetitive, and O'Brien's topographical and sociological flourishes don't help. Nor does his remorseless vanity: one girl calls him 'king-size', another can't prevent herself from handing it out free, and almost every one of the whores he runs into finds something about him she admires.
Interestingly, from the Cynthia Payne angle if no other, O'Brien's most vividly recorded encounter is with a dominatrix in Paris who locks him up in leg chains, binds, blindfolds and gags him and then gives him a sound thrashing: 'I felt with each new stroke

only a burst of warmth, spreading, like fat dissolving in a heated pan.' The description goes on for some two pages and, in terms of gratification, is the high point of O'Brien's odyssey. If *All the Girls* fails, he could do worse than put his name down for some kitchen work in Cynthia's old folks' home.

1982

EILEEN McLEOD
Women Working: Prostitution Now
Croom Helm

PAUL BAILEY
An English Madam: The Life and Work of Cynthia Payne
Cape

MARTIN O'BRIEN
All the Girls
Macmillan

TV's World Cup '82

June 25: the first phase of the World Cup ended yesterday with England stumbling to a narrow victory over Kuwait and with Northern Ireland somehow getting through their game against Spain without conceding a penalty. And on Monday, the serious bit starts. A nice moment, I had thought, to venture a few pundit-like predictions for you to scoff at (or admire) in ten days' time. Will grit and 'character' undo the flashy pirouetting of the Argie, the robot-like pre-planning of the Hun? That kind of thing.

The trouble is, though, that like every other British armchair fan I have but a dim notion of the strengths and weaknesses of Britain's opposition. The television coverage so far has been exasperatingly lop-sided. Only four out of the six groups in Phase One have been looked at in any detail. Group Three – the Argentine group – has been contemptuously goose-greened, and Group Two – won by West Germany and Austria – has been pushed to one side because its key games kept on coinciding with appearances by England. The upshot is that no one here has seen two of the Cup's hot favourites in action over ninety minutes – rather as if we had been watching a movie with one third of the screen blacked out. (And in our own Group Four we were denied any sustained view of games between England's competitors: not even chauvinism, it seems, could induce an awareness of the Cup's potency as simple narrative.) It is hard to think of any other major sports competition that would have been 'covered' in this way – could it be that someone did not expect England to get beyond the first phase of the competition and therefore saw no point in 'weighing up' the opposition?

Certainly, there has been something odd about the BBC's role in all this. Usually tenacious of its Number One spot in the World of Sport, the Corporation has thus far been remarkably offhand about events in Spain. So offhand, indeed, that my *Radio Times* World Cup Wallchart (an insert in the *RT*'s £1 per copy World Cup Handbook) is packed with dreadful howlers. It has the winner of Group Four (England) scheduled to meet the runners-up in Groups One and Three (i.e., Italy and Argentina). West Germany are thus about to face Northern Ireland and Brazil, and Spain will shortly tangle with the Russians. And so on. Interestingly, the *Mail on Sunday*'s 'Where and When' guide (6 June) carried identical mistakes. Again, it was as if nobody could bring himself to believe that Phase Two would have anything to do with us.

Grumbles of this sort aside, though, it has been a marvellous World Cup, and not least through the efforts of those 'tiny' nations who were expected to lower the high standards of the competition. At first, countries like Algeria, Honduras and Kuwait were talked of as cuddly little items whose 'sheer' (i.e., childlike) 'pleasure in the game' was exemplary but whose 'technical deficiencies' would be horribly exposed by the strolling midfield narcissists of teams like Italy and Yugoslavia. 'Happy as Sand Boys,' declared the *Mail* of the Kuwaiti squad, and there was many a chuckle when *The Times* carried a half-page advertisement on 17 June – the day of Kuwait's first appearance in the competition – which 'pronounced forth upon your ears that we shall proceed forward with the Kuwaiti football from its local and regional environment to comprehensiveness and universality'. Ho ho. Next day, though, after Kuwait had splendidly held Czechoslovakia to a draw, *The Times* sports page made a graceful back-allusion: 'Carefree Kuwait are at home on the world stage.' And over the first week of the competition there was much similarly frozen mirth as Algeria beat West Germany; Honduras held Spain (eleven players and a referee) and Cameroon gave Poland a fair fright. A pity that it all had to end with the Kuwaitis mumbling about a FIFA fix, the Algerians accusing Austria and Germany of rigging the result of Group Two's deciding match, and Honduras denouncing the 'standard of refereeing' after being eliminated by a last-minute penalty – in fact, one of the few penalties in the World Cup so far which it would have been hard for the referee not to award.

Now, of course, the line on 'tiny' countries is that, although they do seem to have learned to play a bit, they still lack the maturity which instructs seasoned soccer pros never to use words

273

like 'bent' or 'fix' on-camera. Perhaps, by the time the likes of Honduras and Kuwait have achieved wisdom of this type, they will also have learned how to do some bending and fixing of their own. If so, I can't say I would blame them.

On the subject of maturity, I hope that none of these already ireful coloured persons gets to hear the ITV soundtrack on which the following exchange took place. Commentator: 'The Cameroon goalkeeper learned his trade from the great German, Sepp Meier, and that is why he wears those black track-suit trousers. Meier gave them to him.' Expert (chuckling): 'I didn't realise he *was* wearing track-suit trousers.' The jester here was Ian St John, who from the very start has worn the air of a man who has been given a bum posting – his Group having, in the main, gone in for timid goalless draws. Sad, this, because St John is one of the few 'experts' who really does seem to have some expertise, who now and then sees things we don't see, spots interesting players we might otherwise have overlooked, and so on. Lawrie McMenemy is similarly valuable (McMenemy is also possessed of a rare television gift – he seems able to think and talk at the same time, and to talk in a voice that almost certainly belongs to him). Some of the other studio sages, however, have been notable merely for over-acting whatever personae the powers-that-be have (it would seem) decreed that they pursue: Brian Clough complacent and sardonic, Jimmy Greaves wayward and impish, Mike Channon impetuous – or is it 'coltishly inarticulate'?

The worst of this lot is the bejewelled, coiffeured John Bond (I was gratified the other day by a newspaper reference to Bond's 'Lady Di' hair-do – surely, after *that*, he'll get it cropped?). Bond has described himself on television as 'flamboyant', which he seems to think has something to do with champagne, cigars, sheepskin, Malcolm Allison and 'being myself, I can't help it, that's the way I'm made'. Sulky, yokelish and thumpingly dogmatic, Bond cuts an unappealing figure, to be sure, but we might still expect him to know more than we do about soccer. And perhaps he does. On-screen, though, he keeps his wits well hidden. Whatever the topic – be it a matter of tactics, individual performance, or even just 'the way the game is going' – Bond's response is invariably both commonplace and hypothetical: 'Why can't they get more men forward? Why can't they get more men wide? For the life of me I can't understand why they can't just go at (or through) defending players . . .' He must have used the formula two dozen times these past two weeks, but there is always a mad indignation in the way he says it, as if the umbrage was acutely personal, as if Bond really does believe that those twenty-two poor brutes out in the Spanish sun are somehow disobeying *him* whenever they decline to 'get more bodies in the box', or 'reach the byline and get crosses in'.

Perhaps John Bond, along with one or two other people I can think of, is suffering from alexithymia, a newly discovered ailment I was told about last week. Derived from the Greek, alexithymia means 'no words for feelings', and now that it has been discovered, American psychiatrists are finding there's an awful lot of it about. Alexithymics are, quite simply, bores. 'They have a difficulty in labelling and experiencing their emotions,' according to a doctor quoted in a recent *Newsweek*. 'Their descriptions of life's events are inevitably dull, focusing on mundane details with no colour or imagery.' Unlike neurotics, who are usually full of labels for their emotions and who can draw on rich reserves of fantasy, the poor old alexithymic never knows what, if anything, is on, or underneath, his mind. He gets headaches, ulcers and the like, but it never occurs to him to connect such symptoms with, say, the car crash he had last week or the terrible marriage he comes home to every day. Boringly, he just thinks he has a headache. According to *Newsweek*, the doctors are beginning to wish they'd never diagnosed the wretched thing:

Some psychiatrists, as might be expected, trace the origins of the condition to early childhood. The mother may have failed to help the child sort out and label feelings, or perhaps the father avoided the discussion of emotions. Alexithymics can sometimes be helped to establish good relations by acting as though they had feelings. 'They learn to infer what they can't discern – like colour-blind people,' says Dr Henry Krystal of Michigan State University. Unfortunately, they may be so boring that psychotherapy is of little use. 'After a while,' says Krystal, 'there's no point in listening.'

Personally, I'm not at all sure that your average Alex (if I may) *would* be more boring than the neurotic abundantly equipped with 'words for feelings'. Certainly, in America today, you can win more listeners for a run-down on your current physical condition than for any dated guff on 'where your mind is at'. Indeed, Alex might be quite a social hit, with his recurrent headaches, and his ulcers, and his healthy refusal of any facile psychic cop-outs. Most intellectuals would probably hand him a pair of running shoes and tell him to get into shape.

And this encourages me to pass on a health warning that should cheer the fairly sick – i.e., those of you who don't jog, diet or 'work out', who have managed not to give up smoking, drinking, carbohydrates, who still cling bravely to poor posture, short breath when climbing stairs, that nagging cough. I was having lunch in New York recently with a glowingly re-juvenated former drunk. He was talking 'gymnasiums' throughout, and after a bit my shamed eye came to rest on the label of his sugar-free low-calorie Tab Cola bottle. The small print legend read as follows: 'Use of this product may be hazardous to your health. This product contains saccharine which has been determined to cause cancer in laboratory animals.' Being a bit alexithymic myself from time to time, I still haven't been able to work out why I should have discerned in this message a small ray of hope.

1982

On the Boundary

August 24. I am writing this during a patch of rained-off play at Lord's Cricket Ground and I can already feel my prose style being drained of zest. Out on the field, the wicket has been covered with low, corrugated sheds and a dozen burly groundsmen have just finished carpeting the surrounding turf with huge lengths of grey tarpaulin. Up on the pavilion balcony, the Middlesex captain stares irritably at the heavens, which are also grey. And a grey, or going-grey, trickle of spectators moves pensively towards the exit gates . . . See what I mean? There *is* something about cricket grounds, and cricket, that enervates the language. Perhaps it is because cricket writers are for ever straining to catch the kind of leisured exactitude that the game itself is noted for, and end up sounding merely sleepy and pedantic. Or maybe they too do their writing in the rain. Whatever the reason, I think I'll continue this at home . . .

August 25. It has been a rough week for Lord's one way and another. First, they get told (by the *Mail on Sunday*, of all people) that their collection of priceless cricket pics is full of – shall we say? – misattributions. Then, for the first time in living (and probably every other kind of) memory, the Long Room which houses said misattributions is flooded in a brief but accurately local thunderstorm. And in between these two dire blows, members have had to sit and watch Middlesex all but surrender three trophies that might easily have been theirs: the three trophies they have been playing for all season. All this in a single week. By Wednesday, those hideous orange and yellow ties really did look as if someone had set fire to them. To complete the general air of spookiness, the three key games had been lost to the same team: Somerset. Somerset's captain for the week was Ian Botham, who still remembers what those ties looked like when the gents of the pavilion silently (and with near-hatred) acknowledged his two ducks against Australia in 1981.

Marylebone's week of torment had begun with the semi-final of the Nat West Cup. It was a marvellously exciting game (and Botham won it almost single-handed), but at the end I found myself almost envying those who had watched it on television. The one-day game has brought 'atmosphere' to cricket, we are often told; you really have to 'be there' to savour the extraordinary new passion that has been engendered by the certainty of an outright result. As it turns out, all this means is that cricket fans have begun imitating soccer fans: the gear is the same, the chants and songs are the same, even the faces – slack-jawed and aggrieved – could have been shipped over from the terraces at White Hart Lane or Upton Park. Umpires get booed, boundary fielders get bombarded with obscenities, and opposing fast bowlers run up to a crescendo of oohs just as goalies do when they prepare to take a goal kick.

The difference is that a soccer game lasts ninety minutes; a one-day cricket match can take anything up to nine hours. 'Atmosphere' simply can't be sustained that long without a certain artificiality creeping in: the celebrated 'passion' becomes a kind of duty. At Lord's, after the first hour or so, the chanting and the whistling began gradually to disconnect itself from events on the field, and the rival groups of fans began staging their own sport: of chant and counter-chant, oath and counter-oath. A mightily struck six or a spectacularly broken wicket might manage to tug their attention back to the detail of the play for a few minutes, but anything that bordered on the cautious or the subtle would induce a fresh upsurge of off-stage tumult. By the end of the game, one faction was shouting 'Liverpool-Liverpool' and the other was yelling 'Come on, you Whites.' By that stage, sundry gallons of Strongbow and Carlsberg had worked wonders and the once-virile clamour had become thin, tired and piping. There was a sour, thwarted note there too. The revellers seemed to have finally realised that they had come to the wrong place, and that it had all taken too long.

Two days after the Nat West match, I was back in the same seat at Lord's for the first day of Middlesex's Schweppes County Championship match with Somerset: a three-day affair, and featuring almost exactly the same players as before. Botham,

Richards and Garner were there for Somerset; Gatting, Emburey and Cowans for Middlesex – big stars indeed, and the stakes too were pretty high. If Middlesex failed to win they would fairly certainly surrender their leadership of the Championship table to Essex; and this after having at one stage of the season held a 48-point lead. Somerset needed to win too, if only because they hardly ever do. I got there early, vowing this time to spot the worst yobs from the outset and then make for whatever corner of the ground was furthest from them.

I need not have bothered. The ground was almost empty, and the thousand or so human shapes sprinkled round the terraces seemed to have taken near-arithmetical pains to keep out of each other's way: there was a minimum three rows of empty seats between each tiny group of fans. 'Fans', though, was hardly the word. There was no one who was not under ten or over fifty. There were fathers with sons, the sons often bespectacled and with gigantic scorebooks on their knees; there were benign-looking pensioners, many of them accompanied by wives with thermos flasks and knitting; there were sad-faced scoutmaster types with binoculars, *Daily Telegraphs* and sandwiches that could only have been packaged by a mum no other woman had ever managed to displace. And there was silence, or near-silence. Voices were lowered even when they didn't need to be.

At eleven o'clock, the two umpires trotted down the steps of the pavilion. There was a restrained, but thoroughly cordial round of applause. Then came the fielding side (more claps) and then the two opening batsmen (from the home team, but the claps were at the same level and lasted not a second longer than before). Let play commence. And so it went on throughout the day: at some time or another, everyone got clapped – bowlers for maidens, fielders for good throws, batsmen for shrewd singles. There was always a reason to be clapping. The first fifty was clapped, the first fifty partnership was clapped, and there were minimally prolonged claps for the first fifty by an individual. Late in the afternoon, someone near the Taverners' Bar launched into a slurred rendering of 'There's only one Ian Botham.' Nobody clapped *him*, and he soon returned to staring vengefully at his beer.

All day long, between claps, the near silence was broken only by the sound of bat on ball (like in the books) or – now and then – by the voice of Philippe Edmonds coarsely berating his fielders, the umpire, the opposing batsmen, Fate – well, it sounded like Fate (as in 'For Fate's Sake'). I have never been able to find out why the England selectors are always supposed to be looking for reasons to leave Edmonds out of the team, why he rarely gets taken on overseas tours, why Middlesex declined to make him captain after Brearley even though, on paper, he was the most likely candidate. After studying him in conditions of near-silence, I'm a shade less puzzled. He's a one-day man, to be sure, and full of atmosphere.

Still, one can hardly blame cricketers for getting a bit testy, so to speak, from time to time. A lot of them spend large lumps of their lives either standing in the field watching cricket or sitting in the pavilion watching cricket. In one innings at Lord's the fielder nearest me touched the ball three times in something like three hours. When his turn came to bat, he was out first ball. And that was him finished for the day. He was a thoughtful-looking fellow, much taken to running his index finger down one side of his nose. Sometimes he would not do this but instead begin studying his fingernails, one by one. When the bowler ran up to bowl, he would bend forward, hitch his trouser-legs and put his hands forward in a welcoming posture. After each ball he would straighten up, and resume work on his nose, or fingernails. He did this some five hundred times during the course of the day. What was he thinking? Did it ever seem strange to him that destiny had brought him to this pass? What did he do in his spare time – indeed, what view of time permitted him to think of some bits of it as 'spare'? As with the ducks, what did he do in winter?

On this last point, there is a handy guide – *The Cricketers' Who's Who*, compiled each year by the ex-MP Iain Sproat. As well as the expected cricket statistics, there are sections on Jobs Outside Cricket, What I did in the Close Season, Nicknames, Opinions on Cricket, and so on – good gossipy stuff to nose about in between overs. In winter, it seems, cricketers simply carry on playing cricket – and a large number of them (I haven't counted but it must be over half) do this in South Africa. South Africa also figures prominently in the Opinions section, with every player I looked up deploring the banning of Gooch, Underwood and Co. 'If Barclays Bank can make money out there, why can't we?' was the familiar theme, and there was mention too of Allen Lamb's inclusion in the England side. Jobs Outside

Cricket ranged from 'horse-breeding' to 'installing fruit machines in pubs'; there is a postman, a window-cleaner, a lorry-driver, an 'ex-steel-worker' and a surgical shoemaker. Mostly, though, cricketers turn out to work as school-masters, civil servants or sales representatives. There are fewer university degrees than one might have expected; indeed, fewer O Levels. And the public school component is small.

On the subject of educational qualifications, my favourite reply came from the South African Robin Smith, who attended Clifton Primary School and Northlands High School, Durban. Where others nervously list their meagre O's and A's, Smith – who seems to have neither – boasts as follows: 'Highly qualified with regard to my educational studies.' Smith's nickname is 'Judge' and under Cricket Superstitions he lists: 'Always have a big night out before a game.' It is already being predicted that he will be the third South African-trained white to find a regular place in the England team (perhaps, with his brother Chris, replacing Gooch and Boycott).

On Sunday, I deserted Lord's for a few hours and sneaked off to Tottenham for Bill Nicholson's Testimonial. Nicholson was Spurs' manager during the team's great period during the sixties, and this was to be his final pay day: Spurs v. West Ham, with Nicholson collecting the proceeds. The real attraction for me, though, was the afternoon's promised curtain-raiser: a forty-minute set-to between Spurs players of the past, players last seen at White Hart Lane as heroes, some twenty years ago. Again, I am not sure that I am glad I went. No sporting heroes are ever quite so worshipped as those of one's own generation; whatever happens afterwards, these remain always 'the real thing'. One gasped at their skills because one was still (in fantasy, at least) young enough to learn them or suddenly, by magic, to find that one had had them all the time. On Sunday, I found myself gasping for somewhat different reasons. There, out on the field, were my heroes, just as they used to be. But this time they were wearing grizzled make-up, pepper and salt wigs, and had cushions stuffed inside their shirts. And they were somehow moving in slow motion. I don't know what I had expected – after all, I knew how old they were. And it was not as if they were in bad shape, considering their age. On the contrary, none of them collapsed, or ran to the touchline to throw up; indeed, their stamina and eagerness could not be faulted. It was just that . . . well, Cyril

Knowles doesn't *have* white hair, and Alan Gilzean is not *completely* bald, and Cliff Jones (as I've been telling everyone for years) really *is* the quickest left-winger in the business. After about half an hour, my sixteen-year-old son (who was there to watch the 'main match') asked me if I felt depressed. I said I didn't, that it was really nice to see the lads again after so many years.

1983

Irving Scholar's Spurs

It's 3 p.m. on Wednesday, 31 March. Instead of writing this I could/should be watching England's World Cup game with Turkey live on my public service BBC TV. As it is, I will have to wait until 10.10 tonight to get the highlights. Between now and 10.10 tonight I will also have to not buy the *Evening Standard*, not watch the *Nine O'Clock News* and not pay my usual early-evening visit to the pub. All information outlets must be shunned. Some public service.

On the other hand, if the World Cup means so much to me, why don't I do what several thousand other armchair fans have had to do this season – sign up with Sky TV? On Sky, I would get not only the World Cup but also the pick of the Premier League action, plus Eurosoccer by the yard, plus *The Boot Room*, *The Footballers' Football Show*, Andy Gray and all manner of other soccer-goodies. With Sky, I need never walk again.

Why don't I then – sign up? A few months ago, when it was announced that a deal had been struck between the BBC, BSkyB and the Premier League, my answer would have been: 'Why should I?' I might even have adopted a principled position. As I understood it, the new arrangement – by which the BBC yielded to Sky nearly all the most interesting fixtures – was something of a stitch-up: the three parties had conspired to cut out ITV. For the BBC this had presumably been in the interests of revenge; a few years earlier ITV had stitched *them* up. But why should we be made to suffer, made to pay? Turkey v. England should surely be a licence-holder's inalienable right – like the Budget or the Boat Race.

Thus spake the average fan, one to another, and at the beginning

283

of the season there did seem to be a feeling that the whole deal might collapse under the weight of public indignation. There was even talk of ITV's Greg Dyke taking the issue to court. Perhaps he did; perhaps he still intends to. No one any longer seems to know or care. In soccer, indignations are short-lived; they have to be. Within a matter of weeks, Sky's obnoxious 'whole new ball game' has become as familiar as Man United's new away strip. And meanwhile, the Norway game has come and gone, not to mention the home tie against Turkey and the great San Marino massacre. And Holland will be happening quite soon. With two-thirds of the season gone, a dozen other major contests have been lost to view. It's getting serious. I'm weakening. I think I'll sign.

If I do, it will no doubt feel like a defeat – albeit a narrow one, in extra time. And my cave-in will remind me yet again that there are few scruples strong enough to do battle with my soccer-lust. It has been wisely said that viewers of football can be divided by the Heysel test, by their responses to that night eight years ago when, having tuned in to watch the soccer, they found themselves watching people die. Some viewers switched off in horror and disgust. Some claimed that they would never again watch a football match. Others stayed on to get what they had come for – Liverpool against Juventus. The game kicked off as soon as all the corpses had been cleared away and, as I remember it, not one of the group I was watching with showed the slightest inclination to switch off. One or two looked uncomfortable, but another one or two (including me) carried on wanting Liverpool to – well, not exactly *crush* the Eyeties, but . . . It was indeed a night of shame.

'For alarmingly large chunks of an average day, I am a moron,' wrote Nick Hornby in his excellent *Fever Pitch* last year. The people who run football, run TV, know that most fans are moronic, that they will put up with just about anything that's thrown at them provided that they are allowed to keep their fantasies intact, provided that they get to see the game. Hornby is an Arsenal supporter so maybe the worst he has to put up with is that he *does* get to see the game; for others, though, fan-loyalty is more variously tested and disdained.

At Spurs, for instance, 'my own team', the last few years have brought an almost unbroken series of humiliations and embarrassments, most of them to do with low-level money-grabbing schemes that have gone wrong: the executive box mania, the flotation, the diversification into 'leisure industry' pursuits, the Saatchi ad campaign, the computerised ticketing, the Spurs credit card, the 0898 Hotline, the Hummel shirt fiasco and numerous other flashy brainwaves – most of them issuing from Irving Scholar in his Monaco tax haven. When Spurs sold Chris Waddle to Marseilles for four and a half million pounds, fans large and small whinged in the streets, or on the East Stand scaffolding, and they whinged some more when it was revealed that the Waddle loot was needed to offset the losses of a Spurs-owned ladies' fashion-wear concern, but even at this, the darkest hour, these same whingers managed to cling on to their belief that Tottenham Hotspur was the team to follow if you wanted style, flair, art for art's sake, and so on. For believers such as these, the business flops could soon be regarded as endearingly Spurs-like – good up front and leaky in defence. If Irving Scholar had been chairman of Arsenal, no doubt his crappy brainwaves would have worked.

And it is this tenacity, if that's the word, that also makes it easy for Spurs fans to forget that when Alan Sugar saved the club from bankruptcy, he surely had other scenarios in mind. Sugar's Amstrad company manufactures the satellite dishes used by Sky subscribers and, as it turned out, Spurs' pro-Sky vote was crucial in the Premier League deal. But we fans have forgotten this and we've forgotten, too, that it was Terry Venables, Sugar's partner-in-salvation, who helped to draw up the Spurs takeover package that sent Paul Gascoigne off to Lazio. El Tel genuinely wanted to keep Gascoigne but he knew that the Midland Bank would never allow a near-insolvent company to hang on to its prime asset. However, he also knows the fan-mentality, and he has somehow managed to persuade us that Irving Scholar was to blame for letting Gazza go. In fact, poor Scholar was busy with Gazza-saving schemes right to the end. Unluckily, his only source of finance was Robert Maxwell: another good reason for Sugar, Rupert Murdoch's friend, to have moved in when he did.

Irving Scholar is now seen as a typical loadsamoney illusionist of the eighties, and is taken to be the architect of all Spurs' financial cock-ups in that decade. His book, *Behind Closed Doors*, is a lengthy, often turgid plea for the defence. In it, he denounces his directors, his legal advisers, his managers – and in particular El Tel. At first Scholar was in awe of Terry's 'silver tongue', his charisma, his fame, his entrepreneurial restlessness. He liked to think they were two of a kind: chirpy guys from nowhere who knew how to make today-things happen. All is sourness now, though, and Scholar – ousted by Venables and Sugar – is anxious to hit Terry where it hurts. The trouble is, he is not sure how to do it. Thus, he tells of Venables blubbing in the lav after a Cup defeat at Bradford, yet on another page he asserts that Tel cares more for money than he does for what happens on the field. According to Scholar, Venables habitually refers to his playing staff as 'stock' – 'as if he was a stall-holder selling ladies' underwear in Petticoat Lane': an unfortunate jibe when we remember where the Waddle money went. And yet elsewhere Venables is said to be habitually reluctant to turn stock into ready cash, even when the stock has had its day: 'Like all managers, he liked to have lots of players around him – it seems that the presence of physical bodies gives him a sense of security.'

From the fans' point of view, Scholar's most provocative charge is that Venables had some responsibility for wrecking Gascoigne's knee in the 1991 Cup Final. Scholar, who spent most of that Final, by his own account, making a big impression on the Royals, says now that 'even before the foul I had the feeling that Gascoigne had been wound up specially for the match . . . Later I was to learn that Venables had turned the key on the young player to get him psyched up for the occasion.' Scholar hates it when players are called 'stock' but is happy enough, it seems, to think of them as clockwork toys. How Venables 'turned the key' we do not learn.

Venables was of course originally hired by Scholar, who jetted to Florida to snap him up, while others dithered. And it was lucky that Spurs had a vacancy when they did – a vacancy created by the resignation of Tel's predecessor, David Pleat. Pleat had been fingered by the *Sun* as a kerb-crawler and there was much bar-room speculation at the time about tip-offs, fit-ups, *Sun* stringers on the Met. The first *Sun* revelations came in July 1987, and Pleat survived these. The second round came in October; this time Spurs sorrowingly sent him on his way. Scholar, who primly never says what the Pleat scandal was about, can now recall:

Curiously, when David's problem first surfaced in the summer I had received a telephone call from a very keen Spurs supporter, who I knew was very friendly with Terry Venables . . . He chit-chatted for a couple of minutes, and then he suddenly said: 'I've got Terry's number on holiday, and he would be very interested in hearing from you.' I politely declined the offer.

What is the point of this anecdote? Are we meant to connect it with Scholar's repeated sneers about Venables's cosy relations with the press? Jeff Powell of the *Daily Mail* is said to have 'got' Venables his earlier big job at Barcelona and is named here as one of Terry's 'sycophants' – the others are Kevin Moseley of the *Express* and Martin Samuel of the *Sun*. Scholar suggests that – on the matter of Pleat – he knows more than he is saying, and no doubt he does: after all, it was he who chose to accept Pleat's resignation. 'I was particularly upset, as I had believed he was going to be Spurs' manager for many years to come.'

Scholar's own methods with the media are simple: he gets on with them, but not too well. 'I have never cultivated the press,' he says, even though 'when you want to be a mover and a shaker in the industry you've also got to establish an identity.' His own faults, if they can be called faults, have tended to be the opposite of El Tel's. Whatever mistakes Scholar made, he made them 'for the glory game' – something that he felt 'meant nothing' to Venables. Scholar loves Tottenham and hints that Venables does not (he remembers how El Veg was barracked for not trying when he played for Spurs in the late-sixties). At one point, Scholar compares himself to Gatsby: 'His dream must have seemed so close that he could hardly fail to grasp it.' And he is forever boasting of his polished Euro-know-how, his multilingual communication skills. Peter Shreeve, who preceded David Pleat, was probably the sort of manager he would have wished Terry Venables to be, or to become:

It was this reference to the French that was to produce a curious postscript. Peter Shreeve had just taken over as manager. That afternoon he came to see me and said: 'Sorry to bother you. I just wanted to know what you said about the French team in your speech.' As I looked a little bemused he continued: 'You know, er, about how they play.' 'You mean *joie de vivre*, Peter?' 'That's the word. What does it mean?' I explained that it was a Gallic expression that stood for gay abandon, and Peter nodded his head, obviously taking it in.

It has to be confessed, though, that underneath all the bogusness, the boasting and the spite, Scholar is what he says he is: a Spurs fan through and through. His 'greatest fault', his co-writer Mihir Bose attests, has been 'to love Tottenham and football to excess'. According to Chris Horrie's *Sick as a Parrot* – a witty account of Spurs' tragicomic decade – Scholar is 'a bottomless repository of soccer trivia – "Ere, I've got one for you," he would say and out would come a question about who was the first Tottenham player to score more than one hat-trick in the FA Cup or something equally arcane':

Social events in his house in Chester Square [*sic*] in posh Regent's Park, where the perfectly proportioned Georgian rooms were cluttered up with mountains of tacky Spurs memorabilia, were a nightmare for anyone not interested in football. Conversation would quickly be pulled around to Spurs and out would come treasured souvenirs such as old match programmes, signed photos or the new invention of videoed collections of great goals.

Biographical data of this sort makes Scholar seem less on top of things than he, in his book, pretends. He wants us to admire him as a lethal wheeler-dealer but he is also pitiably keen to prove his fanhood. And he doesn't want us to laugh when he recounts how, on becoming chairman of Spurs, one of his first acts was to pull on a first team shirt and get stuck into a kickaround with Ossie, Archie, Garth and all the lads: within minutes Scholar snapped an Achilles tendon and thus spent the early weeks of his chairmanship with his leg in plaster – a symbolic crippling that would have been made much of by F. Scott Fitzgerald.

All in all, Scholar has good reason to feel undervalued by the terrace diehards. Fan of fans, he brought to Spurs great players like Waddle, Gascoigne and Lineker. None of them is still there of course but even so. Perhaps a club chairman cannot be a fan. In the case of Waddle, and to some extent of Gascoigne, the terraces ended up feeling they'd been conned. They learned to love these players only to find that they were not really theirs to love. With Lineker it was different. The fans liked him well enough and they were grateful for his goals, but he never quite seemed to belong at White Hart Lane. The revelation that Scholar had secretly borrowed the transfer-money from Maxwell contributed to the notion that this hero was just passing through.

But then Lineker always seems a little detached from the teams he represents. With his good-boy looks, his modest demeanour, his unflagging courtesy etc, he seems to have been packaged for some other role in life, beyond the field of play. To love Gascoigne, you *have* to love football. Lineker's appeal is, in Scholarspeak, more broadly based. It would be wrong to mock his niceness because he almost certainly *is* nice, but after reading this new biography, one can see why he sometimes gets up the noses of his colleagues.

Lineker dislikes training, we are told, and so while others sweat and groan, he is to be found lying in the bath, getting ready for his next TV-call. And on the field, what does he *do*? He drifts into good positions, he attacks space, he gets on the blind side of defenders, he thinks quickly, and so on. No mention of the ball. And then he scores. It isn't fair. And Lineker half-feels this too – he now and then looks sheepish when he scores. And he also has the knack of scoring when it matters most: the hat-trick in Mexico, the face-saver against Poland, the equaliser against West Germany in the World Cup.

When you think about it, we owe him quite a lot, and the blood boils when we remember how he was humbled by Graham Taylor in his final game for England: taken off with half an hour to go and a Lineker-style goal desperately needed. The liveliest section of this otherwise pretty tame account of his career comes at the end when Colin Malam gets Taylor and Lineker at each other's throats. Lineker is characteristically oblique and Taylor characteristically confused but the animosity is clear. Taylor comes out of it the worse, seeming envious, petty and two-faced.

But this is Lineker's book, not his. Colin Malam's chief inform-
ant throughout was Jonathan Holmes, Lineker's smooth-talking
agent, and Taylor's chief gripe seems to have been that Lineker
listened to Holmes when he should have been listening to Taylor.
Although he is not always sure of what he wants to say, Graham
Taylor does like to be listened to. So, Saint David Platt, beware.

1993

IRVING SCHOLAR AND MIHIR BOSE
Behind Closed Doors
Deutsch

CHRIS HORRIE
Sick as a Parrot: The Inside Story of the Spurs Fiasco
Virgin

COLIN MALAM
Gary Lineker: Strikingly Different
Stanley Paul

Lennox Lewis: A Profile

When I first met Lennox Lewis he was dressed up as Father Christmas and he had a gold crucifix hanging from one ear. A six-foot-six man-mountain, he was encircled by a small congregation of admirers: a dozen or so disabled infants from the Freddie Mills Boys' Clubs, each of them kitted out in a T-shirt made by SPX, the clothing firm that sponsors Lewis and exclusively supplies his gear – though not, one guessed, the ill-fitting scarlet cloak that he was sporting on this day, nor the cotton-wool whiskers that he was having such trouble securing to his chin. As Lewis moved among the damaged kids, sparring up to one or two of them, tousling heads, dropping the odd word, his expression was properly benign and Santa-like. But it was also detached and self-aware. After all, was this not the 'charity work' that all topflight celebrities went in for? Lewis looked as if he had been doing it for years.

The occasion was the Skysports Christmas Party, pre-recorded on 29 November, less than a month after this same Santa had savagely clubbed Razor Ruddock to the canvas at Earls Court – clubbed him not once but three times: Ruddock, who had gone the distance with Mike Tyson! It was on that day, November 1st, that Lewis had become a bona-fide British star. A one-time Canadian Olympic champion, the London-born heavyweight could now be safely hailed as a phenomenon not granted to this country since the last years of the nineteenth century: a genuine world-championship contender, a puncher who could hang in there with the New Yorkers and the Philadelphians. To us, it no longer mattered that Lewis had learned to box in Canadian gymnasiums and been groomed in the hills of Pennsylvania. He still had a British passport and 'with one hammer blow, lethal Lennox – the kid from London's East End – had punched his way into the hearts of the nation'.

So said the *Sun* on the morning of November 2nd. And there was Lennox over two pages, wielding a champ-sized Union Jack and managing to look both gratified and faintly scornful, as if to say: you lot may be surprised but I'm not. Lewis knew well enough that if he had lost to Ruddock, as several papers thought he might, it would have been a different story. He would still have been ours, sort of. But we would almost certainly have been reminded that, passport or no passport, he had lived on these shores as an adult for a mere three years. Words like 'carpetbagger' and 'flag of convenience' had already been whispered in the prints, and there was never much chance that Lewis would fit into the lovable-loser bracket that we reserve for the likes of 'Enery Cooper and Dame Bruno. As it was, with Ruddock pole-axed, none of this needed to be said. We were now more than happy to lay claim to all of him.

And all of him is quite a lot. Stripped of his Santa costume, Lewis at once seems more authentically gigantic, but with none of the 'air of menace' that boxers reputedly like to 'exude'. Even at weigh-ins, which are often stage-managed rehearsals for the coming storm, Lewis wears the look of one who is running a bit late for some other, more peaceable appointment – a modelling gig, maybe, or a session with his business associates. Close-up, he has little about him of the pug: no broken nose, no vulnerable scar-tissue. His skin looks more pampered than pummelled. At first, the stare he greets you with seems meant to disconcert but it's actually quite neutral. It's a celebrity stare, the stare of one who expects to be stared at. At the same time, though, the eyes are rather kindly and amused. The message seems to be: Relax, shorty, I only *use* all this muscle-power when I'm at work. Off-duty, I'm just another extraordinary guy.

Lennox Claudius Lewis was born twenty-seven years ago in Forest Gate, East London. His parents split up when he was six and at the age of twelve Lennox was removed to Canada. His mother Violet took him and his older brother Dennis to settle in a small town just outside Toronto. His mother has recalled: 'Things got difficult and I couldn't manage to have the boys with me, so I sent them back home to their aunt in London. It was a very difficult decision . . . All my friends called me the weeping mother – I used to cry all the time when I was apart from the boys. I phoned them every day . . . (but) when Lennie returned

292

to Canada, he was angry with me. Somehow that anger always seemed to be in him.'

Lennox's anger found an outlet in the playground. He was a big boy and was growing fast. At his school in Kitchener, Ontario, he came in for a lot of teasing: he was the school's only black and he had a Cockney accent. 'I was at an awkward age,' says Lewis. 'I was an outsider. They didn't treat me badly but I did run into, you know, certain different cases there, and I used to get into a lot of fights. My school principal, after the third time giving me the strap, we got on pretty well because of the fact that he understood, you know, my language thing and that I looked at things differently. So we became good friends and he encouraged me to go into a contact sport, which is boxing. He told me where to go. It could have been basketball – that's a sport at which I always thought I would go far – but I excelled so much at boxing.'

Lewis was coached at the local Police Recreational Center and was soon winning local and then national tournaments. At sixteen, he won the World Junior Championship in Santo Domingo and 'after that, I thought I'll see how far I can actually go'. Under the guidance of Romanian coach Adrian Teoderescu, he progressed to become the world's best Intermediate (under twenties) and represented Canada at the Los Angeles Olympics. He lost there in the quarter-finals but four years later, after lifting the 1986 Commonwealth Games title, he won the gold at Seoul. His opponent in the final there was Riddick Bowe.

The offers to turn professional poured in, but Lewis already had a money problem. In the run-up to the Olympics he had had no income apart from a miserly $450 a month stipend from the government agency Sport Canada. With Teoderescu's assistance, but with no professional advice, he entered into a punishing loan agreement that left him owing more than $160,000 by the time he won his medal. $100,000 of this was a penalty for late repayment: the small print had required him to repay what he owed four months *before* the Games. Originally, the loan company had said they would write off the debt if Lewis won a medal and signed up with them, but when it came to a hard offer there was no mention of wiping out the debt. It was a standard managerial proposal, 65–35 in favour of the management, plus a modest signing-on fee of $25,000. Lewis courageously refused to sign: 'When they offered me that, I said to myself, "Holy smoke, man." I looked at the medal and said this didn't really mean anything at all.'

Lewis hired a lawyer and put his services to auction. 'I wanted to not take any chances. I wanted to get involved with the right people. I wanted to give everybody an opportunity to get to know me, and for me to get to know them, to find out if I could trust them to, let's say, nourish the champion with the pedigree, 'cos a lot of people don't know how to bring up a champion, or how to bring up a boxer. So I was going on a lot of past things, basically looking at their record and going around and meeting them. And the funny thing about that is that they all sounded the same, they all sounded so good, and I said, "Boy, where are all the *bad* ones that people hear about?" I know one guy I wanted to stay away from was Don King. I wouldn't say keep away from him. I was always waiting to see when he would come out, you know.'

Even before his triumph at Seoul, Lewis had toyed with the idea of returning to England. There was the British title to go for, and also the Commonwealth, the European. In Canada he felt neglected. In the States, he feared that he would be exploited, then neglected. England 'just seemed like the best place' from which to make a start. Happily, it turned out that the English offer, when it came, topped anything that had been tabled from the States. Bankrolled by the Levitt financial services group, which was then – according to the business press – 'moving aggressively into sports management', the deal guaranteed a $200,000 signing-on fee (enough for Lewis to dispose of his Canadian debt), a company house, a company car and the hire of a tutor to help Lewis with his reading, never his strong subject when he was at school. The split would be 75–25, but Levitt would cover all expenses, including the salary of a full-time trainer. And, most important of all, says Lewis, 'They also gave me control of my own career. I realised that I would be used in professional boxing, but I didn't want to be used a lot. I wanted to be the founder of my own destiny.'

But wasn't he taking a bit of a chance, cutting himself off from the big-time transatlantic scene? 'I believed I could do it from the English side. They don't really have a heavyweight champion. To have an entire country behind me instead of like, let's say, New York or Canada or whatever. That's what I wanted. The English really stand behind their athletes. They support them – emphatically.' Stripping Canada of its status as

294

an 'entire country' seems to indicate that Lewis really will be here
to stay. Significantly, his recent triumphs have rated somewhat
terse mentions in the Canadian sports pages.

By the time the Levitt group collapsed, in December 1990, Lewis
had already moved to England and had won some fights. He is now
backed by a London accountant whose speciality is liquidation
and, says the *Independent*, 'by another backer who doesn't even like
his name mentioned'. His brother Dennis serves as his 'financial
adviser' and his mother also seems to have a formidable say. And
Frank Maloney, his original Levitt contact, has been retained as
manager. A former amateur flyweight, this amiable hustler runs a
pub in Crayford and has contacts in the murky world of 'small-hall'
boxing. He has worked for Frank Warren and Micky Duff, both of
whom presumably now view him with some envy. Duff is said
to have sneeringly predicted that Maloney would do a Cecil B.
de Mille on Lewis, in reverse: he would take a star and turn him
into an unknown.

Maloney may be inexperienced but he has sense enough to
recognise that 'I'm only in the position I'm in because of Lennox
Lewis . . . I work for Lennox, Lennox doesn't work for me.'
Maloney has been mocked for giving Lewis too much control
of his own destiny but looking at the pair of them, the eagle
and the sparrow, Maloney all fuss and bother and Lewis so lordly
and composed, it is pretty obvious who is, and has to be the
boss. Maloney's account, to *Boxing Monthly*, of the build-up to
the Ruddock fight well captures how the power seems to be
balanced:

. . . I walked over to Lennox's hotel and went up to his room
and he was just sitting there, laughing. I said, 'In a minute
you're going to have the hardest fight of your life.' But he
just shrugged his shoulders and said: 'I'm going to win, don't
worry. Relax. Meditate.'

I stayed with him for about twenty minutes then I went to
the arena. When I got there you could sense the build-up and
everything, people coming up and asking how Lennox was. It
was tense. But the atmosphere in Lennox's dressing room was
so calm. I've been in a lot of big fighters' dressing rooms in
America, but I'd seen nothing like this. It was just like sitting
in a front room. Lennox was just sitting there with his dark

glasses on and the camp were just talking amongst themselves. That's what Lennox injects into people. Calm. You can't have all this excitement around a fighter's dressing room. I tend to stay away from him because I'm a bit excitable, to be honest.

Lennox knows about this 'calm' and values it. He calls it 'being focused' and speaks of himself as a 'foreseer'. Before the Ruddock fight he was, he says, tuned into the 'low heartbeat' of Bob Marley's 'Chase Those Crazy Baldheads out of Town'. By the time he got into the ring, even his movement was linked to Marley's bass-line. 'That's what you call rhythm,' said Lewis; or did he mean: 'That's what *you* call rhythm'?

Watching Lennox go about his saintly business for Skysports, I could more or less see what Maloney meant. Lennox managed to beam out some deep cool even from behind his silly whiskers. Was it a rare brand of moral authority that gave him this thoughtful, somewhere-else demeanour, or was it just that he rather badly wanted to *be* somewhere else? Whatever it was, he responded fairly well to the show's frantic and inane demands. His smile was never more than a half-smile but he did what he was told. He fooled about in a bouncy rubber boxing ring, he exchanged blows with a legless robot, he bantered in near-Cockney with one or two of his 'old mates' – including Arsenal's pugilistic Ian Wright – and he was politely indulgent to John Conteh and Billy Walker, two bruisers from the past who were brought on at the end as the party's 'mystery guests' and may well have been as mysterious to Lennox as they were to most of the assembled audience. Lewis was required, as a climax to the show, to fun-fight one of these illustrious has-beens in the bouncy ring, and it was rather sad to overhear a now less-than-husky-looking Conteh getting ready to do combat: 'Maybe,' he said, 'I'll catch him with a lucky punch.'

He didn't, but then so far no one has. Lewis has had twenty-two fights as a professional and has won all of them, eighteen by a K.O. It is true enough that his opponents, pre-Ruddock, have been more nuisances than threats but even a Mike Tyson can get knocked out by a nuisance. Lewis, however, is no brawler; he leaves nothing much to chance. At school, he was nicknamed The Scientist – 'because I'm the kind of guy who likes to sit back and observe things' – and he still rather relishes the label. He speaks of his adversaries as 'puzzles to be worked out', and to date he has had no trouble coming up with the right answers.

In the ring, Lewis uses his high-speed, high-precision left to keep his opponent at arm's length, to wear him down with stinging jabs and also – while he's at it – to measure him for the forthcoming kill. There is a marvellous arrogance in the way Lewis now and then freezes the action, shoves a squashy left into his victim's nose and holds it there for just long enough to take a glance along the length of his own arm. It is as if he is rechecking the arithmetic, the angles. And the sums usually look good. Lewis has an eighty-two inch reach.

The kill is likely to happen when the other man presumes to land a punch, or a near-punch. Flicked by an opponent's hopeful glove, Lewis appears to snap out of a studious half-dream: who *is* this guy that he should so interrupt my calculations? He has been riled by an impertinence, but mostly he seems keen to get this last, messy bit settled as quickly as he can. A ferocious three-punch combination tends to do the job. If it doesn't, and Lewis has to batter his opponent on the ropes, there is no discernible blood-hunger. The attitude seems more to be one of sorrowing contempt: can't this man *see* that the puzzle has been solved?

It was probably this failure of blood-lust that led people to assume that Lewis, for all his stylish ringcraft, had no killer punch. The guys he knocked over were described as journeymen, bill-fillers, Mexican roadsweepers and the like. The forty-year-old Mike Weaver, the punchbag Tyrell Biggs (who beat Lewis at the Los Angeles Olympics, when Lewis was nineteen), the immobile Gary Mason: these were name-fighters, names enough, anyway, to generate real money from TV, but none of them was reckoned to be hard to floor. Pre-Ruddock, Lewis's cerebral approach was still thought of as a liability, OK for the Olympic Games but unlikely to upset a mongrel pro.

For a time, under his former trainer, the American Marine John Davenport, Lewis was encouraged to exhibit more animal aggression, to rush out from his corner at the bell and act very, very angry. In this role, he looked – and no doubt felt – a bit ridiculous, and against the short, squat, flailing Levi Billups he came close to getting caught. The Billups fight taught Lewis a few lessons: 'I did more fighting than boxing. I should have boxed more, moved backwards, analysed it. That's why I changed my trainer, because he was making me get into a fight when I didn't need to. I've got enough mobility in my feet to stay on the outside and just work it out that way.' Under his new coach, Pepe Correa (who used to handle Sugar Ray Leonard), he is always urged to 'work it out', to have a 'gameplan' and to be ready to make 'sacrifices' in the interests of a chosen strategy – in other words, to take no notice when the critics accuse him of being passive or switched-off.

The other lesson Lewis learned from Billups is that he should never go into a contest without having done his homework on the opposition. Billups was a late replacement for Tony Tucker and Lewis had but three days' notice and no videos. Today he would refuse to take this kind of risk. Before Ruddock, 'I watched so much tape on Razor that I had it all stored in my head. I could see him box in front of me, exactly the way he boxes. So when I went out there and presented him with something he wasn't used to, he starts doing things that he *doesn't* do, and then I take advantage.'

Like Mike Tyson, Lewis spends a lot of time watching boxing videos, but Lewis believes his interest in the past is more constructive than Tyson's: 'Tyson is not a student of boxing, he is a student of boxing *history*. When I watch an old Ali fight, for instance, I try to incorporate his style into my style. I try to memorise some of the tricks that Ali did, his methods of holding on, what he would do, where he would move in the ring. It's like looking things up in a book. What did *he* do under these circumstances? And then I put it in my training regimen.'

Against Ruddock, this kind of scholarship certainly paid off. Lewis and Correa worked it out that Ruddock had one genuinely fearsome weapon, his big left, but that when he wasn't using it he kept it hanging low. The gameplan seems to have been for Lewis to keep moving clockwise, to avoid the left, and force Ruddock to attack his body. It was this that Razor 'doesn't do'. To body-punch, Ruddock was obliged to bend into his opponent and thus set himself up for Lewis's pulverising right, which – when it came – must have seemed to have dropped on him from the sky. 'Razor wasn't expecting me to be so quick. He threw a couple of hooks and I wasn't there. Not only my anticipation was good, but my balance was too. Ruddock was too sure of himself. The press believed he was going to knock me out. They didn't realise that I thrive on the thrill of competition.'

Certainly, Lennox doesn't seem all that competitive. His
Christmas video is subtitled 'I'm British and I'm Bad' but
Lewis doesn't usually pitch as the snarling type. When it comes
to the routine pre-match slag-offs, he prefers on the whole to
let the other side spit venom. 'My insults', he says proudly,
'are reality-insults. When I said Gary Mason had a big head, I
meant that he had a big head. My insults are meant.' But why
bother with that sort of thing; why not say nothing? And why
all this preening and parading that goes on before a fight? 'You
say those things to pester, to get under a guy's skin. It's part of
the psyche-game. And the parading is an animal instinct that
comes out in us, in the almost ape-ian side of us. All animals
do that. The human animal is not known to do that and yet
it is, if you want to look at it in true respect. We all kind of
parade. We want to impress, what do we do? We've gotta walk
right, whether we model or whether we're athletes in front of
our audience. You have the Eubanks that does this [he mimes
the Eubank strut], or you have the Lennox Lewis who does a
little dance before the fight.'

Many sports heroes speak of themselves in the third person,
but Lewis does it more than most, as if to acknowledge a
discrepancy between the real man and the packaged star. He
talks unblushingly of Lennox Lewis's marketable attributes: the
looks, the personality, the mid-Atlantic accent. 'People find me
easy to talk to. I don't look like boxers are supposed to look
like – rough guys that cause trouble and fight all the time. In
one sense, I'm an ambassador of my sport in the way I know
how. Plus with the help of my mother bringing me up the right
way.' And what about his life when he retires? 'It should be filled
with me touching people's lives in different ways. Whether it's
as a sporting champion or whether it's as business man. I think
I spread a certain kind of positive energy around. I want when
people talk about me for them to say, yeah, he's a good solid
person.'

It is this kind of piety which has led Lewis's enemies to deride
him as a softy, a 'hairdresser' – and it must be said that his flat-top
is almost pedantically well-groomed – or to chuckle about his pet
poodle (name of Tyson), his tropical fish, his mother-love. When
asked about his 'outside interests', Lennox is likely to assume that
the question has to do with money: after all, he once took a

course in business studies. And when he does name his hobbies and pastimes, there is always a sense that the list is meant to sound impressively unboxerlike: he plays chess a lot (because it teaches him to be 'cunning') and when he reads, he reads usefully: 'I don't read fiction. I like things that educate you, that you can learn and put to work. I'm studying black history because a lot of things weren't taught to us in school. You read about Christopher Columbus and all of those things but you don't read about Africa, where we originated from – those kind of things. After a time, you have to start educating yourself – for instance, when I get married and have kids I'm going to be part of the programme of educating my children.'

Get married? Lennox is not known to have a girlfriend, and if he does he's not telling. When the *Evening Standard*'s Daisy Waugh tried to cajole him into a confession on this topic, the exchange went as follows:

Wasn't his girlfriend jealous of his relationship with his mother?
Lennox: 'I guess a girlfriend *would* get jealous.'
Was he ever teased for being a mummy's boy?
Lennox: 'Would *you* tease me?'

Violet is often in residence at Lewis's small, mock-Georgian house in Bexleyheath but on the day I visited she was away. It was easy to tell this because the living room was a shambles of scattered videos, remote-control guns, tracksuit tops, newspaper cuttings, mail. There was no tea or coffee left and Lennox was touchingly triumphant when he unearthed a bottle of Asti Spumante from the fridge. Violet, we know, is a stickler for tidiness and a terrific cook. There are photographs of her on the walls and Lewis invariably speaks of her with reverence. When I ask about his father, he cuts me short: ask mother. Does Violet mind him being a boxer? 'No. She sees me travelling the world, not getting hurt, and she knows where I am.'

Will Lennox Lewis get hurt? Quizzed about Mike Tyson, he is uncharacteristically tentative. He has seen the bull-man dismantle quite a few well-trained defences and he knows that Tyson's headlong style would be difficult for him to cope with. 'If ever I was to go against Tyson what old fight would I turn back to? Ali–Frazier. But I believe I can knock anybody out, including

Tyson. If they just stand there for one second and let me generate all my body-mechanics.'

Before Tyson – if that fight ever happens – Lewis's body-mechanics will presumably have to apply themselves to Riddick Bowe. When I interviewed Lewis last December, the haggling over Lewis–Bowe had just begun. The insults were flying: Lewis was calling Bowe a 'chicken', Bowe was calling Lewis a 'faggot', and so on. Shortly afterwards, Bowe contemptuously surrendered his WBC belt – in a waste-bin. Lewis picked it up, the press cheered – a world champion at last! – but everybody knew that it was really Bowe who held the crown: he was the man who beat the man who beat the man.

The fear was that by isolating Lewis and the WBC (Bowe held on to his three other titles), the Bowe handlers had outmanoeuvred Frank Maloney. Certainly they seemed to have achieved what they wanted: an indefinite postponement of the Lewis–Bowe match (thus freeing Bowe to milk his title against a procession of no-hopers). How could Lennox as WBC champ go up against Bowe, who had denounced the WBC prize as 'dishonoured, a piece of tainted trash'? Must Lennox relinquish *his* title in order to win Bowe's?

If these doubts have substance, Lewis can look forward to some domestic entertainment but not to a real breakthrough in the States – at least not yet. There will be Lewis–Bruno, Lewis–Foreman, Lewis–Stewart and maybe even Lewis against Tony Tucker, which will mean that Don King, who handles Tucker and is cosy with the WBC, will be getting a piece of Lennox after all. By the time this article appears, one or another of these fights may well have taken place.

For Lewis, though, the big one will be still to come, and for him at the moment the big one is without doubt Riddick Bowe, the *real* world champion, the man he has already floored. As so often before, though, Lennox believes he has the psychological advantage: 'Yeah, Bowe's gonna have to second-guess himself. I don't. He has to remember. I don't have anything against Riddick Bowe. He's just someone I'm competing with. Whether he wants to turn it into a grudge match and call me names, that's his prerogative, but it's a waste of energy on his part.' At this, Lennox sprawled back, gave a contented yawn and then hoisted his massive size-fifteens on to the coffee table. He had wasted enough energy today. 'I'm only saying something that is reality, you know. I don't think he has enough heart to hang with me. All the things I say I believe.'

1993

A Note on the Author

Ian Hamilton has published two collections of his own poetry and his books include *Robert Lowell: A Biography*, *In Search of J.D. Salinger*, *Writers in Hollywood*, *Keepers of the Flame*, and most recently *Gazza Agonistes*.